CHANGING THE ECONOMIC SYSTEM IN RUSSIA

Edited by Anders Åslund and Richard Layard

St. Martin's Press

New York

First published in the United States of America in 1993

Library of Congress Cataloging-in- Publication Data

Changing the economic system in Russia / edited by Anders Åslund and
Richard Layard
      p. cm.
    Includes index.
    ISBN 0-312-09581-3
    1. Russia (Federation)--Economic Policy--1991- 2. Russia
(Federation) -- Economic conditions--1991- I. Åslund, Anders, 1952-
. II. Layard, P.R.G. (P. Richard G.)
HC340.18.C43 1993
330.947'0854--dc20

                           92-43673
                              CIP

ISBN 0-312-09581-3

Printed and bound in Great Britain

Contents

Part III Privatisation

Part IV Money and Foreign Trade

Contributors

Anders Åslund, Professor, Director, Stockholm Institute of East European Economics, Stockholm School of Economics; Economic Adviser to the Russian government.

Maxim Boycko, Dr., Institute of the World Economy and International Relations (IMEMO), Russian Academy of Sciences, Moscow University; Economic Adviser, State Committee for State Property Management of Russia (Goskomimushchestvo).

Peter Boone, Dr., Jeffrey D. Sachs & Associates, Inc. and Harvard University, collaborator of the Russian government.

Anatoly B. Chubais, Dr., Deputy Prime Minister, Chairman of the State Committee for State Property Management of Russia.

Marek Dabrowski, Dr., Centre for Social and Economic Research, Warsaw, MP, Chairman of Council of Ownership Changes; Former First Deputy Minister of Finance of Poland; Economic Adviser to the Russian government.

Michael Ellam, London School of Economics; collaborator of the Ministry of Labour of Russia.

Boris Fedorov, Dr., Deputy Prime Minister of Russia for Finance and Economy.

Ardo Hansson, Dr., Research Fellow, Stockholm Institute of East European Economics, Stockholm School of Economics.

Contributors

Mark Horton, John F. Kennedy School of Government, Harvard University.

Simon Johnson, Dr.,Assistant Professor, The Fuqua School of Business, Duke University.

Heidi Kroll, Dr., Visiting Fellow, Russian Research Center, Harvard University.

Richard Layard, Professor, London School of Economics; Economic Adviser to the Russian government.

David Lipton, Dr., World Institute for Development Economics Research, Economic Adviser to the Russian government.

Alexei V. Mozhin, Dr., Head of Department for Interaction with International Financial Institutions, Council of Ministers of Russia.

Jeffrey D. Sachs, Galen I. Stone Professor of International Trade, Harvard University; Economic Adviser to the Russian government.

Andrei Shleifer, Professor, Harvard University; Economic Adviser, State Committee for State Property Management of Russia.

Sergei A. Vasiliev, Dr., Economic Counsellor, Centre for Economic Reform, Council of Ministers of Russia.

Maria Vishnevskaya, International Centre for Economic Transformation, Moscow.

Acknowledgements

The papers included in this book consitute a selection of papers commissioned by the Stockholm Institute of East European Economics. They were all discussed and reviewed at a lively and intensive research conference held at the Stockholm School of Economics, 15-16 June 1992. The authors have subsequently revised their papers.

Apart from the authors of the papers included, gratitude should also be expressed to the active participants in the discussion of the papers (in alphabetic order): Hans Aage, John Andersson, Mikhail Berger, Erik Berglöf, Anders Bornefalk, Wlodzimierz Brus, Julian Cooper, Rudiger Dornbusch, Rolf Eidem, Richard Ericson, Alan Gelb, Torun Hedbäck, Terhi Kivilahti, Georg Kjällgren, Elena Kolokoltseva, Vladimir Kosmarskii, Mikhail Leontiev, Sten Luthman, Silvana Malle, Randalf Karl Morck, Leif Mutén, Susanne Oxenstierna, Pavel Pelikan, Paul Quinn-Judge, Marian Radetzki, Per Ronnås, Jacek Rostowski, Lennart Samuelsson, Wolfram Schrettl, Peter Semneby, Nikolai Shmelev, Alexander Shokhin, Örjan Sjöberg, Michael Sohlman, Ulf Stange, Joakim Stymne, Pekka Sutela, Anna Tiagunenko, Andrei Vavilov, John Williamson and Michael Wyzan.

Marion Cutting has provided extensive and vital editorial assistance as well as administering the editorial process. Gun Malmquist has offered eminent secretarial services.

The book as well as the conference have been generously financed by the Ministry for Foreign Affairs of Sweden, the Jan Wallander & Tom Hedelius Foundation, the Royal Academy of Sciences of Sweden, ,and the Prince Bertil Foundation. Their support is gratefully acknowledged. Finally, we want to express our great appreciation of Dr. Frances Pinter and her excellent and always so friendly staff.

Notwithstanding the numerous people who have kindly contributed to the production of this book, the ultimate responsibility for any remaining errors must fall upon us, the editors.

Anders Åslund, Richard Layard
Stockholm and London, November 1992

Introduction

Anders Åslund and Richard Layard

At the end of 1991, Russia faced a horrendous economic crisis. The imminence of Gehenna hang in the air. Shops were more empty than at any time after World War II. In spite of regulated prices, massive repressed inflation was swiftly turning into open inflation. The consolidated state budget deficit was at least 20 per cent of gross national product, and public finances were on the verge of collapsing altogether. Production was falling at an annual rate of some 20 per cent, and there were fears of an outright collapse of production. In December 1991, the Soviet Union had run out of foreign reserves and had to cease fulfilling its foreign debt service. The Soviet Union was no longer a real entity, and its process of dissolution could result in unnamed horrors. Widespread fears prevailed both in Russia and abroad of imminent famine, widepread freezing to death, and mass emigration. It was a truly formidable economic crisis.

However, there was one bastion of hope — the democratically-elected Russian President. In June 1991, Boris Yeltsin was elected President of Russia with 57 per cent of the popular vote, to the great dismay of the non-elected first and last President of the Soviet Union, Mikhail Gorbachev. The old Soviet institutions were broken by their involvement in the failed coup in August 1991. The former Soviet republics were allowed to go their own way, and in Russia the road lay open to democratic rule.

A couple of months of confusion ensued, but they were not wasted. At least five alternative teams presented themselves as government options to President Yeltsin. There was intense competition between the various economic programmes being prepared in Moscow and the nearby dachas. On 28 October 1991, President Yeltsin made a speech to the Supreme Soviet of Russia in which he outlined a radical liberal reform, leading to an ordinary market economy based on private property (Yeltsin, 1991). To the insiders this signalled that the team headed by Gennadii Burbulis, Yegor Gaidar and Aleksandr Shokhin was on the road to victory, and on 8 November they and their collaborators were appointed by President Yeltsin to the top jobs in the Russian government. The work on the change of economic system could start in earnest.

The Gaidar team, as it is generally called, comprised the best and the brightest of Russia's young economists. They were based in economics research institutes in Moscow and St. Petersburg, though several had also had some government experience. All had been involved in the extensive Soviet discussion on economic reform, but not much in the actual writing of programmes before the summer of 1990, partly because they were too young to be allowed to emerge by the old Academicians, partly because they were more liberal in their market orientation. Several of them attracted public attention as members of the Shatalin group (named after its chairman Academician Stanislav Shatalin), that presented the so-called 500-day programme in the summer of 1990 (Åslund, 1992b). As soon as the Soviet Union had opened to the West in the late 1980s, these young Russian economists had forged links with a variety of Western economists. For years we had been discussing how the transition to capitalism could and should be undertaken in the Soviet Union.[1]

In 1991, two sharp cleavages opened up among Russian economists. Increasingly, Russian economists realized that the relevant entity of economic transformation was not the Soviet Union but Russia. This realization could be related to different economic views, and in the autumn of 1991 President Yeltsin was offered economic programmes ranging from the recreation of a Soviet-type economy in Russia to laissez-faire. The previously prominent young economist Grigorii Yavlinskii fell out of the competition by insisting on the preservation of the Soviet Union long after this had ceased to be a feasible option.

The other divide among Russian economists concerned the goal and nature of economic transformation. This was largely a question of something as simple as knowledge of economics. The older generation of Soviet economists of the age above 40 was largely ignorant both of foreign languages and ordinary economics as it is known in the West, being stuck in the mindset of Marxist-Leninist political economy. The good young Russian economists, on the contrary, had learnt English and they had utilized their knowledge to devour Western economics literature largely without assistance from their Soviet professors. As a result, the alienation between the young and old Russian economists was almost complete. The old Russian economic Academicians knew hardly anything of relevance for the transition to capitalism, while their pretences were staggering, pampered as they had been by privileges under the old hierarchical and gerontological system. The young Russian economists realized that neither their number nor their knowledge were sufficient.

The natural consequence was that their Western economist friends, with whom they had kept in touch all along, turned up and offered their assistance, and that assistance was accepted when and where it appeared relevant and appropriate. This volume is one of the many results of this cooperation between the bright young Russian economists who have assumed major government responsibilities and Western economists anxious to support the development of democracy, market economy and private ownership in Russia, that will eventually lead to the kind of social and economic welfare that we are used to in the West. We are convinced that social scientists can and should contribute to the amelioration of society. But should academics run society? Not in general. But academics can be especially useful when a country is about to change track, when its old experiences are of limited relevance for its future course. Russia and Eastern Europe are going through such a period. Domestic and foreign academics can help to suggest what the essentials of the new society should be. When everything is up in the air, it is no easy feat to establish what is cause and what is effect. For instance, should production or prices be stabilized first? In order to answer such a question a proper theory is required and that is indeed the domain of academe. The traditional Russian practitioner would answer that production should be stabilized first, while modern economics of any branch says prices, if extreme inflation is at hand.

Another use of academics is to provide knowledge from other countries and times that is of relevance for the current situation. In the current Russian transition to capitalism, it is particularly important to analyse and draw the appropriate lessons from the attempts at change of economic system in other former socialist countries. Poland has become the most extensive source of relevant experience, because it suffered from a similar degree of destabilization and foreign debt problem and was generally very complicated politically and economically (Lipton and Sachs, 1990; Blanchard et al, 1991; Åslund, 1992c). For fighting hyperinflation, Latin America provides many useful insights. As the change of economic system proceeds, one new problem after another emerges. The immediate question that arises is: Where has such a problem appeared before and what was done to solve it? Applied science should be able to provide the answers to such questions. But if suitable representatives of such knowledge are not at hand, the country tends to go through the same mistakes that other countries.

A third role of foreign academics may sound somewhat surprising, namely to provide insights into the functioning of the old communist economic system. To live in a system is not the same as to understand it, because life and intellectual comprehension are very different things. Arguably, the best analysis of the communist economic system has been written by Janos Kornai (1992), an academic economist from Hungary who has combined his empirical insights into the working of communist societies with his extensive knowledge of Western economic theory. The Marxist-Leninist straitjacket was devastating to social sciences in the USSR. Few economic books were published there that contained fundamental insights. If they were cited, it tended to be as sources of facts on the Soviet Union. Significantly, one of the best Soviet academic books in economics was written by acting Prime Minister Yegor Gaidar (1990).

As it happens, the Western economic advisers who have been involved in the initial stages of the change of economic system combine between them these three kinds of knowledge. The intellectual leadership of Jeffrey Sachs must be recognized as anyone is aware who has worked with him. The status of a foreign economic adviser is so loose, that it can only be maintained if a person can provide useful answers to relevant questions reasonably swiftly. Characteristically, there is a strong US domination and a substantial UK representation among the foreign advisers, with some representatives from Poland and Sweden. Contrary to what many think, we take very different political stands in our own countries. With regard to Russia, however, we have a perfect consensus that our common aim is to assist in taking Russia into the ballpark of market economies as soon as possible. Only later could relatively marginal issues, such as arguments between social democracy and liberalism, take precedence. After the fundamental questions have been answered and the replies transformed into legislation, the demand for independent intellectual advice is likely to fall, and administrators of the ordinary kind are likely to retrieve their tasks from the academics, if the latter have not been transformed into politicians and civil servants.

This book is a joint venture between members of the Russian government and its foreign economic advisers, although we take upon ourselves the full responsibility for the editing. Five of the chapters have been written by senior members of the Russian government, five by foreign economic advisers, while two pertain to other parts of the former Soviet Union. This is certainly a partisan book. The authors of ten of the twelve chapters have been deeply involved in the elaboration of the change of economic system in Russia. We are driven by a belief that it is fully possible to build a democracy and a market economy based on private property in Russia, and this is our great passion. Still, all the authors are also academic economists, who believe in critical analysis, and we have insisted that this must be an academic book. The reader might be surprised by how critical the assessment of the initial reforms is in the first two chapters, but if we do not face up to reality, we shall not be able to correct the many flaws. Has anyone ever thought that the change of economic system in Russia would be a piece of cake? The chapters contain both analysis and policy statements to varying degrees. It is natural that the forward-looking chapters, notably on privatisation, have the form of policy statements. The reader may notice that occasionally the word "we" refers to both the authors and the Russian government, because of the positions the authors occupy.

The book is divided into four parts. The first part is an assessment of the initial reforms; the second part discusses government strategies in broad terms; the third part is devoted to privatisation; while the final part concerns money and foreign trade. Our natural intention has been to focus on key issues of the transition to capitalism. Since we have commissioned the papers, the choice of topics has been in our hands.

Marek Dabrowski provides a broad assessment of the first half year of Russian transformation, looking both into what was intended and what the actual outcome has been. His general assessment is that both the liberalisation and the macroeconomic stabilization have been half-hearted. The concept of the reform was not sufficiently comprehensive and radical, and the outcome has been considerably worse. Dabrowski emphasises that the initial conditions were so difficult that the problems are rather understandable, but many more lessons should have been drawn from the Polish experience.

Anders Åslund starts on the same note, but turns to the question of how prominent academic economists and interest groups have responded to the various problems. The dominant impression is that the vocal opposition has opted for a programme based on a mixture of Marxist remnants, ignorance and populism that would lead to hyperinflation. The only means to curtail these strong pressures appears to be parliamentary elections.

Michael Ellam and *Richard Layard* look into what has happened to the standard of living. They ask why prices have risen so much relative to wages, and why inflation has remained so high. After a thorough statistical investigation, they conclude that a central problem has been insufficient macroeconomic stabilization. Excessive credit emission causes excessive inflation, but also excessive stockbuilding since enterprises are neither forced to sell nor have any positive incentive to do so. The result is that the standard of living falls more than necessary.

Russia's negotiations with the IMF have been controversial. *Alexei V. Mozhin* has been one of the major Russian negotiators. He goes concisely through the main issues at stake during the first half of 1992, looking into the demands of Russia and the IMF, respectively, what commitments Russia made, and to what extent it has complied with them. This lucid exposé does away with many of the myths that have arisen around these negotiations. One of the crucial early disagreements was that Russia insisted on a quick movement to a pegged exchange rate, for which it required a clear statement on a stabilization fund. The IMF finally agreed. Alas, the whole process took too long, and before the exchange rate could be pegged, the whole stabilization effort had been undermined.

To any economist, it is evident that political institutions are vital for any economic accomplishments. *Sergei Vasiliev*, who is head of the Russian government's Working Centre for Economic Reform, is a central strategic thinker in the Russian government. He goes through all the social, political and economic intricacies and his conclusion is that, on the one hand, the preconditions for building a market economy are meagre; on the other hand, there is no alternative to the market economy. Hence, Vasiliev suggests that this contradictory situation will lead to a long-lasting crisis in Russia. In particular, he doubts that macroeconomic stabilization can be successful before substantial institutional changes have been undertaken, including the development of democratic institutions, privatisation and a market infrastructure. He does not believe that this will occur swiftly.

Deputy Prime Minister *Anatoly Chubais* and *Maria Vishnevskaya* present the main features of the Russian privatisation programme. The reader will be struck by the consistency in the government's privatisation policies. This degree of correlation between the government programme, legislation and its implementation is rare in Russia.

Maxim Boycko and *Andrei Shleifer* take up a key part of the privatisation programme, namely the mass privatisation through the free distribution of vouchers to the population. They lead us through the intricate problems of principle involved in voucher privatisation and explain the motive of the choices made by the Russian government. The informed reader will notice the similarities with the Czechoslovak privatisation scheme, but also that the Russian programme has been made simpler and more decentralized for the important reason that the Russian state administration performs worse than the Czechoslovak administration.

Boris G. Fedorov draws on experiences from promoting foreign investment in the St. Petersburg area. This is an insightful empirical study of all the problems that a foreign investment in Russia encounters in the early stage of the transition. But Fedorov also explains how most of these problems can be solved.

The monetary system was one part of the Russian economic system that was much less developed than in Eastern Europe, when the transition to capitalism started there. *Jeffrey Sachs* and *David Lipton* have made a thorough analysis of all the peculiarities of the Russian monetary arrangements in 1992 and suggest comprehensive solutions. A key issue is to clarify the extent of the ruble area and its monetary regime. This substantial article offers the outline of a whole new monetary system for Russia.

At this point, we found it necessary to leave Russia for a digression into Estonia. The reason is that Estonia was the first former Soviet republic to introduce its own fully-independent currency. *Ardo Hansson* who was a member of the three-man monetary reform committee in Estonia clarifies the principles, the implementation and the tentative outcome of the Estonian monetary reform and draws out the broader lessons from the Estonian experience for other former Soviet republics.

Our second digression outside Russia takes us to Ukraine. We find it of vital importance to understand how this multitude of new commercial banks actually function, and it appeared to be much easier to get a proper empirical overview in Kiev than in Moscow with its 500 commercial banks. This pioneering study has been carried out by *Simon Johnson*, *Heidi Kroll* and *Mark Horton*. Are the new commercial banks real banks or Potemkin villages? Not surprisingly, the answer turns out to be that they are a bit of both, and that they fall into different categories, some of which are more like banks and other that are more like channels of cheap government money to parasitic state enterprises.

In 1992, an overwhelming pessimism has prevailed over Russia's ability to boost its exports in the near future. However, in Eastern Europe, we have seen how one country after the other has swiftly seen its exports surge after a change of economic system. *Peter Boone* has looked into these experiences. With more formal economics than in the other papers and a scrutiny of the statistics, he has made a quantitative assessment of Russia's balance of payments prospects. He concludes that they look pretty reassuring, if only the reform programme is implemented as planned.

At present it would be foolhardy to claim that the Russian economic reform has been a success. But even so a lot has been achieved. However things turn out in the future, it is important to assess clearly the outcome of the first phase, and to understand how some of the key policy-makers were thinking at the time.

Anders Åslund, Richard Layard
Stockholm, Moscow, London

References

Åslund, Anders (ed.) (1992a) *The Post-Soviet Economy: Soviet and Western Perspectives*, London, Pinter.
Åslund, Anders (1992b) 'A Critique of Soviet Reform Plans' in Åslund (1992a), pp. 167-180.
Åslund, Anders (1992c) *Post-Communist Economic Revolutions: How Big a Bang?*, Washington, DC, Center for Strategic and International Studies.
Blanchard, Olivier, Rudiger Dornbusch, Paul Krugman, Richard Layard and Lawrence Summers (1991) *Reform in Eastern Europe*, London, MIT Press.
Gaidar, Yegor T. (1990) *Ekonomicheskie reformy i ierarkhicheskie struktury*, Moscow, Nauka.
Kornai, Janos (1992) *The Socialist System. The Political Economy of Communism*, Princeton, N.J., Princeton University Press.
Lipton, David, and Jeffrey Sachs (1990) 'Creating a Market in Eastern Europe: The Case of Poland', *Brookings Papers on Economic Activity*, no. 1, pp. 75-147.
Peck, Merton J., and Thomas J. Richardson (eds.) (1991) *What Is To Be Done? Proposals for the Soviet Transition to the Market*, New Haven and London, Yale University Press.
Yeltsin, Boris N. (1991) 'Vystuplenie B. N. El'tsina', *Sovetskaya Rossiya*, 29 October, pp. 1, 3.

Note

[1] The first important conference occurred in Györ in Hungary in 1988. In 1990 and 1991 a number of important conferences took place, notably in Sopron in Hungary (organized by the International Institute for Applied Systems Analysis in Vienna; Peck et al, 1991) and in Kiel in Germany at the Institute of the World Economy in June 1991. Possibly the most immediate precursor of the new Russian government and its programme was the conference held at the Stockholm Institute of Soviet and East European Economics in June 1991 (Åslund, 1992). The cooperative project that attracted the greatest public attention was the 'Grand Bargain' that was worked out in Cambridge, Massachusetts, in the summer of 1991. Its Soviet side was headed by Grigorii Yavlinskii and no single person from his team joined the new Russian government. However, two leading Western economists in this undertaking, Jeffrey Sachs and David Lipton, became advisers to the new Russian government.

Part I
Assessment of the Initial Reforms

1 The First Half-Year of Russian Transformation

Marek Dabrowski

In the beginning of November 1991, the new Russian government started its policy of radical economic reforms. Its declared aims were the transformation from planned to a market economy and macroeconomic stabilization. This paper will examine the first half-year of the Russian transformation. I shall discuss the economic and political conditions at the outset, the different possible approaches to reform that were available, the results of the first stage of the reform process, the situation in spring 1992, and possible scenarios for the future. Having the advantage of being an active participant in the Polish transformation process[1], I shall analyse the Russian course of events from the point of view of the Polish experience. Therefore I shall try to compare the initial conditions in Russia with those in Poland, and, formulate a few lessons Russia can take from Poland's experience and finally show how the current Polish debate can be illuminated by the Russian experience.

Economic conditions at the outset of reform

The economic conditions in which the Russian transformation was to begin in the autumn of 1991 were extremely difficult. The economy of the former USSR and of the Russian Federation was in the deep disintegration typical of most post-communist countries in Central and Eastern Europe. In such an economy the central planning system has already ceased to work as a mechanism of microeconomic discipline and macroeconomic coordination. Nor has a new market mechanism yet assumed this role. We have the typical syndrome of a non-planned, non-market economy, without sufficient microeconomic motivation or the means to achieve elementary macroeconomic equilibrium. Moreover, the government is weak in the sense that it does not have political support, and it is prepared to buy temporary social peace in exchange for inflationary money. This scenario is not unique to the former USSR in 1989-1991. It was also evident in Poland in 1987-1989, in Romania after the collapse of Nicolae Ceausescu's dictatorship, in Bulgaria, and in Albania. Only East Germany, Hungary, and Czechoslovakia were able to avoid macroeconomic chaos in the transition period.

The last two years of the former USSR were marked by a constant decline in output and an uncontrolled increase of the monetary overhang. In the past the money supply in the Soviet economy (as in other countries with traditional command economy) was permanently excessive by standards of a normal market economy. For example, in 1981-85 the average annual rate of growth of the money supply (M2, measured as cash, plus current and deposit accounts) amounted to 7.5 per cent (IMF et al., 1990, p. 49).

This excessive supply of money combined with predominantly fixed prices contributed to the repressed inflation and forced savings, which seem to be a quite normal phenomenon in a traditional command economy. In the former USSR, however, the level of repressed inflation was probably traditionally higher than in some other socialist countries like the GDR, Czechoslovakia and Hungary. The monetary overhang was mitigated to some extent by the internal (or commodity) inconvertibility of the ruble, especially in the enterprise sphere, because of the thorough rationing system with administrative allocation of material resources and investment goods, as well as rigid monitoring of different kinds of expenditures (such as the wage fund, investment money, etc.) of state-owned enterprises (McKinnon, 1991).

In the second half of the 1980s the monetary disequilibrium started to worsen gradually. The traditional discipline of the central plan began to crumble because of the partial political and economic liberalisation of the perestroika period. The money supply also increased. According to IMF estimates, the M2 annual rate of growth was 8.5 per cent in 1986, 14.7 per cent in 1987, 14.1 per cent in 1988, 14.8 per cent in 1989, and 15.3 per cent in 1990 (IMF et al., 1990, p. 49). The rising fiscal deficit was the main reason for this monetary expansion. It amounted to 2.4 per cent of GDP in 1985, 6.2 per cent in 1986, 8.4 per cent in 1987, 9.2 per cent in 1988, and 8.5 per cent in 1989 (IMF et al., 1990, p. 10).

At the same time, partial economic liberalisation increased the level of internal convertibility of the ruble (by giving enterprises more flexibility in using their financial assets), thus increasing money velocity. This is also a standard effect of the deregulation of the traditional socialist economic system (McKinnon, 1991).

The second half of the 1980s was also a time of significant deterioration of external balances. Current account balance in convertible currencies had been positive until 1988 (US$ 2.3. bn in 1986, US$ 6.7 bn. in 1987 and US$ 1.6 bn. in 1988), but decreased radically in 1989 (US$ 3.8 bn.) and in 1990 (US$ 10.7 bn.) (IMF et al., 1990, p. 10). Consequently, the gross external debt rose from US$ 28.9 bn. in 1985 to US$ 54.0 bn. in 1989 (ibid., p. 50). These developments were connected both with the growing level of internal macroeconomic disequilibrium (budget deficit and monetary expansion) and with the sharply worsening terms of trade, especially on the oil market (IMF et al., 1990, p. 50). Declining oil export revenues and oil profits, resulting from a steady decrease in oil production, also contributed to fiscal difficulties since oil exports had been a significant source of budget revenue.

The level of repressed inflation continued to increase because of monetary expansion, increasing money in circulation, and the continuing price controls. Until the beginning of 1991 the official consumer price index (CPI) was rather stable. The CPI in state retail trade rose by 2.4 per cent in 1989 and 5.2 per cent in 1990.

The retail price increase in co-operative trade was recorded as 0.5 per cent in 1989 and 5.2 per cent in 1990. The same indicators for the kolkhoz market were 7.4 per cent in 1989 and 34.3 per cent in 1990 (IMF, 1992, table 11). These figures illustrate indirectly the increasing level of repressed inflation and forced savings. Carlo Cottarelli and Mario I. Blejer considered that "at the end of 1990 the amount of wealth accumulated in monetary form by Soviet households as a result of forced savings was around 170-190 billion rubles, close to 20 percent of GDP and around one third of the existing financial assets" (Cottarelli and Blejer, 1991).

After 1 April 1991, and the price reform of Valentin Pavlov,[2] inflation started to have a more open form. The average price level in state retail trade was 89.5 per cent higher in 1991 than in 1990, and the state retail price index rose by 146.1 per cent from December 1990 to December 1991. The consolidated retail price index rose by 152.1 per cent, and the kolkhoz market price index by 281.2 per cent (IMF, 1992, table 11). Inflation (and later hyperinflation) in the second half of 1991 showed up partly in the form of open price increases, partly in the form of rising market shortages.

The rising budget deficit, financed exclusively by credit from the USSR State Bank (Gosbank) was a key cause of hyperinflation in 1991. According to IMF estimates, the total budget deficit of the Russian Federation in 1991 (including the consequences of taking responsibility for the former all-union budget) reached a level of 31 per cent of GDP (IMF, 1992, p. 13). The sources of this huge fiscal deficit were ever-increasing state subsidies to support administratively controlled prices, the decrease of output, and poor tax discipline.

This weakening of the financial discipline at the micro level brought about the fast growth of nominal and the "real" wages in the second half of 1991. In the last quarter of 1991 the "real" wage in industry was 33 per cent higher than its average level in 1990 (IMF, 1992, p. 11).[3] This contributed to the significant decrease in the real profits of enterprises.

In the years of perestroika, the economic growth of the USSR and the Russian Federation was lower than in the preceding decades and was gradually decreasing. The net material product (NMP) of Russia increased only by 2.4 per cent in 1986, 0.7 per cent in 1987, 4.5 per cent in 1988, and 1.9 per cent in 1989. In 1990 the NMP started to decrease: by 3.6 per cent in 1990 and by 11.0 per cent in 1991 (preliminary estimates, see IMF, 1992, table 4). In the same period, gross industrial output grew by 4.5 per cent in 1986, 3.5 per cent in 1987, 3.8 per cent in 1988, 1.4 per cent in 1989, and fell by 0.1 per cent in 1990 and 8.0 per cent in 1991 (IMF, 1992, table 5).

The main reasons for the 1990-1991 recession were the crisis of the central planning system, the motivational crisis in state-owned enterprises, the disintegration of trade relations between Eastern European countries after the collapse of CMEA, as well as the gradual weakening of trade links between former USSR republics. After the political dictatorship and terror were gradually dismantled under perestroika, the system of central planning lost its capacity to mobilise resources for economic growth. For example, the rate of investment decreased in the second half of the 1980s. Also lost was the ability to guarantee elementary macroeconomic balance and microeconomic discipline. The deep recession in the former USSR supports the hypothesis that a deep fall in output is unavoidable in post-communist economies even before the start of a real stabilization and liberalisation.

Russia's starting point: similarities and differences with Poland in 1989

Many Russian politicians and economists as well as foreign observers and advisers tend to view market reforms in Russia as an imitation of Balcerowicz's programme in Poland. One of the aims of this paper is to examine this popular view. I shall try to answer two questions: is Russia really following the Polish way, and can Russia copy the Polish experience? Let us look at how Gaidar's starting point was similar to that of Balcerowicz. The main economic similarity seems be the deep macroeconomic disequilibrium (Poland in 1989 and the USSR in 1991) which had almost the same source in both countries. However, the extent of the budget deficit and monetary imbalance in the former USSR at the end of 1991 was worse than in Poland in September 1989. The major difference is the level of "marketisation" of both economies. In 1989 the Polish economy had already seen eight years of semi-market reforms. These reforms were not effective from a macro- or micro-economic point of view. They nevertheless created portions of a market infrastructure and prepared the Polish society for the new rules of game. At this time, Poland already showed the strong beginnings of a private sector. This was evident even outside of agriculture, which in 1989 made up 28 per cent of GDP. (Polish agriculture was never collectivised.) Russia and the other CIS states have no significant capitalist traditions. On the contrary, for 60 years they have lived under a rigid planning system. This is an important difference from Poland and other Central and Eastern European countries.

Turning to the political aspects, both the Mazowiecki government in Poland and Boris Yeltsin's cabinet in Russia were the first non-communist, democratic organs of executive power in these countries. The revolutionary atmosphere after the collapse of the coup d'etat in Russia in August 1991 was not unlike the political atmosphere in Poland after the "Solidarity" victory in the June 1989 general elections.

Tadeusz Mazowiecki's government received nearly the full support of all serious political parties and movements in Poland. His cabinet was able to create national unity around the programme of economic and political reform, partly by virtue of Solidarity's political position and influence. This atmosphere lived on until the summer of 1990 when the "War at the Top" and the presidential election campaign started to dissolve the post-Solidarity political camp.

In Russia, strong political and intellectual opposition against market-oriented reforms appeared at the very beginning, and has been stronger than in Poland. The Yeltsin-Gaidar government has met strong resistance to its programme both in the Supreme Soviet and in the Congress of People's Deputies.

The new Russian government also inherited a powerful industrial and agricultural bureaucracy from the old command system. In Poland this bureaucracy gradually lost political influence during the semi-market reforms in the 1980s. Thus the number of industrial ministries in Poland had been decreased to 3 in 1981, and to one Ministry of Industry in 1987. Traditional industrial trusts (ob"edinenie) were abolished in 1982 and replaced primarily by voluntary associations, and sometimes by compulsory ones. But even these were phased out from 1987 to the first half of 1989. After eight years of partial labour-management in state-owned enterprises, the state and party bureaucracy were no longer capable of interfering in the day-to-day activities of enterprises to the same extent as earlier. During these eight years economic actors had the opportunity to gain a certain market mentality. When Balcerowicz's programme was put into action at the end of 1989, resistance from the old apparatus was no longer the main political barrier to reform. Nevertheless, it still existed, and it created constant interventionist pressure (Dabrowski, 1992a).

In Russia this anti-reform lobby is considerably stronger than it was in Poland in 1989. The process of concentration of many industrial ministries in Russia really got started in the autumn of 1991 when the "reform" cabinet was nominated. Even after this, and after the dissolution of the all-union government, the number of different sectoral ministries and committees remains higher than in Poland, Czechoslovakia or Hungary. Some ministries such as the Ministry of the Economy, Ministry of Trade, and Ministry of Foreign Economic Cooperation are heavily involved in protecting the structures and instruments inherited from the previous system. At the end of May and the beginning of June 1992, three rather conservative (in the Russian sense) representatives were appointed to positions as new industrial Deputy Prime Ministers, creating a fear that the anti-reform lobby would gain hold inside government.

Different branch structures such as trusts, concerns, and associations still survive, and they provide an organisational base for various lobbies, which are very active in the Russian parliament. The military-industrial complex seems to be the most influential lobby on this scene. Old staff in the state administration also continue to play an important role.

The Yeltsin-Gaidar government has also met with difficulties that Poland luckily did not have. First, the political crisis of the former Soviet Union and the problem of cooperation between the former Soviet republics have seriously hampered macroeconomic policy-making in the first half-year of the Russian transition. Until the beginning of 1992 nobody knew who was responsible for the monetary and fiscal policy on the former USSR territory.

Neither the "nationalisation" of the former USSR Gosbank by Russia nor the decision to grant to the Central Bank of Russia the role of a central monetary authority over the ruble area have solved all these problems. Up to mid-June 1992 the coordination of the monetary, fiscal, trade and custom policies inside the ruble area has been too loose to guarantee a stable macroeconomic policy and effective market transformation.

This political situation has created a very strange monetary system - a monetary union of 15 independent states with 15 independent central banks who are not willing to cooperate between themselves (see Sachs and Lipton, 1992). Many trade barriers, mostly illegal, still exist between CIS countries, contributing to the economic disintegration of the ruble area. It seems that the lingering mentality of the shortage economy is the main cause of these continued barriers.

Second, the Russian government is also faced with serious inter-ethnic conflicts both inside the Russian Federation and in the other CIS countries, undermining these countries' political and economic stability. The Russian federal system too is a source of many political problems.

Alternative concepts of reform

As the authors of the EPICENTR report (Yavlinskii et al., 1992) correctly noted, the Yeltsin-Gaidar cabinet never published any clear formulation of the government programme. President Boris Yeltsin and Vice-Prime Minister Yegor Gaidar had only made general statements in their public presentations. But this is not to say that the new government had no comprehensive concept for economic reform at the onset. Indeed, the concept was drafted by Gaidar's "team" just before its nomination to government. In October and early November 1991, a special working group, appointed by President Yeltsin and headed by Gaidar, gathered in a government dacha in Arkhangelskoe (near Moscow) to perform this task.

Stabilisation and Reforms, the name of the unofficial working document prepared by this special group (Russian Government, 1991), proposed a gradual stabilization and liberalisation package to be implemented over the course of one year. In the first stage, most prices were to be deregulated and foreign economic relations were to be partially liberalised: foreign exchange auctions were to be introduced, and export and import transactions were to be partially liberalised. However, this was to be done without convertibility for the ruble and without a unified exchange rate. After 8-9 months, the next stage of reform was to be implemented, namely, currency reform. A new Russian ruble convertible to Western currencies was to be introduced.

The group's proposal was widely criticised by foreign experts, including this author (Dabrowski, 1991b) on the following counts:

First, the proposal aimed to transform hidden (repressed) hyperinflation into open hyperinflation for a period of at least half a year, risking that inflation would get out of control altogether.

Second, under hyperinflation, the indexation of wages and other incomes creates a very strong inflationary thrust making it difficult to break the hyperinflationary spiral.

Third, a longer transition period means that undesirable compromises must be made, such as maintaining the system of administrative allocation of resources.

Fourth, the continuing macroeconomic crisis, combined with plans to

7

introduce the new currency will contribute to the disintegration of the ruble area, which can run counter to the economic and political interests of Russia.

Fifth, currency reform is a very complicated operation technically, and very risky politically. Reducing effective nominal money balances through currency reform, while it is a frequently used means of monetary adjustment in countries with hyperinflation (Dornbusch, 1991, pp. 174-176), seems difficult, given the current Russian circumstances.

Sixth, political and social support for a new government will not be long-lived. Therefore it is better to apply one big shock than a series of shocks over an extended period. Otherwise, the government may lose political support before embarking on the decisive phase of monetary reform. Moreover, gradual implementation of reform can provide the traditional bureaucracy with a better opportunity to consolidate anti-reform forces.

The concept Gaidar and his colleagues sought to follow was the Polish transformation step-by-step. First, partial liberalisation and the "opening" of repressed inflation would take place, as under the Rakowski government from the end of 1988 until August of 1989. Only afterwards would they move on to full liberalisation, monetary and fiscal adjustment, and the introduction of current account convertibility, as in Balcerowicz's programme (see Dabrowski 1991a, pp. 121-122). However, it is important to note that this sequence of events in Poland was a result of the political situation rather than of a conscious plan for transformation. Moreover, Poland had certain political reserves: Mazowiecki's government was available to start the second, decisive stage of liberalisation and transformation. Russia seems to be in another situation — the first post-communist government is already under fire.

Most foreign experts (Dabrowski 1991b) advised implementing one single complex shock operation which would contain:

1) Elimination of the huge monetary overhang through price liberalisation and restrictive monetary policy.
2) Deregulation of prices for all goods and services except railway and electricity rates and housing rents. However, prices remaining under administrative control should be increased significantly.
3) Elimination of the budget deficit through a sharp reduction of subsidies (made possible by price liberalisation) and comprehensive tax reform.
4) Unification of the exchange rate, introduction of current account convertibility for the ruble, and radical liberalisation of foreign trade.
5) Massive demonopolisation of industry and trade, including the administrative "de-concentration" of all cartel-like branch organisa-

tions, free entry for all enterprises to each specific product market, and elimination of all existing barriers to enterpreneurship.

Incomes policy was a controversial point in discussions among experts. A number of them, like Stanislaw Gomulka and Richard Layard (see Gomulka, 1991), considering Polish experience, proposed to retain wage control using tax instruments. Other advisers, such as Jacek Rostowski and this author, were more hesitant about recommending incomes policy in Russian circumstances.

Results of the first half-year

Starting at the end of November 1991 the Yeltsin-Gaidar cabinet began to implement measures for liberalisation and stabilization. But despite the warnings of foreign experts, the scenario of gradual changes proposed in the *Stabilisation and Reforms* document was chosen. The one important deviation from this proposal was the abandonment of the currency reform idea. Instead, they intended to tackle monetary adjustment through a corrective inflation.

The results of this policy seem to confirm my reservations regarding the two-stage scenario. By mid-June 1992 Russia had accomplished only a partial domestic liberalisation, and neither monetary stabilization nor the elimination of the shortage economy had taken place.

Price liberalisation

The main effort in the first half-year was focused on price liberalisation, a crucial step on the way to a market economy. This is a very difficult operation politically, especially difficult in a country like Russia where for sixty years almost all prices have been controlled by the government. The liberalisation of prices at the beginning of January 1992 was extensive, but in June 1992 it is still not complete. Two important targets have yet to be achieved, namely, the elimination of a shortage economy and the introduction of market allocation of goods.

Unpublished statistical data from the Centre for Economic Reform of the Russian Government show that most food products became more readily available in retail trade in February and March of 1992 compared to the last months of 1991. However, the number of cities with shortages of specific goods was still high. A survey of 132 cities taken on 25 February 1992, when the market situation was at its best for the first half of 1992, shows that specific shortages were experienced. Three per cent of cities had a shortage of eggs, 4.5 per cent of milk, and 9 per cent of potatoes. Moreover, in more than 50 per cent of cities, acute shortages existed in the case of wheat flour, macaroni, rice, rye bread, cheese, milk powder, tinned fish, and sweets. According to the same data, from the end of February to the end of May, the situation *per saldo* did not improve. In the case of some goods (meat, milk and some flour products) the number of cities with shortages decreased slightly. However there are also product markets (especially for fruits and vegetables) where the situation worsened since the end of February.

Turning to the allocation mechanism, we can still observe the administrative system of goods rationing, compulsory regional and inter-enterprise barter, and different forms of inter-regional trade restrictions (Yavlinskii et al., 1992). This situation should be viewed as evidence of the survival of the shortage economy and of the shortage mentality among economic actors.

There are many reasons why the shortage economy lingers on. First, not all prices were deregulated, in particular oil and energy prices, and transport rates. Second, administrative control of many prices (bread, milk, margarine, and some transport rates) was simply decentralised to the local level (Yavlinskii et al., 1992). Third, anti-monopoly price controls are repeatedly applied too widely. Fourth, monopolist producers are not interested in selling at market equilibrium prices. They prefer barter transactions and "producer diktat". Fifth, high inflation and powerful inflationary expectations have stimulated speculative behaviour (hoarding goods in expectation of price increases). An accommodating monetary policy reinforces such behaviour.

Far more limited results have been accomplished in the external liberalisation. Most import barriers have been removed, and all enterprises have had access to foreign currency through the auction system, direct transactions with exporters, or central allocation. But the Russian economy in the first half of 1992 was still a closed economy. The main reason was the extremely high exchange rate of the US dollar (and other convertible currencies) vis-a-vis the ruble.

The overvaluation of the US dollar against the ruble has been caused by several factors. First, expansionary monetary policy has undermined faith in the ruble. Second, the system of multiple exchange rates has caused the main free-market exchange rate to rise further than it otherwise would. Third, many export barriers such as export duties, regulations requiring enterprises to surrender part of their foreign currency, export licences, and quotas have limited possible export revenues and worsened the current account balance of the Russian economy. On the other hand, the real overvaluation of the dollar has been decreasing since December 1991. The free market nominal exchange rate of the ruble was rather stable from the beginning of 1992 to the middle of the year, while domestic prices and wages increased several times during this period.

Fiscal policy

A second area where relative success has been achieved, at least in the first quarter of 1992, is in fiscal policy. In this period the cash deficit of the consolidated state budget did not exceed 2 per cent of GDP if one uses the official Russian methodology (data of the Ministry of Finance of the Russian Federation). According to international statistical methods the level of the first quarter deficit is higher - about 5-6 per cent of GDP. This is still not high compared to the situation in 1991 (especially in the fourth quarter). Moreover, according to the official reports of the Ministry of Finance, the budget was almost balanced in April 1992 as well. However, some negative signals in this area are evident for the future, namely, a number of wage concessions in the budgetary sphere and tax exemptions (see below). The government did not pay all its obligations in the first months, and thus part of them will have to be paid later.

The second accomplishment in the area of fiscal policy is in comprehensive tax reform. On 1 January 1992 the Russian government introduced an entire package of tax instruments typical to a real market economy: a value-added tax, an excise tax, personal income taxes, and corporate income taxes — an impressive achievement from a legislative point of view! But the organisational difficulties of tax collection remain unsolved. The Russian tax authorities have had great difficulties trying to collect VAT and export duties for the first months of 1992. The problem of tax collectibility can become more dramatic in the future when privatisation and demonopolisation will have advanced further. Here also there are lessons to be learned from Polish experience.

The tax policy has other weak points. First, there is poor coordination between CIS states, especially in VAT collection. Second, the government often gives in to pressure for tax exemptions. This is an unfortunate ailment of the late communist economy, and it is now threatening Russian public finances. New tax exemptions were allowed at an increasing pace in the second quarter of 1992, as a direct result of several political concessions of the government towards the industrial and agricultural lobby. Third, the VAT rate is extremely high (28 per cent) in comparison with other countries, where the maximum does not usually exceed 20 per cent. This high rate makes it even more difficult to withstand pressure for exemptions. It would be desirable to decrease this rate to around 20 per cent in the near future.

Monetary policy

Given the absence of wage control and of a fixed exchange rate, monetary policy should play a key role in the stabilization process. Aside from these two potential nominal anchors, the Russian government has only one feasible option for stabilization - a money-based orthodox program.

According to the monetary statistics of the Central Bank of Russia, money supply was truly restrictive only in January 1992. From February 1992 both base money (see table 1) and M3 began to grow quickly again. In the balance sheet of the Central Bank of Russia, credits to commercial banks, net credit to the government, and credit to other republics (through their correspondent accounts in the Central Bank of Russia) were the main sources of base money increase. In the consolidated balance sheet of the commercial banks, the rapid increase of short-term credits to enterprises is the cause of monetary expansion (see table 2).

Table 1 Base money December 1991-April 1992

Date	Amount in bn rubles	1 Jan 1991 =100	Previous month = 100
1 Dec 91	301	100.0	x
1 Jan 92	382	126.9	126.9
1 Feb 92	327	108.9	85.6
1 Mar 92	451	149.8	137.9
1 Apr 92	617	205.0	136.8
1 May 92	832	276.4	134.8

Source: monetary statistics of Central Bank of Russia

Table 2 Short term credits of commercial banks

Date	Amount in bn rubles	1 Jan 91 = 100	Previous month = 100
1 Dec 91	366	100.0	x
1 Jan 92	394	107.7	107.7
1 Feb 92	474	129.5	120.3
1 Mar 92	635	173.5	133.9
1 Apr 92	767	209.6	120.8
1 May 92	848	231.7	110.6

Source: monetary statistics of Central Bank of Russia

This is a reaction to the rapid increase of inter-enterprise arrears and to a kind of political hysteria connected with these arrears.

The result of fluctuations in monetary policy is the continuing high inflation rate of 10-20 per cent monthly, shortages of goods, the passive market behaviour of most state enterprises, and the overvaluation of the dollar. The latter problem is also compounded by a negative real interest rate. While the nominal interest rate was increased gradually from 6-9 per cent a year at the end of 1991 to 20 per cent in January, 50 per cent in April, and 80 per cent in May 1992, it is still considerably lower than the level of inflation. It is not enough to increase the demand for domestic money balances and to limit the demand for credit. The increase in reserve requirements to 20 per cent for demand deposits and to 15 per cent for time deposits also came relatively late - at the beginning of April 1992. All these attempts at discipline, however, are repeatedly being undermined by political pressure for special credit lines to specific sectors and industries, such as the agro-industrial complex and the energy sector. A number of decisions taken in the end of May 1992 on these matters could be a dangerous precedent.

The huge shortage of cash is yet another aspect of the monetary problem. It was brought on by several factors: the huge credit expansion, and some technical and organisational mistakes, including the Supreme Soviet's refusal to print banknotes of higher denominations at the end of 1991. The government must begin to ration cash between CIS states and regions of Russian Federation as a means of political bargaining and pressure. The cash shortage has been disastrous for the effecting of monetary settlements. The black market exchange rate of the cash ruble against the credit ruble was as high as 1: 2 in some regions at the end of May. Some other CIS states such as Ukraine and Belarus have introduced coupons as money surrogates, which has compounded the monetary and trade disintegration of the former USSR territory. The Russian government must also give special compensation to employees who have not received their wages and salaries on time.

Two scenarios of further developments

After half a year of economic transformation the Russian government must again make a fundamental choice — either to quickly make a decisive stabilization effort or to continue a policy of "controlled" high inflation. The two other options are: to accept open hyperinflation or to return to overall price and wage control (Russian Government, 1992). Neither of these scenarios are desirable and should not be considered. Both economic theory and the empirical experience of other countries tell us that only through quick and consequent stabilization can the Russian economy change into a real market system and have a lasting recovery. Nevertheless, there are some Russian economists and politicians who would rather see a variant of "controlled" inflation for a longer period, such as a year (Yasin, 1992).

A few good arguments against a scenario of "controlled" inflation come to mind. The danger of indexation, inflationary inertia, and political impatience were named above. In addition, high inflation is very difficult to stabilise, especially in a post-communist economy. At any moment it can turn into hyperinflation. It is also naive to expect that chronic high inflation can protect an economy from deep recession, enable state enterprises to adjust to the new market economy, or stimulate private enterpreneurship. Instead, it would be likely to prolong uncompetitiveness and pathological behaviour. It would make it very difficult to introduce effective current account convertibility for the ruble. All chances of reaching an agreement with the IMF and receiving Western financial support would probably be forfeited.

The road to quick stabilization must start, however, by solving the crucial economic and political problems. The first of these is to quickly reach an agreement with the other CIS states and with the Baltic states to either form a coordinated monetary policy inside the ruble area, or to divorce these states from the ruble (Sachs and Lipton, 1992). The second task is to liberalize oil and energy prices. Third, negotiations with the IMF must be completed quickly to make a stand-by loan and stabilization fund available to the Russian Central Bank and the government of Russia. Fourth, monetary policy, and also to some extent fiscal policy, needs significant tightening, which is closely dependent on the previous point.

Polish and Russian transformation: mutual lessons

Although there are many differences in the economic and political conditions for transition to a market economy in these two countries, Polish experience can be very useful for Russian reformers. The limited scope of this paper does not allow a comprehensive analysis, but I shall name a few specific conclusions.

First, it is important to make optimum use of the "political credit" and time given to the reform government to go as far as possible in reform policy. This amount of political credit is only available to the first really post-communist government, and it lasts for a limited time only. This necessitates shock therapy rather than a gradualist approach.

Second, the Polish experience shows that most of the painful decisions should be built into the initial decisive stabilization and liberalisation package. There are plenty of examples where important reforms were put aside in the end of 1989, and have still not been implemented. These postponements have in turn delayed necessary budgetary policy changes and structural reforms. I have in mind reforms such as the deregulation of the coal, energy, and transport industries, of the housing sector, wage indexation in the "budgetary sphere", and elimination of several branch privileges.

Third, monetary policy plays an absolutely crucial role in the process of stabilization and liberalisation. There is a lesson to be gained here from the Czechoslovakian experience of 1991. The importance of incomes policy (wage control) is rather secondary and controversial from a microeconomic point of view. But, the refinance interest rate of the central bank is a key instrument of monetary adjustment in a post-communist economy, at least in the first stage of transition. The high nominal interest rate in the first two months of Balcerowicz's pro-gramme, together with the radical fiscal adjustment were the main rea-sons for the success of the stabilization effort in early 1990. The lack of similar measures in Russia has made the Russian results far more limited.

Fourth, if drastic anti-inflationary measures are relaxed too early, the results of stabilization can be quickly undermined. Take, for example, the Polish experience from the second half of 1990 (Dabrowski, 1992b) when monetary, fiscal and income policies were relaxed too early and brought on the next wave of inflation.

Fifth, it is absolutely necessary to adopt a long-term approach in fiscal and other accompanying policies (especially in the social safety net). The main budgetary troubles will come in the second and third year of the transition process.

Sixth, macroeconomic stabilization and domestic liberalisation must be combined with at least current account convertibility and with signif-icant external liberalisation. Otherwise results will be limited.

Seventh, Central and Eastern European experience so far shows that deep recession is unavoidable after the collapse of a Communist eco-nomic system, even without stabilization and external liberalisation measures. There are no trade-offs between recession and inflation. Deep institutional changes and quick privatisation, while they do not bring immediate results, appear to be the only way out of a transformation depression.

Eighth, Polish, East German and Hungarian experience also prove the necessity of pragmatic, non-ideological attitudes toward privatisation. A multi-facetted approach, with a significant role for decentralised deci-sion-making, seems to bring faster privatisation. Russia still has a chance of avoiding some of Poland's mistakes made in the first year of the Balcerowicz programme.

And finally, Russian experience has at least one lesson to offer Poland. Many Polish economists and politicians still argue that Balcerowicz's programme was too restrictive in the sphere of monetary, fiscal and incomes policy, and that this made the recession unnecessarily deep (Kolodko, 1992). These critics of Balcerowicz's policy argue that a softer stabilization package with more gradual liberalisation, especially in the external sphere, and with more government interventionism, would have given better results in terms of the level of the GDP, and no worse results in terms of macroeconomic equilibrium. The results of the Russian transformation in the first half of 1992 cast great doubt on this approach. In fact, this kind of gradualism can only lead to a closed economy with continued high inflation and the lingering traits of a shortage economy, coupled with deep recession and growing social impatience. The critical task of reform is to radically change market behaviour and the economic mentality, and this task still lies ahead.

References

Cottarelli, Carlo, and Mario I. Blejer (1991) 'Forced Savings and Repressed Inflation in the Soviet Union: Some Empirical Results' (IMF Working Paper, June), Washington D.C.

Dabrowski, Marek (1991a) 'The Polish Stabilisation Programme: Accomplishments and Prospects', *Communist Economies and Economic Transformation*, 3:1, pp. 121-133.

Dabrowski, Marek (1991b) 'Stabilizatsiya i liberalizatsiya rossiiskoi ekonomiki. Skorost' i sekventsiya nuzhnykh shagov' (unpublished memo), Moscow, 15 November.

Dabrowski, Marek (1992a) 'Interventionist Pressures on a Policy Maker During the Transition to Economic Freedom (Personal Experience)', *Communist Economies and Economic Transformation*, 4: 1, pp. 59-73.

Dabrowski, Marek (1992b) 'The Polish Stabilisation 1990-1991', *Journal of International and Comparative Economics* (JOICE), 1 (forthcoming).

Dornbusch, Rudiger (1991) 'Strategies and Priorities for Reform' i P. Marer and S. Zecchini, eds., *The Transition to a Market Economy*, Paris: OECD, vol. I, pp. 169-183.

Gomulka, Stanislaw (1991), 'The "Gaidar Plan" and the "Letter of Intent"', (unpublished memo), Moscow, 4 December.

IMF, The World Bank, OECD and EBRD (1990), *The Economy of the USSR. Summary and Recommendation* (A study undertaken in response to a request by the Houston Summit), 19 December.

IMF (1992), *Economic Review. Russian Federation*, Washington D.C., April

Kolodko, Grzegorz W.(1991) 'Transition from Socialism & Stabilization Policies: The Polish Experience', IMF Seminar Paper, Washington D.C., 11 June.

McKinnon, Ronald I.(1991) 'Financial Control in the Transition from Classical Socialism to a Market Economy'. (Paper prepared for the IPR-IRIS Conference "The Transition to a Market Economy - Institutional Aspects"), Prague, 24-27 March.

Russian Government (1991) 'Stabilizatsiya i reformy. Ekonomicheskaya politika Rossii v perekhodnii period (noyabr' 1991- dekabr' 1992 gg).' (unpublished working document), Moscow, November.

Russian Government (1992) 'Srednesrochnaya programma (kontseptsiya)', (unpublished working document), Moscow, May.

Sachs, Jeffrey, and David Lipton (1992) 'Making the Rouble Area Work' (unpublished memo), 11 May.

Yasin, Evgenii G. (1992) 'Liberalizatsiya i stabilizatsiya ekonomiki' (unpublished manuscript), Moscow 11 May.

Yavlinskii, Grigorii A. et al. (1992) 'Reformy v Rossii, vesna-92', *Moskovskie novosti*, no. 21, pp. 9-16.

Notes

1 From 15 September 1989 until 21 September 1990 I held the position of a Secretary of State in the Ministry of Finance (First Deputy Minister of Finance). Since April 1991 I hold the post of Chairman of the Council of Ownership Changes, advisory body to the Prime Minister of Poland. Since 25 November 1991 I have been a member of the Sejm (the lower house of the Polish parliament).

2 It was in principle the typical administrative price reform, but with some liberalisation components, especially in the sphere of producer goods. In the subsequent months, effective price control weakened due to the political decomposition of the all-union government.

3 I use quotation marks around the word "real" to show that I mean it in the formal, statistical sense. In reality the increase of "real" wages does not produce an equal increase in welfare market equivalent due to increasing market shortages.

2 The Gradual Nature of Economic Change in Russia

Anders Åslund

At the beginning of 1992, Russia launched its daring transition to a market economy. The government sought to undertake a comprehensive and swift transition, and much of the criticism suggests that it has done so. However, in reality the opposite has taken place. To a greater extent than in Eastern Europe, the systemic changes have been introduced one after the other with little apparent coordination. It is a myth that Russia has been subjected to a big bang or "shock therapy". The problems that have arisen are instead often caused by excessive gradualism.

The purpose of this paper is to pinpoint the major shortcomings in the initial reform strategy, as it was in fact applied, and to contrast our perception with the current Russian debate and the demands of major vested interests there. This review of the first half year of systemic change can help us to suggest the present direction of events. The immediate tasks in systemic change in a formerly socialist economy are liberalisation and macroeconomic stabilization, to which the two first sections of this paper are devoted. Privatisation is a process that requires ample time, as the experiences of all countries to date have proved. The policy-making process falls outside the scope of this paper. In a third section, I shall contrast my own assessment with the gist of the Russian public criticism of the government's reform programme. In a fourth section, I single out the main vested interests and appraise their effects on economic policies. In my conclusions, I shall sum up and assess the balance of the current economic dilemma, the policy debate and the impact of pressure groups.

Liberalisation has been too gradual

In his original speech on the change of economic system on 28 October 1991, President Yeltsin (1991) left the reader with the impression that a truly big bang was under way, although much of the strategy was merely outlined. The focal point was the concomitant liberalisation of prices and the abolition of the chronic budget deficit. Most of this did take place at the outset of 1992.

Price liberalisation was far-reaching. The standard assessment is that the prices of 90 per cent of the retail trade volume and 80 per cent of the wholesale trade volume were liberalised on 2 January 1992 ('Russian Economy', 1992; 'Memorandum', 1992).[1] A substantial liberalisation of wholesale trade took place, and from 29 January a blanket decree issued by President Yeltsin permitted free trade in anything almost anywhere.

While all this was very impressive, it is also important to note what did not happen. Initially, the intended *liberalisation of foreign trade* did not occur. While imports were liberalised, export regulations on the contrary became more restrictive. They were the greatest impediment to a true liberalisation of the economy. The export regulations were so unreasonable that they had to be altered every month, each time in a more liberal direction. In effect a gradual deregulation of exports was taking place until the summer of 1992. The most damaging kind of foreign trade regulations persisted. Their crucial characteristic was that export licences and quotas were distributed by fiat by central state organs. These licences were of great commercial value. As could be expected, massive corruption evolved around export licences, since the procedures for the allotment of licences are not very transparent. Not surprisingly, imports grew thanks to the liberalisation and humanitarian credits (by 15 per cent in the first quarter of 1992 in comparison with the first quarter of 1991), while exports declined by 20 per cent (Goskomstat, 1992). Consequently, a Russian foreign trade surplus during the first quarter of 1991 was turned into a deficit in the first quarter of 1992.

A second major problem was that *energy prices* remained regulated and extremely low by international standards. A small rise occurred in the middle of May, but given the auction exchange rate of the ruble, the price of oil stayed at around one-sixth of the world market price. As a consequence, Russian enterprises hoarded and squandered energy as before. Throughout the winter, the dominant complaint from enterprises was not shortage of demand but shortages of energy inputs. Amazingly, the phenomenon of prolonged price controls on energy alone appears to have preserved the characteristic command economy features of the Russian economy.

A third severe shortcoming was the *limited internal liberalisation* of both prices and trade flows. A surprising number of regulations persisted. Up to 40 per cent of inter-enterprise distribution remained subject to centralised allocation, and centralised distribution was usually connected with price controls. Only 2-3 per cent of the commodity flows went through the commodity exchanges ('Srednesrochnaya', 1992). For agricultural produce, 25-45 per cent of output was supposed to be sold compulsorily to the state at fixed prices far below market level, which provoked a massive refusal by state and collective farms to sell to the state in the summer of 1992. State trade organisations were restricted in their pricing, being allowed a mark-up of only 25 per cent. While the federal government deregulated prices and commodity flows, many regional authorities continued to enforce price regulations and rationing. In June 1992, meat was not for sale in half the 132 biggest Russian cities because of various local regulations (Zhagel', 1992). In fact, many features of the old regulatory system remained, either at the federal level or at regional level or just informally.

In Moscow for example, from the end of April 1992, the city police started regulating street trade severely by restricting the traders to minute zones. A large number of traders kept doing business in prohibited areas, but the character of trade had gone through a metamorphosis. The re-introduction of restrictions instantly benefited organised economic crime, whose role was to have been diminished by far-reaching liberalisation. Established traders with tables and kiosks took over, notably the flower trade that is reported to be thoroughly controlled by criminal networks.[2] The very idea of the liberalisation of street trade issued by President Yeltsin on 29 January had been swept aside by the Moscow city authorities.

Fourth, *inter-republican trade* remained essentially regulated by state orders as in the old command economy, since there was no agreement about deregulating it. However, prices were not determined in the state orders. It remained difficult to conclude trade agreements in a highly uncertain environment, and the actual outcome was that the inter-republican trade gradually collapsed. This development was hastened by massive arrears or outright non-payment of debts between enterprises in different republics.

Fifth, *freedom of enterprise* was not really established. Interviews made in St. Petersburg suggest that an ordinary bribe for having a new private enterprise registered was 30,000 rubles at the end of April 1992. Even the acquisition of premises provided ample opportunities for bribery.

The picture that arises is one of substantial but incomplete liberalisation. In no single instance was there a truly general liberalisation, although deregulation tended to proceed, notably price liberalisation.

The lingering regulations benefitted the old rent-seeking strata who could exploit arbitrage between low regulated prices and high free prices. Any regulation favoured corruption, which flourished in exports and the real estate business. These problems are typical of a gradual deregulation and illustrate why swift liberalisation can be so beneficial.

Limited stabilisation

From the outset it was plain that inflation would be the main problem in the short term. The consolidated state budget deficit was no less than 20 per cent of the Russian GNP in 1991. In spite of substantial price regulation, the official retail price index rose by 152 per cent in 1991. The combination of a substantial monetary overhang and essentially free wages from October 1991 guaranteed massive inflation, and 'the longer the delay the more dramatic the inflationary explosion' (Dornbusch, 1992, p. 22).

The focal point of the Russian government's stabilization efforts was to *balance the budget* in the first quarter of 1992. Their very impressive attempt succeeded amazingly well. The consolidated state budget was even overbalanced by 4 per cent of GNP in cash flow terms during the first quarter of 1992, while it showed a deficit of 5 per cent on commitment basis.[3] The balancing of the budget was essentially achieved thanks to massive cuts of subsidies (almost eliminated), of defence expenditures (arms purchases down by some 70 per cent), and of investment financed by the state budget.

The endeavours on the revenue side were less impressive. The profits tax (32 per cent of profits), the payroll tax (38 per cent of the wage bill allocated to the pension fund, the social security fund, and the employment fund) and the small incomes tax (from 12 per cent rising progressively to a maximum of 60 per cent) existed already and were collectible from state enterprises. The two innovations were a value-added tax (VAT) and various export duties.

The *VAT* was a good idea, since the old turnover tax had to be replaced by a proportional tax which would limit economic distortions and would rise in pace with inflation. It would have been very difficult to collect a pure sales tax at the sales outlets, and thus it is preferable to collect an indirect tax primarily at the large state production enterprises. Moreover, a VAT system had been under preparation by the Ministry of Finance for a couple of years and the administrative procedures were considered to be reasonably reliable. Generally, the world is moving in the direction of VAT as one of the most broad-based and least distortive taxes. One problem, however, was that the initial tax rate was set as high as 28 per cent, which presumably rendered the tax harder to collect and instantly unleashed various demands for differentiation and concessions.[4] In addition, a few of the old turnover taxes were retained, such as excise taxes on products that are usually subject to higher tax in the West, notably liquour and cars. This was also a reliable source of income. The principles for the VAT seemed right, and tax receipts rose quickly. The VAT contributed no less than 30.6 per cent of state budget revenues during the first quarter of 1992. The VAT had proved itself. However, demands for a reduction seem reasonable, and a formal lowering of the VAT rate may actually lead to larger revenues being collected.

The other novelty was *taxation on exports*. This system was excessively complicated and originally some of the taxes were confiscatory. Forty per cent of export revenues were supposed to be surrendered to the government at an exchange rate of 55 rubles per dollar; 10 per cent of export revenues were to be surrendered to the government currency reserve at a rate of 100 rubles per dollar; and for the rest a large export tax was to be paid to the government at a special rate set for each major export commodity. These rates changed about once a month, but were not standardized. The result was that enterprises did not export until they had been granted exemptions from the export tariffs, and the resulting payments in hard currency were usually kept abroad so that little hard currency was surrendered to the government (Yavlinskii et al, 1992). Besides, the surrender system entailed that two additional, artificial exchange rates were preserved. On top of that, 600 currency coefficients were maintained for centralized imports with an average exchange rate of 5 rubles per dollar, bringing about both a great loss of potential state revenues from imports, and awarding enormous profits in state funds to central trading houses in Moscow for no good reason.

The budgetary outcome of these high and differentiated foreign trade taxes was that foreign trade revenues dwindled to as little as 2.9 per cent of state budget revenues. Thus, not only did the foreign trade regulations block the liberalisation of the economy, they were also a complete fiscal failure. In short, they were indefensible, and little reason remained to delay a move to an ordinary tariff system. An export tariff can be justified as an easy means of collecting revenues, and the prices of the main export commodities, notably oil, had to rise sharply in any case. The Russian government's memorandum to the IMF stated that an export tax of 20 per cent of the currency income should be paid, either in rubles or hard currency ('Memorandum', 1992), which seems a suitable solution.

While the budget was balanced in the first quarter, the budget for the second quarter caused much greater problems. It was rejected by the

Supreme Soviet as too severe, and was never adopted. Even so it contained a deficit of some 8 per cent of the GNP. On the one hand, social expenditures were catching up, after having been extremely low in the first quarter. This was a necessary adjustment. On the other hand, state revenues were not raised accordingly. The foreign trade tax system was not fixed, and the VAT rates for certain products were cut. The original intention, as expressed in the Russian government's memorandum to the IMF in late February, had been to achieve a consolidated state budget surplus of 1.4 per cent of the GNP from April to December 1992. An important source of additional income that was supposed to be tapped was the freeing of energy prices, that would be subject to a substantial tax ('Memorandum', 1992). But this did not occur, and other tax revenues also appeared to be lower than expected, leaving the budget with a substantial deficit. Under conditions of high inflation, there was no possibility to finance the budget deficit with loans, rendering it highly inflationary. Regardless of the exact size of the budget deficit, it was large, and the budget for the second quarter of 1992 implied that the government was forced to give up its stabilization efforts for the time being.

The second plank of the Russian stabilization policy was a strict *monetary policy*. The Russian Central Bank's reserve requirements rose gradually to 20 per cent of the assets of the commercial banks from 1 April 1992, and the re-finance rate increased from 2-9 per cent in 1991 to 20 per cent in early 1992, to 50 per cent in April, and 80 per cent in May. Even so, this amounted to little but a give-away since the price level was officially about 1300 per cent higher in March 1992 than a year earlier. The aim of the Central Bank had been to ration credits to commercial banks and to expand credit by only 15 per cent in the first quarter of 1992. In fact, these credits increased by 92 per cent and total ruble money supply (M2) increased by 46 per cent in this period ('Russian Economy', 1992). Thus, the monetary policy was not at all as strict as intended.

An additional problem was *arrears* on payments between enterprises. At the end of June, these arrears had reached 3.2 trillion rubles — substantially more than the total money supply. There were many causes of the arrears. Their origin was that the amount of money as a ratio of GNP was falling sharply. With a penalty interest rate of only 14 per cent per annum on arrears, the delayed payment of a bill amounted to the cheapest credit at hand. The Central Bank had changed its clearing system and caused substantial delays because of its extraordinary centralisation and slow clearing of payments. The payments and settlements system for trade between the former Soviet republics was breaking down, causing ever longer delays. While only 15 per cent of enterprises were deemed unprofitable, loss-making banks and enterprises could hide their predicament behind arrears. No serious consequences arose when an enterprise did not pay its bills. Wages were paid in any case. There were no bankruptcy laws or bankruptcy procedures. No enterprise directors appear to have been sacked at this time. Ultimately, the arrears signalled a refusal by state enterprises to accept that money was becoming scarce. Rather than lowering their prices, they demanded even higher prices and hoarded final output. Outstanding examples are the paper and pharmaceutical industries which had jacked up their prices to an extremely high level. Their nominal profitability was enormous, but they did not sell much, preferring to wait until their clients accepted higher market prices. In the meantime, these enterprises lobbied for cheap state credits.

Neither the *exchange rate* nor any *incomes policy* have been utilized to battle inflation. The Russian government intends to peg the exchange rate after it has been unified and when sufficient reserves for a pegging have been gathered, under the assumption that the budget balances and the monetary policies are reasonable. As long as the exchange rate remains unpegged, the government finds it impossible to pursue any incomes policy. Thus, wages have been essentially free during the initial stages of the systemic change.

Contrary to the government's intentions, stabilization policy has become far too weak. While a serious effort at macroeconomic stabilization was made by balancing the budget during the first quarter, little remained in the second quarter. The lowest official monthly inflation rates were 245 per cent in January 1992, 24 per cent in February, 21 per cent in March, 15 per cent in April, 11 per cent in May and 13 per cent in June, though these rates are disputed and subject to substantial revisions. Even so, it is obvious that inflation has stayed very high. Given the weak stabilization policies and additional energy price hikes to come, it seems more likely that inflation will speed up again, unless very serious renewed stabilization efforts are undertaken. The underlying inflation appears to be about 15 per cent a month, that is, 450 per cent a year, and Russian society is getting used to very high inflation. As Dornbusch (1992, p. 24) puts it: 'In the process of high inflation all institutions break down.' 'As a result more sizable adjustments in the budget are required, and more dramatic measures are necessary to create the confidence that stabilization will, in fact, last.' On the other hand, there is little doubt that this high inflation will sweep away most of the command economy institutions as well. The failure of stabilization will be costly to society, but it can hardly stop the liberalisation, as old state institutions are collapsing.

Alternative suggestions in the Russian debate

The Russian public discussion on economic reform has been intense.[5] Professional economic arguments, political ambitions and vested interests have been naturally intertwined. A number of different camps can be distinguished. We shall leave aside the hard communists and nationalists, who simply demand a strict command economy, continued state ownership, price and wage controls, and more autarky with no sales of the national wealth of Russia, that is, raw materials. This line of thought has hardly anything new to offer, and does not seem to carry significant political weight.

One notable critical group in the discussion has been the old academicians Nikolai Petrakov, Leonid Abalkin, Georgii Arbatov, Oleg Bogomolov, Yurii Yaremenko and their collaborators.[6] Their criticism has been very sharp, focusing on the costs of transition, and suggesting that some third way would be possible, without using that term. While they seem to think that they have departed from socialist thinking, their ideas are still heavily influenced by old Marxist values, such as the extraordinary emphasis on production. Looking back on their previous publicised views, they are simply showing that the views they expressed were more heartfelt than many would have believed.[7] Another group of older economists, such as Academician Stanislav Shatalin and Professor Evgenii Yasin with collaborators harbour intermediary views.[8] They share most of the government's views, but accept some of Petrakov's criticism, while presenting a lot of detailed constructive criticism. Grigorii Yavlinskii and his Centre for Economic and Political Research tend to take a critical view of the government, but the essence of their criticism is that the government should be more consistently liberal, although there are also other political tilts to their position.[9] A group of neo-liberal critics spearheaded by Larisa Piyasheva, also including Vasilii Selyunin and Boris Pinsker, has focused on swift privatisation through free distribution and push for as far-reaching liberalisation as possible with low taxes.[10]

Among politicians, certain traditional socialist ideas blend easily with straight-forward populism. A good example of this is the speaker of the Parliament, Ruslan Khasbulatov.[11] Vice President Aleksandr Rutskoi originally took a similar stand, though he has gradually moved in a more reformist direction, criticising the government from a liberal point of view on the privatisation of land and the liberalisation of foreign trade.[12] It is often impossible to distinguish what is populism and what are socialist relics, for instance the idea that finances are irrelevant or unrealistic claims for a higher standard of living.

The government has to fend for itself both politically and in formulating the economic arguments. First Deputy Premier Yegor Gaidar has made an abundance of speeches and interviews; other ministers push their policies; the economic spokesman of the government, Aleksei Ulyukaev, has a general responsibility to explain policies,[13] though various officials and intellectuals defend the government line as well.[14] The official government documents are the IMF Memorandum of 27 February[15] and the Medium-Term Programme of May 1992.[16]

In the following, my main interest is to discern in what direction the various critics have tried to push the government. I shall focus on differences of systemic relevance, while leaving aside issues such as relations with the other former Soviet republics. In this section, the criticism of leading economists and politicians with substantial backing of professional economists is to be analysed, while the nature of vested economic interests is discussed in the next section. The themes selected are the ones that seem to have attracted the greatest controversy. An underlying assumption is that the public debate is of great importance. A general experience from large macroeconomic stabilizations is that it is essential to have the population understand the necessity of the belt-tightening that they inevitably will have to go through. The policy needs to be explained over and over again. Thus, it is a great problem if most senior economists do not possess even elementary insight in the functioning of a market economy. They will offer both reckless populist politicians and representatives of vested interests welcome arguments for bad causes.

The domestic debate has evolved swiftly. Before the price liberalisation on 2 January 1992, and soon afterwards, critics tended to be highly categorical, arguing that if things were not done perfectly in one regard or the other there would be a catastrophe. Much of the discussion centred on *sequencing*, especially the time of privatisation. A broad political opinion maintained that "economic subjects" had to be created before prices were liberalised, that is, demonopolisation and privatisation should come first. Such a stand had already been taken by the Shatalin group that wrote the 500-day programme in the summer of 1990, and Yavlinskii maintained this position. It was also heralded by Larisa Piyasheva (1992, p. 6): 'Did the reformers not know that the liberalisation of prices is only possible under one condition: when free commodity producers sell their products at free prices in private shops that compete among themselves for the consumers.'

Vice President Rutskoi (1992) forwarded a related view: 'The liberalisation of prices without the existence of a civilized market requires strict price control... in all civilised countries such strict control exists.' Rutskoi argued that it was a myth that market relations were impossible without private ownership, at the same time as he insisted on the creation of "economic subjects". Monopolies should be controlled administratively.

Many emphasised the importance of a quick land reform: 'No market economy and no liberalization of prices is possible as long as land is fully owned by the state.'[17] Thus, radical liberals wanted *swift privatisation*, while hesitant reformers, such as Rutskoi, used the absence of a large private sector to argue for a variety of regulations, notably price regulations for a wide range of monopolies. Nobody seemed to notice that reform governments in Hungary, Poland, Czechoslovakia, and Romania had tried to start with demonopolisation and privatisation before price liberalisation, but that no one had succeeded, which is easy to understand. Privatisation is a complex and politically controversial process. Moreover it requires the creation of property rights, which by nature presuppose liberalisation. Property rights are severely restricted if both trade and prices are as regulated as in the old system of state orders. In addition, if there are no market prices, it is impossible to see who will gain and lose from some form of privatisation, and this arouses tremendous suspicion. In the old command economy system, state monopolies are natural, though not necessary. Since prices were controlled anyhow in the old Soviet system, there was little popular reaction against the monopolies. As soon as prices are liberalised, however, the consumers feel and notice the effects of monopolies. Only then does it appear politically feasible to break up the politically powerful monopolies, if we judge from the East European experiences.

However, *Russians have shown little interest in the experiences of other countries that had changed economic system.* The ignorance here was palpable. Moreover, many participants in the debate argued that Russia was unique and that the experiences of others were irrelevant. For instance, Nikolai Petrakov et al (1992) stated: 'But our situation is different. It cannot be described by general rules.' Similarly, Georgii Arbatov (1992) and Oleg Bogomolov (1992) dismissed the relevance of the Polish experience on the grounds of various differences between Poland and Russia. Rutskoi (1992) suggests that to try to undertake macroeconomic stabilization in Russia is 'the worst kind of utopianism', if one does not 'consider the real situation in Russia and her regions' (whatever that might mean). Khasbulatov reinforced this reasoning: '...since the foundation of economic reforms must be laid not on abstract and extremely simplified models, but decisions derived from real life, considering the real situation in the economy, the population of the country and the experiences of the whole political and socio-economic history of Russia.' ('Programma dlya Khasbulatova', 1992). Typically, the significance of the "uniqueness of Russia" is not discussed analytically but presented as the ultimate argument when all other arguments have been exhausted. It serves as a convenient excuse for, and defence of, ignorance and anti-intellectual attitudes. It is sad to see how widely it is used in the supposedly intellectual debate.

In the beginning of the price liberalisation, a variety of people (Petrakov et al, 1992; Fedorenko et al, 1992; Rutskoi, 1992; Arbatov, 1992) argued that *the costs of transition were simply too high*. Prices had gone up too much; more than 90 per cent of the population was allegedly living below the subsistence level; mass unemployment and mass bankruptcies were supposedly around the corner; production was seen as falling too sharply. The reformers were accused of ruthlessness.

But what was the alternative? From the outset, there was a surprisingly broad consensus among the economists over the age of 40, or those outside the government, that *stabilization was not important, while production was*. Similarly, an extraordinary contempt for trade and services prevailed. The mindset of Marx's labour theory of value is most deeply ingrained in Rutskoi's (1992) outrage over 'the uncontrolled growth in the number of intermediary structures, exchanges and commercial banks'. He went on to state: 'The most important activity of the state under the conditions of shortages in the market is the struggle against speculation...'

Petrakov et al (1992; Fedorenko et al, 1992) were most explicit on their alternative. They advocated a return to a *fully regulated and centralised economy*. The stabilization would be sorted out through a comprehensive regulation of prices and wages together with a currency reform, which would be followed by limited convertibility. However, the exchange rate should not be unified. A very high exchange rate should be set for energy, while a lower one should apply to other goods. Exports of energy and raw materials should be restricted so that the market would be saturated. Credits should be rationed at a low interest rate, since the state was to pursue an active investment policy. Foreign investments should be encouraged. Petrakov et al (1992) insisted: 'Only under the conditions of sufficiently strong state regulation can a transition to the market take place'. In the meantime a state programme was to ascertain the establishment of a market infrastructure. Fedorenko et al (1992) maintained: 'Financial stabilization cannot precede the stabilization of production...' They harped on Roosevelt's new wave, stating: 'As long as the fall in production does not turn into sustained growth, it is necessary to abandon any attempt to balance the state budget.'[18] They were the old Soviet market advocates whose intellectual collapse and ignorance had become evident in the face of a real transition to a market economy, but they refused to accept being superfluous, and their extensive writing undoubtedly influenced public opinion. Presumably it was only ignorance that hindered them from invoking John Maynard Keynes, as has become commonplace in Eastern Europe (though inappropriate since Keynes would never have suggested a budget deficit in a situation that was characterised by over-heating).

Similarly, a study directed by Leonid Abalkin *refuted the primacy of financial stabilization* without the simultaneous formation of market subjects, and went on to argue that 'the history of the two last centuries shows that not a single strong state has had a budget without a deficit'. Moreover, 'given the conditions of already existing inflation, it is even theoretically impossible to have a budget without deficit... a budget deficit cannot be reduced by an increase in taxes. Their rise will lead to price hikes and the reduction of production volumes...' (Institut, 1992). Arbatov (1992) simply repeats that it is impossible to balance the budget, implying that therefore it should not be tried. Khasbulatov urged the government to refute the idea of balancing the budget, though accepted that the deficit should be limited to 3-5 per cent of GNP ('Programma dlya Khasbulatova', 1992). Rutskoi wanted massive credits to stimulate production.

Piyasheva and her allies were also disinterested in stabilization, because their first priority was to keep taxes low and the economy as liberal as possible in a supply-side reasoning that neglected the stability of currency. Yavlinskii et al (1992) provide a substantial criticism of the failures of the government to undertake a consistent stabilization and liberalisation, but, possibly out of political opportunism, they concluded meekly that 'economic policy should be redirected toward a long-term financial stabilization.'

Beneath this contempt for stabilization it is easy to detect the old Marxist scorn for, or ignorance of, finance and money. Hardly anyone outside the government seemed to have the most elementary insights in macroeconomics. Since the critics did not understand macroeconomics, they could not understand the importance of a balanced budget or a strict monetary policy. They had no idea of the implications of hyperinflation. Facing such a phenomenon, a whole row of economists of all kinds of political inclinations turned to the idea of a currency reform that Lenin had pursued from 1922 to 1924, apparently because it was the only example of a victory over high inflation they were reasonably acquainted with.[19]

In particular Rutskoi and Petrakov combined their dislike for stabilization with their *desire for a gradual transition to the market* with strict state regulation. Rutskoi (1992) wanted 'a regulated transition to a market economy' and distanced himself from 'the macroeconomic regulation propagated by Ye. Gaidar, which in practice means the absence of any management'. With fright Petrakov et al (1992) noted: 'The government has lost control over the economic processes.'

Rutskoi and Petrakov felt *no hesitation about the extensive and predominant role of the state*, believing it should be deeply involved in the running of the economy. The most self-evident role of the state was to pursue structural and industrial policy. Rutskoi (1992) did not believe much in the market as an equalising force: 'The main function of the state under shortage conditions has become to give tax breaks to those who increase the production of commodities in short supply...' 'can the state really not control prices on monopoly production? Of course it can if it wants to.' The demands for industrial policies through the selective distribution of cheap credits is also to be found in writing stemming from Shatalin and Yasin. Moreover, even the First Deputy Minister of Foreign Economic Relations Sergei Glaz'ev (1992ab) takes a positive view of some kind of industrial policies, though they appear more general than what the older generation prefers.

As the fear that reforms would bring on the end of the world began to fade away, the *demands for structural and industrial policies* tended to grow stronger. In particular the demands for selective credits grew, because it was easier to present them as market-conform, while they were in fact heavily subsidised. Still, the mainstream of the debate became more market-oriented during the spring of 1992.

Not all demands in the debate have been drawbacks to the old system. One focal point of liberal arguments has been *corruption and the malfunctioning of the state apparatus*. The most principled argumentation was presented by Boris L'vin (1992) who pursued a fully Hayekian line. Yavlinskii (1992), Shatalin and Assekritov (1992) and even Rutskoi ('Programma dlya Rutskogo', 1992) advocated not only an amelioration of the performance of the state apparatus but also the generalisation of retained regulations and substantial liberalisation. These demands were clearly growing stronger as the costs of the bureaucracy became more exposed to public criticism. As Yavlinskii et al (1992) put it: 'the liberalisation of markets is far from completed'. Another group of demands advocated a lowering of taxes. The taxes that were most criticised were the new export taxes and the value-added tax.

The role of vested interests

Far more important than intellectual arguments are a number of vested interests that are prominent in the Russian debate. The state enterprise directors appear to possess amazing political weight. However, they benefit greatly from the sorry state of the political and intellectual debate, because it makes it easier for them to present their demands as if they were based on principles or of a fundamental nature, and not simply a reflection of the greed of a ruling rent-seeking stratum. Their main demands are *cheap state credits and lower taxes* of all kinds, notably export taxes and VAT. Their slogan is that production, not finances must be stabilised first.[20] Furthermore, these directors and to a lesser extent their workers demand the right to the enterprises in which they work, with or without actual ownership. In particular, the military-industrial complex is demanding subsidised state credits to facilitate their conversion to civilian production. In addition, it is pushing for the right to export arms.

The commodity exchanges have swiftly lost standing with the liberalisation of prices, but they insist on the preservation of low state prices, so that they can buy goods cheaply and sell them dearly, preferably abroad. They also want lower taxes and more liberalised foreign trade. Similarly, the commercial bankers are strongly urging large and cheap credits from the Central Bank of Russia. The chairmen of kolkhozy and the directors of sovkhozy are demanding large state credits at highly subsidised interest rates and price controls for their inputs, while they want agricultural produce to be sold freely at free prices. Their nightmare is the privatisation of land and the establishment of family farms.

In short, all the main vested interests of the Russian economy behave like rent-seekers rather than profit-seekers. They are completely unabashed in their demands for massive state support and, on top of that, they insist that they possess extraordinary competence as business people. A special feature of Russia in comparison with Eastern Europe is that the vested interests of the old system have retained much of their influence after the initial change of economic system. Curiously, the state enterprise directors' main organisation, the Russian Union of Industrialists and Entrepreneurs has established a political party, the All-Russian Union of Renewal, which considers they have the right to take over government because of their knowledge and connections, but also because they claim to have control over the workers and allege they could bring out the workers on strike.[21]

The influence of the state enterprise directors is an anomaly. It is odd that they can get away with the claims that they know how to run the economy. First, former Prime Minister Nikolai Ryzhkov and most of his ministers were former state enterprise directors. Rarely has the Soviet economy been as misunderstood and mismanaged as under his leadership. Thus, the domestic experience shows that it is extremely dangerous to appoint Soviet state directors to ministerial posts. Second, in most market economies and democracies few enterprise directors become ministers, for a number of reasons. Managing an enterprise is far different from managing the state, and it is important that a minister is not motivated by personal monetary gain in some enterprise. Third, the Russian state enterprise directors focus entirely upon their own vested interests and want to extract as much as possible from the state to their own and their enterprises' benefit, while they are little concerned with the welfare of the population. Fourth, all these vested interests are strikingly disinterested in stabilization. To let them take over policy-making would be a virtual guarantee of hyperinflation. Fifth, when a society is to change system, it is vital to bring in people who feel a distance to the old society. In Latin America, reforming governments are typically dominated by young academic economists with a good U.S. education, that is, exactly the same kind of people who have taken the lead in the Russian government. Hence, the Russian state directors seem to have all the characteristics that one would like to avoid: they have little knowledge of economics; they are firmly moulded by the old Soviet command economy; they know nothing of the outside world; their purpose for coming into power is to gain wealth for themselves and their narrow constituency. It is difficult to imagine any grouping that would be less suitable for governing a country in transition, and it is strange that these obvious arguments have not won the Russian debate.

One explanation for the persistent political clout of the state directors also clarifies what needs to be done to provide the economic reforms with satisfactory political support. Their role is quite natural, if we recall Mancur Olson's (1965) ideas of the logic of collective action. Russian society is virtually atomised. A civil society has yet to emerge. Apart from the coal-miners, Russian workers are poorly organised. The political parties are rudimentary, and the communist *nomenklatura* does not function as an organisation in the old manner. The private sector remains too tiny to be a power base as yet. Thus, it is natural that the state enterprise directors would be the first group that is able to constitute a strong political pressure group. However, they would be well advised not to forget how few they are. The first threat against them could come from the workers, whom they daringly consider their constituency. Any organisation of the workers could bring the directors' power to an end.

The ultimate response to the directors' lobby, however, is likely to be the formation of ordinary political parties, the probable result of new parliamentary elections under a new constitution. Then, politicians inside and outside the Russian government would become acutely aware of how few votes the directors possess. Shrewdly, the leader of the state directors, Arkadii Volskii, is opposing any referendum or early elections. Instead he advocates a roundtable conference. The state directors are likely to generate neither national economic achievements nor votes, only personal fortunes. Therefore, it seems plausible that the current swell of directors' power is a brief parenthesis, approximately as was the case in Poland just before the fall of the last communist government of Mieczyslaw Rakowski. Still, it is doubtful that a stabilization is politically feasible before parliamentary elections have taken place.

Conclusions

The starting point of this paper is that the Russian liberalisation and stabilization have been far more gradual and piecemeal than has been generally understood. In fact, the Russian transition appears an eminent
example of a gradual transition to a market economy. Thus, the problems are not so much caused by swift change as by the tardiness of the
transition. The examples of harm caused by gradualism in the transition
are ample.

The qualified Russian debate, however, has been stuck in the old
mindset of Marxism and the socialist command economy. These ideas
have blended well with ordinary populism. This has been true both of
leading politicians outside the government, such as Rutskoi and
Khasbulatov, and most of the old reform economists. They have insisted
that privatisation must come before the liberalisation of prices, although
such a course of events has not succeeded anywhere. They are not the
least interested in the transition processes in other countries, because
they have convinced themselves that Russia is unique and that no general economic laws apply to it. They have expressed outrage at the cost of
price liberalisation, but refused to acknowledge that they had no viable
alternative. Instead they have longed back to old command economic
regulation of prices, wages and credits. Since finances and money are of
little relevance in Marxist economies, the old economists disregard the
need for stabilization, apparently not realising that they are in fact arguing for hyperinflation. While ignoring the stabilization of the currency,
these economists favour the stabilization of production, although much
of current industrial output is not at all in demand. They desire as strong
a role as possible for the state, a gradual transition to the market, and
intrusive industrial and structural policies.

Even so, there is an important and growing tendency in the debate to
criticise corruption, malfunctioning of the state, excessive regulation and
high taxes. It is becoming ever more difficult to advocate far-reaching
regulation. It is significant that leading politicians outside the government, such as Rutskoi and Khasbulatov, have become more market-oriented in their reasoning. This is particularly true of Rutskoi. On the
whole, however, it appears as if economics in Russia will need a complete change of generations, if market-oriented economics is to take
over.

The predominance of lingering Marxism and the calls for state intervention have been very advantageous for the stratum of state enterprise
directors, who currently enjoy a rare position of political strength, since
few other groups in society have got organised as yet. Their interests
are, on the one hand, to get as large subsidies as possible from the state,

on the other, not to be impeded by the state in their rent-seeking. Therefore, the interests of the state directors appear to coincide with the outcome of the intellectual debate. In spite of resistance, the liberalisation process is gradually proliferating. However, stabilization is enjoying neither intellectual nor political support, since this presupposes some familiarity with macroeconomic theory, which barely seems to be found outside of the government in Russia today. Moreover, stabilization and a stable currency are beneficial to the population at large, while the current dominant stratum of state enterprise directors is typically rent-seeking. Thus, the combination of continued gradual liberalisation and very high inflation will likely persist until a parliamentary election can introduce a more representative political body capable of launching a full-scale macroeconomic stabilization.

References

Arbatov, Georgii (1992) '"Gaidarizm" - eto reaktsiya na svoi sobstvennyi marksizm', *Nezavisimaya gazeta*, 13 March, p. 4.

Bogomolov, Oleg (1992) '"Net ni vremeni, ni effektivnoi vlasti"', *Nezavisimaya gazeta*, 7 February, p. 4.

Dornbusch, Rudiger (1992) 'Lessons from Experiences with High Inflation', *The World Bank Economic Review*, vol. 6, 1:13-31.

Fedorenko, N., N. Petrakov, V. Perlamutrov, V. Dadayan, and D. L'vov (1992) 'Shturm rynochnykh redutov poka ne udalsya', *Izvestiya*, 18 March, p. 3.

Fond 'Reforma'(1992a) 'Memorandum Rossiiskogo Pravitel'stva ochen' interesen', *Nezavisimaya gazeta*, 21 March, p. 5.

Fond 'Reforma'(1992b) 'Ob ekonomicheskikh preobrazovaniyakh v Rossii', *Nezavisimaya gazeta*, 29 February, pp. 1 and 4.

Glaz'ev, Sergei (1992a) 'Liberalizatsiya tsen nel'zya nazvat' udachnoi', *Nezavisimaya gazeta*, 21 May, p. 4.

Glaz'ev, Sergei (1992b) 'Reshat' problemy iskhodya iz imeyushchikhsya resursov', *Nezavisimaya gazeta*, 23 May, p. 4.

Goskomstat (1992) 'Sotsial'no-ekonomicheskoe polozhenie Rossiiskoi Federatsii v pervom kvartale 1992 goda', *Ekonomicheskaya gazeta*, no. 17, April, pp. 14-15.

Institut ekonomiki Rossiiskoi Akademii Nauk (1992) 'Ekonomicheskaya reforma: rezultaty i perspektivy', *Ekonomicheskaya gazeta*, no. 21, May, pp. 14-16.

Khasbulatov, Ruslan, and Anatolii Milyukov (1992) 'O dal'neishem razvitii ekonomicheskoi reformy v Rossii (material dlya obsuzhdeniya)', mimeo., Moscow, April, 54 pp.

Korov'ev, Fedor, and Bogdan Skibchevskii (1992) 'Koroli i gvozdiki', *Nezavisimaya gazeta*, 27 March, p. 6.

Leont'ev, Mikhail (1992) 'Stabilizatsiya proizvodstva na trupe finansovoi sistemy', *Izvestiya*, 23 July, p. 2.

L'vin, Boris (1992) 'Kak delat' revolyutsiyu', *Nezavisimaya gazeta*, 10 March, p. 5.

Maiminas, Efrem (1992) 'Alternativa - za predelami rynka', *Nezavisimaya gazeta*, 19 March, pp. 1 and 4.

'Memorandum Pravitel'stva Rossii' (1992) *Nezavisimaya gazeta*, 3 March, pp. 1 and 5.

Olson, Mancur (1965) *The Logic of Collective Action*, Cambridge, Mass., Harvard University Press.

Petrakov, N., V. Perlamutrov, Yu. Borozdin, and V. Manevich (1992) 'Pravitel'stvo utratilo kontrol' nad ekonomicheskimi protsessami', *Nezavisimaya gazeta*, 6 March, p. 4.

Piyasheva, Larisa (1992) 'Priznanie komissara ekonomiki Presidentu Respubliki', *Moskovskie novosti*, no. 5, pp. 6-8.

'Programma dlya Khasbulatova' (1992) *Nezavisimaya gazeta*, 3 April, p. 5.

'Programma dlya Rutskogo' (1992) *Nezavisimaya gazeta*, 3 April, p. 5.

'The Russian Economy in the First Quarter of 1992' (1992) mimeo, Moscow.

Russian Union of Industrialists and Entrepreneurs, Expert Institute (1992) 'Russian Reform: The First Step', mimeo, Moscow, January, 49 pp.

Rutskoi, Aleksandr (1992) 'Est' li vykhod iz krizisa?', *Pravda*, 8 February, pp. 3-4.

Shatalin, Stanislav, and Stanislav Assekritov (1992) 'Chinovnik mozhet pogubit' i reformu', *Izvestiya*, 28 April, p. 3.

'Srednesrochnaya programma (kontseptsiya)' (1992) mimeo., Moscow, May, 31 pp.

Sutela, Pekka (1991) *Economic Thought and Economic Reform in the Soviet Union*, Cambridge, Cambridge University Press.

Ulyukaev, Aleksei (1992) 'O "sovetakh postoronnikh"', *Nezavisimaya gazeta*, 27 March, p. 2.

Vasil'ev, Sergei (1992) 'Strukturnyi krizis - podgotovka k rostu', *Nezavisimaya gazeta*, 27 May , p. 4.

Williamson, John (ed.) (1991) *Currency Convertibility in Eastern Europe*, Washington, DC, Institute for International Economics,.

Yaremenko, Yurii, Viktor Ivanter, Aleksandr Nekrasov, Marat Yzyakov, and Vyacheslav Panfilov (1992) 'Nado li otpuskat' tseny na toplivo?', *Nezavisimaya gazeta*, 1 April, p. 4.

Yavlinskii, Grigorii, et al (1992) 'Diagnoz: Reformy v Rossii, Vesna - 92', *Moskvoskie novosti*, no. 21, pp. 9-16.

Yeltsin, Boris N. (1991) 'Vystuplenie B. N. Yel'tsina', *Sovetskaya Rossiya*, 29 October, pp. 1 and 3.

Zhagel', Ivan (1992) 'Sderzhannyi optimizm pri spade proizvodstva', *Izvestiya*, 20 July, p. 2.

Notes

1 Henceforth statistics used are derived from the official government report 'The Russian Economy in the First Quarter of 1992', if nothing else is indicated.

2 Korov'ev and Skibchevskii (1992).

3 'Russian Economy' (1992). Alternative assessments abound and the variations depend on the periodisation of different items, the choice of exchange rate for the external debt service, uncertainty about the exact surplus of the pension fund which is outside the purview of the Ministry of Finance but should be included in the consolidated state budget. Similarly, the local budgets showed a surplus which is frequently omitted. A certain confusion between revenues and financing has lingered on.

4 To my knowledge, no country in the world has a higher VAT than Sweden, where it is 25 per cent and also there the rise of VAT to 25 per cent prompted a differentiation in the tax rate.

5 The main forum of the qualified public economic discussion has become the daily *Nezavisimaya gazeta*, while larger tracts are circulated as photo-copies.

6 Arbatov (1992), Bogomolov (1992), Fedorenko et al (1992), Institut (1992), Petrakov et al (1992) and Yaremenko et al (1992).

7 See Sutela (1991).

8 Fond (1992ab), Shatalin and Assekritov (1992) and Russian Union (1992).

9 Yavlinskii et al (1992).

10 Piyasheva (1992) and L'vin (1992).
11 Khasbulatov and Milyukov (1992) and 'Programma dlya Khasbulatova' (1992).
12 Rutskoi (1992) and 'Programma dlya Rutskogo' (1992).
13 A comprehensive article is Ulyukaev (1992).
14 Notable broad articles are Glaz'ev (1992ab), Maiminas (1992), and Vasil'ev (1992).
15 'Memorandum' (1992).
16 'Srednesrochnaya' (1992).
17 Boris Mozhaev quoted in *Moscow News*, no. 22, 1992, p. 11.
18 The absurdity and inconsistency of these views are too obvious to require further comments here. They have been properly dissected and rebuked in the Russian debate by Ulyukaev (1992) and Maiminas (1992).
19 For an appropriate criticism of these ideas, see Williamson (1991), pp. 310-335.
20 For a good criticism of the industrial lobby, see Leont'ev (1992).
21 A good presentation of these demands is an interview with Aleksandr Vladislavlev, First Deputy Chairman of the Russian Union of Industrialists and Entrepreneurs in *Nezavisimaya gazeta*, 2 June 1992, p. 2.

3   Prices, Incomes, and Hardship[1]

Michael Ellam and Richard Layard

In the first four months of 1992, prices in Russia rose 7.5 times. The measured real wage fell to 40 per cent below its 1991 average. And yet in April inflation was still rising at 20 per cent a month. There are thus two central questions that need answering:

(i)   Why did prices rise so much relative to wages?
(ii)   Why, despite this, was inflation still so high in April?

We begin with the second question. The basic answer is that unemployment in Russia is very low. In a free society such low unemployment is bound to generate inflation, and financial policy will only bring inflation under control by increasing unemployment. Some people may question whether wages in Russia respond to employment opportunities. But in fact our evidence shows clearly that wages rise much less fast in industries with poor employment opportunities.

Turning to the first question, the price rise was so high that real sales fell sharply relative to output — and stocks accumulated rapidly. This overshooting appears to be due to high inflationary expectations and negative real interest rates, leading to a preference for holding goods rather than money. The effect has been however a sharp fall in real wages — and in the real value of pensions and other benefits.

Our analysis has five sections. The first provides a general economic framework, with an application to Russia, based on the models used by Layard, Nickell and others in analysing Western unemployment-inflation trade-offs. It also discusses the key issues of how to preserve productivity as unemployment rises. The next section analyses the facts about prices and real aggregate demand, and discusses the reasons for price over-shooting. We then turn to the response of wages to prices, and analyse in some detail the system of wage determination and the pattern of wage behaviour. Next we look at the social safety net and finally summarize our policy conclusions.

General framework

Much of the basic history can be captured in the four phases depicted in Figure 1.

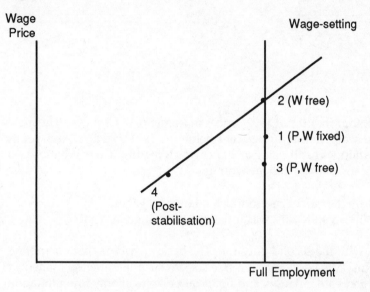

Figure 1 Four phases in the move to the market

In each period the real wage is determined by the way in which prices are set relative to wages. This *price-setting relationship* can be written as

$$\frac{\text{Wage}}{\text{Price}} = \text{Productivity} \cdot \frac{1 + \text{Net rate of subsidy}}{1 + \text{Profit mark-up}}$$

This is so whether wages and prices are controlled or free. The four phases were then as follows.

1. Initially, both wages and prices were controlled, and they together with the rate of subsidy determined the profit mark-up.
2. As state power weakened from 1985 onwards, wages began to break

free, but prices remained controlled. To avoid a wage-price spiral, the state ratified the higher wages by increasing subsidies in order to hold down prices. Real wages rose to an unsustainable level. The subsidies generated a monetary overhang, which forced eventual liberalisation of prices.

3. At that stage net subsidies were cut drastically in order to balance the budget. At the same time the profit mark-up rose sharply, for reasons to be explained. Measured real wages plummeted. But inflation continued, as workers tried to compensate themselves for rising prices.

4. This wage-price spiral is the effect of a free society and will inevitably continue until sufficient unemployment emerges. When wages are free, workers will try to set their wages as a mark-up on the recent price level. But this mark-up will be less if unemployment is higher. There is thus a *wage-setting relationship* which can be written

$$\frac{\text{Wage}}{\text{Lagged price}} = \underset{+}{f(\text{Employment})}$$

If there is a financial stabilisation, the main mechanism through which it will work is unemployment. As the rate of growth of money is reduced, real output will fall (due to the initial inertia of prices). And then the fall in output will reduce the rate of growth of prices. Prices will of course also be affected by price expectations, but it will not be possible to sustain stable inflation without unemployment of Western European levels.[2]

This fall in employment is not a temporary phenomenon. It corresponds to the fundamental need in a free economy for sufficient slack in the labour market to contain inflation. The Russian experience is likely to reflect that of Spain. Under Franco strikes were illegal and there was no unemployment. After his death strikes were legalized and inflation soared. Eventually unemployment had to rise to 22 per cent in the process of reducing inflation, and it is still 16 per cent.

As regards the real wage after stabilisation, this depends strongly on the course of productivity. After stabilisation in Spain (1978) and Germany (1948) productivity rose (see Table 1).

But in the ex-Communist countries it has fallen sharply, since socialist managers only dismiss workers after major falls in output. This is the single main reason for economic hardship in Eastern Europe—the necessary fall in employment has been accompanied by an "unnecessarily" large fall in output. If Russia can privatise fast, it may be able to avoid the problem. We have arrived at this optimistic view by assuming that

Years After Stabilisation	Poland Year 0= 1990		Spain Year 0=1978		West Germany Year 0=1948	
	Industrial Unempl-oyment (%)	Produc-tivity	Industrial Unempl-oyment (%)	Produc-tivity	Unempl-oyment (%)	Industrial Produc-tivity
0	0	100	7	100	4	100
1	3	84	8	102	8	120
2	8	73	11	106	10	140

Table 1 Unemployment and industrial productivity after stabilisation in Poland, Spain and West Germany

Source: OECD, EC

real wages after stabilisation are no lower than before (compare points 3 and 4)[3].

The future pattern of productivity is of the utmost importance since it will be the prime determinant of living standards in Russia. Attempts to sustain employment may cause major hardship by forcing down productivity. Instead workers should be released as soon as output falls, so that they can be redeployed producing something else as soon as possible. There are exceptions to this—especially cases of isolated defence enterprises which could in reasonable time find export markets.

How much unemployment will be needed? In Poland unemployment reached roughly 10 per cent of the workforce within 2 years of stabilisation, in Czechoslovakia and Hungary 5 per cent within 6 months of stabilisation and up to 10 per cent in Slovakia with its large defence sector. It seems inevitable that unemployment will for a time exceed the West European average of 10 per cent.

Some numbers

In the light of this, we can now look more closely at the Russian experience (see Table 2 and Figure 2).

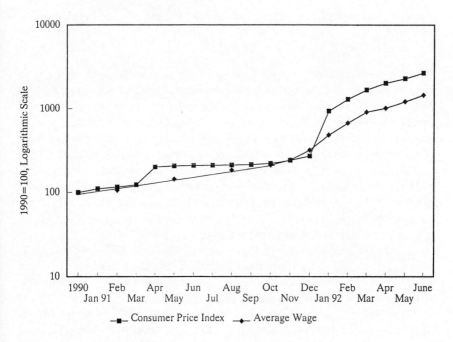

Figure 2 Prices and wages

Table 2 Expenditure and money

R bn.

	Retail sales (p.m)	GNP (p.m)	Household income	Currency in circulation	Household deposits	Ruble M2
1991 Mar	29	62	42	73	228	
Jun	33	94	53	89	235	
Sep	40	93	67	122	266	
Oct	47	94	78	130	275	
Nov	52	102	83	142	282	714
Dec	72	115	122	162	294	783
1992 Jan	74	372	119	119	302	851
Feb	112	513	174	174	307	905
Mar	146	668	226	226	386	1145
Apr	158	777	276	276	392	1207
May	187		275	351	413	
June	209		379	441	432	

Source: Goskomstat RF, Central Bank of Russia and Ministry of Finance of the Russian Federation

Between 1985 and 1990 wages rose by 50 per cent while consumer prices rose very little. This led to increased subsidies and soft credits. To reduce these, Pavlov raised many consumer prices in April 1991 and partly liberalised some other prices of manufactured consumer goods. But this in turn led to further wage rises, which by the autumn had fully restored the real wage to its 1990 level, requiring massive subsidies.

After the putsch in August price controls became increasingly difficult to enforce and a further extension of "contract prices" was allowed.[4] However the main price liberalisation came in January 1992, against the background of a massive monetary overhang generated by previous budget deficits and credits to enterprises.

In January prices rose 3.45 times and wages only 1.55—reducing the measured real wage by more than half. Net subsidies were slashed, and budget balance on a cash flow basis was achieved in the first quarter. After January wages rose roughly in line with prices.

Since money continued to grow rapidly, output fell no faster than it did throughout 1991—an output decline due to supply factors rather than insufficient demand. Inflation continued at a high rate.

Prices, consumption and stockbuilding

However there is more to the story than this:

—Real wages fell by much more than the fall in net subsidies, and (partly in consequence)

—Retail sales fell much more than output, leading to massive stockbuilding.

We shall first document this and then attempt to explain why prices were set so high.

The profit mark-up

Real wages fell more than can be explained by the movement of subsidies and productivity, given a constant profit mark-up. Comparing measured real wages in 1992 with 1990, they have fallen by 47 per cent. At the same time productivity has fallen only 20 per cent and net indirect taxes have risen by only 11 per cent of GNP. Correspondingly there has been a substantial rise in the profit mark-up.[5] This is shown dramatically in Table 3, and raises the immediate question of whether in some sense prices overshot.

Table 3 Wages, profits, productivity and taxes

	Wage Bill++ R bn.	Profits R bn	Labour Productivity	Real Wage+	Indirect Taxes minus Subsidies (as % of GNP)
1985			100.0	100	7 (USSR)
1986			102.4		
1987			103.1		
1988			107.7		
1989			109.8		
1990	292.8	154.0	105.8	133	5 (USSR)
1991	484.0	320.0	94.2	117	
1992 Q1	440.0	570.0	84.8	70	16

+The real wage is computed using the Consumer Price Index
++ Up to 1990 inclusive, the employers wage tax was around 9 per cent of the wage bill and from 1991, 37 per cent. This is not included in the wage bill.

Source: IMF, Economic Review of the Russian Federation, 1992, Tables 4,10,17 and Goskomstat RF.

Demand and stockbuilding

One obvious approach to this is to ask what happened to real sales. These fell far more than output. Prices did not equate the demand for output to the current rate of production. As Table 4 shows, production of consumer goods fell only slightly, while real retail sales collapsed.

The sales data may of course exclude an increased share of sales

Table 4 Consumer market (Dec. 1990 Prices)
Quarterly rate, not seasonally adjusted
R bn.

		Production of Manufactured Consumer Goods	Real Retail Sales
1990		65	69
1991	Q1	64	64
	Q2	66	50
	Q3	64	62
	Q4	65	79
1992	Q1	57	35
	Jan		30
	Feb		36
	Mar		39
	Q2	40	37
	April		36
	May		39
	June		39

Source: Goskomstat RF

through new outlets, though many of the new outlets resell items that have already been sold once through traditional channels and are therefore caught in standard statistics. (Moreover price liberalisation would bring back into normal channels some produce that previously went outside.) A check on the sales data can be got by looking at personal disposable income minus increases in household monetary wealth. This tells the same story: between 1991 and 1992 (Q1) this measure of consumption grew at the same rate as retail sales.[6]

Clearly the very sharp fall in sales in January was partly due to the fact that households had bought heavily in December, anticipating the price rise. But even by April monthly retail sales were still only 55 per cent of the 1991 average. The fall in food purchases was very much less—reflecting the fact that food is a necessity and households were becoming poorer. (Food prices rose at roughly the same rate as other prices—see Figure 3.)

Purchases of meat and dairy products fell only 20 per cent between December and March and the calorie content of purchases in January 1992 was only 14 per cent less than a year earlier.

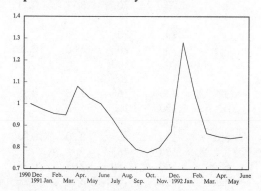

Figure 3 Ratio of food to non – food prices

Of course welfare did not fall by the full amount of the fall in consumer purchases, since the massive reduction in queues represents a major welfare gain. The only point we are making is that the prices that were set led to a massive degree of stock accumulation of consumer goods.[7]

Investment also collapsed, to a level in the first quarter equal to 56 per cent of what it was one year earlier. Since the index of industrial production was down by only 13 per cent, inventories of producer goods also accumulated rapidly. The situation is graphically illustrated in Table 5, which shows the growth of retail sales compared with estimated GNP at market prices.

As can be seen between November and April, nominal GNP (including stockbuilding) rose by a multiple of 7.7, while retail sales rose by a multiple of only just over 3.

The question is therefore "Why were prices set at a level which led to high measured profits and accumulation of stocks?"

Monopoly power

One explanation is monopoly power. According to this theory it is in

Table 5 Wages, incomes and prices (R.p.m. unless stated)

	Consumer prices	Av. Wage	Min. Wage	Min Pension	Av. wage divided by price index	Min. pension divided by average wage	Min. pension divided by price index
1985	86	201	70	50	2.33	0.25	0.53
1990	95	297	70	70	3.11	0.24	0.73
1991							
Jan	106		70	70			0.66
Feb	111	315	70	70	2.83	0.22	0.63
Mar	118		70	100			0.84
April	194		130	165			0.85
May	199	429	130	165	2.15	0.38	0.83
June	202		130	165			0.82
July	203		130	165			0.81
Aug	204	551	130	165	2.70	0.30	0.81
Sept	206		130	165			0.80
Oct	214	634	180	180	2.97	0.28	0.84
Nov	233	726	195	180	3.12	0.25	0.77
Dec	261	950	200	342	3.65	0.36	1.31
1992							
Jan	900	1438	342	342	1.63	0.23	0.38
Feb	1242	2004	342	542	1.61	0.27	0.44
Mar	1613	2705	342	542	1.69	0.20	0.33
Apr	1936	3024	342	642	1.56	0.21	0.36
May	2188	3629	900	900	1.66	0.25	0.41
June	2560	4318	900	900	1.69	0.21	0.35

Note: Average Wages in Feb, May and Aug 1991 are averages for 1st, 2nd, and 3rd quarters respectively.

Source: Goskomstat RF; Ministry of Labour of the Russian Federation

the interest of a monopolist to charge a higher price mark-up over cost than was allowed under price controls—even if in the short run this means that he can only sell a fraction of his output. He must of course be able to finance the stocks, with bank credit or credit from his suppliers. We shall be able to investigate how important this theory is when we see whether profit mark-ups continue in the future at their present level. However there may well be temporary influences making profit mark-ups atypically high. We can now investigate these.

Inflation expectations

If producers expect cost inflation to continue and real interest rates are low, it is rational for them to produce now and sell later. This would lead them to set prices that restricted sales to less than current output. Enterprises faced monthly real interest rates of roughly -35, -25 and -15 per cent in February, March and April, and therefore chose to withhold supplies from the market. Where they could not finance this stockbuilding from bank credit, they forced their suppliers to "lend" them the necessary money. But the scope for storing output was less in the case of food than other goods—hence the lower accumulation of stocks.

In this situation a stabilisation would lead to increased sales of goods and higher real wages. But at the same time output and employment would fall due to the credit crunch.

Monetary imbalances

Another explanation of the stock accumulation is based on the idea that credit was too abundant relative to currency, driving up prices to a level where there was insufficient currency to circulate all the output produced. In simple terms we can take output (Y) as given, and its value as determined by total money (M) according to the relation

$$PY = v_M M$$

Real sales (X) are however determined by currency, since in Russia currency (C) is almost the only means of transaction open to households:

$$PX = v_C C$$

Thus the fraction of output which is sold is given by

$$\frac{X}{Y} = \frac{v_C}{v_M} \cdot \frac{C}{M}$$

If currency is too low relative to total money, stocks will accumulate (X<Y). If in addition L is fixed and $WL = v_C C$, then real wages (W/P) are also proportional to the ratio of currency to money.

How plausible is this explanation? The first piece of evidence is the series of "cash crises" that has occurred, in which there has been too little currency to pay wages and pensions in full. Wage and pension entitlements have been pushed up by high prices stemming from excessive credit, but it has not been possible to meet these entitlements in full.

At this point sceptics will point out that currency has grown as fast as total money. However when real financial wealth falls (and it plummeted after price liberalisation), the demand for real currency falls much less than the demand for real deposits, since there is an irreducible amount of real currency needed to circulate household income. In

Russia workers are paid in currency twice a month,[8] so that the irreducible minimum ratio of currency to monthly household income is
0.25. Between November and April the ratio fell from 1.70 to 1.12. But
the ratio of total money to total national income fell from 7.00 to 1.55—
very much more.

A further piece of evidence in support of this analysis of pricing is the
fact that wholesale industrial prices have risen much faster than retail
prices (see Figure 4). This suggests that the financial position of enterprises has been much stronger than of final buyers.

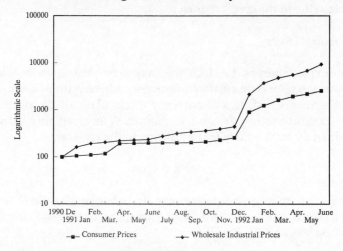

Figure 4 Consumer and industrial prices

Conclusion

We conclude that real wages have fallen more than was justified on
grounds of changes in subsidies and productivity. Given the low level
of real balances, this led to low real aggregate demand, and stockbuilding. The low real wage may be partly a result of monopolistic prices but
also of temporary withholding of supplies and shortages of currency
(relative to credit).

Wage behaviour

We have so far looked at real wages from the side of prices. However it
is time to look more carefully at how wages are themselves determined.

In his speech on 28th October 1991 President Yeltsin announced the
freeing of wages. This was the culmination of a process whereby

throughout the year enterprises in more and more industries were given freedom to set their own wages. There remains a degree of central interference in that wages in excess of 4 times the minimum wage cannot be deducted from revenue when computing profit.[9] Thus these excess wages are subject to the rate of profits tax (a basic rate of 32 per cent).

Until the end of 1991 most wages consisted of a tariff wage for the industry linked to the minimum wage (and therefore changing infrequently) plus a bonus linked to value added (measured in principle in real terms but often in nominal terms). The bonus changed each month. However since January the distinction between basic wage and bonus has largely disappeared, and wages in most enterprises have changed each month.

Wages are now settled entirely at the level of the enterprise. They are fixed at the discretion of managers, who have since 1990 been officially appointed on one-year contracts by some external agency (ministry, kombinat, or concern). Most managers have considerable authority in their enterprises (this is not Poland or Yugoslavia), but of course they want to keep their workers happy. Except in a few industries like coal, the only trade union is the old official trade union, now renamed the "independent" trade union. (In coal a truly unofficial union coexists with the "independent" one.)

At the national level the government has established a tripartite structure of employers, unions, and government to determine the framework for wage settlements. This framework is in turn to be amplified through industrial tripartite agreements. This somewhat German-style approach has considerable promise, but so far the agreements reached have done no more than set the minimum wage in the industry concerned. They have had little effect on outcomes.

The Parliament has also passed a wage indexation law in 1991, but this has so far been side-stepped. Wages in the public sector have been set either by Parliament (in December) or more recently by the government after discussion with the trade unions.

There have been remarkably few strikes, considering the fall in real wages and the still high level of employment. In January the coal miners threatened to strike, but were bought off by the government with a three-fold increase in wages financed by a massive government subsidy. In the first quarter, 90 per cent of strikes were in the budgetary sphere. From January to April, 169,000 workers were involved in strikes with only 1 million working days lost—very low by international standards. For some weeks in April and May many medical workers performed only limited duties, and teachers threatened a national strike. These actions however were averted by concessions involving major pay increases. The main increases in budgetary sector wages were as follows:

	Increase times	Cumulative increase
1991 Dec	1.9	1.90
1992 Feb/Mar	1.45	2.76
May	2.6-2.7	7.2-7.4

The minimum wage was raised sharply in October, January and June, as follows

	Roubles per month
1991 October	180
1992 January	342
June	900

however few workers receive wages anywhere near the minimum wages.

The outcome

In the aggregate outcome, wages fell sharply relative to prices in January and have since risen at about the same rate as prices. There have however been major changes in the wage structure compared with last year. As Table 6 shows, industrial wages have risen much faster than the average wage, and budgetary wages much slower.

Even more striking is the disparity in the rates of wage growth within industry. Across 37 branches of industry the dispersion of average wages more than doubled. The standard deviation of $\log_e$ wages was 0.18 in Jan-Feb 91 and 0.46 a year later.[10] Wages grew much faster where they were already high, so that

$$w_1 = \text{const.} + 1.88\, w_0 \qquad (R^2 = .51)$$
$$(5.7)$$

where w_0 is the original log wage and w_1 the final one.

The changes in wage structure presumably reflect

(a) the movement of relative wages from previously constrained levels towards equilibrium, and

(b) shifts in those equilibrium levels against industries whose relative demand has fallen.

In the first case relative wages rise in industries where there was already high excess demand and fall in those where excess demand was less (or there was excess supply). In the second case wages rise in those

Table 6 Wages by sector, relative to average wage

| | 1991 | | | 1992 | | |
	Q1	Q2	Q3	Jan	Feb	Mar
Industry	1.08	1.04	1.08	1.25	1.28	1.28
Agriculture	0.81	0.71	0.81	0.62	0.52	
Transport	1.15	1.19	1.22	1.42	1.37	
Communications	0.87	1.00	0.95	0.87	0.84	
Construction	1.25	1.27	1.33	1.23	1.29	
Trade	0.86	0.81	0.83	0.71	0.68	
Health	0.76	0.89	0.77	0.63	0.63	
Education	0.81	0.87	0.65	0.76	0.66	
Science	1.23	1.06	1.03	0.74	0.70	
StateSecurity+	1.51	1.72	1.69	1.13	1.17	
StateAdmin.	1.15	1.03	0.95	1.13	1.17	
MaterialSphere	1.03	1.02	1.06	1.09	1.08	
Non-Mater.Sphere	0.86	0.96	0.71	0.74	0.68	
AverageWage(R.pm)	315	429	551	1438	2004	2705

+Excludes armed forces

Source: Russian Ministry of Labour

industries where demand conditions become relatively more favourable, and fall in those industries where demand conditions become less favourable (due for example to cutbacks in subsidies or public procurement). The case of demand shifts is illustrated in Figure 5.

If relative demand falls, this puts downwards pressure on relative wages, and both relative wages and relative employment fall from point A to point B. By contrast, if relative demand rises, relative wages and

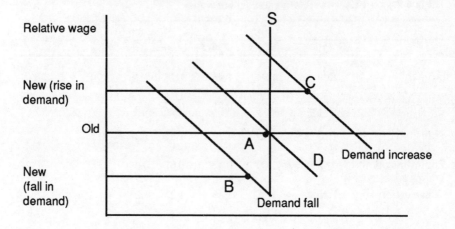

Figure 5 Industry adjustment after demand shift

relative employment rise to point C. Since in the short-run workers can be thought of as "belonging" to an industry, the differences in employment between points B and C corresponds to differences in employment rates. Thus the curve BAC is a kind of Phillips-curve, showing how wages are affected by employment rates (other things equal).

It is therefore interesting to look at the relation between wage changes and employment changes across Russian industries. The basic data for 38 industries are plotted in Figure 6.

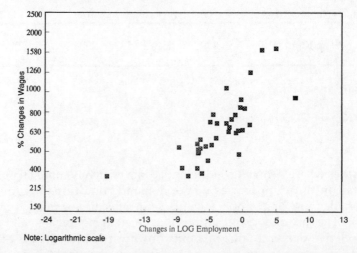

Figure 6 Wage and employment change across industries (Jan–Feb 92 relative to Jan–Feb 91)

For the period Jan-Feb 91 to Jan-Feb 92, the regression of change in log wages (dw) on changes in log employment (dn) is

$$dw = const. + 5.81dn \qquad (R^2 = .57)$$
$$(6.9)$$

This is a very strong effect—stronger than the usual effect of employment rates on wages in OECD countries, which typically involves a coefficient of 1 to 2 (Layard et al, 1991).[11]

Wage growth is uncorrelated with changes in industry prices, presumably because there have been such large changes in subsidies. But, as expected, employment fell in industries whose prices rose. This pseudo-demand relation is

$$dn = const. - 0.06 \ dp \qquad (R^2 = .51)$$
$$(3.5)$$

Across administrative areas (77 of them) there has also been a doubling of wage dispersion, with the standard deviation of $\log_e$ wages rising from 0.23 to 0.44. Again wages have risen fastest where they were already highest:

$$w_1 = const. + 1.63 \ w_0 \qquad (R^2 = .78)$$
$$(16)$$

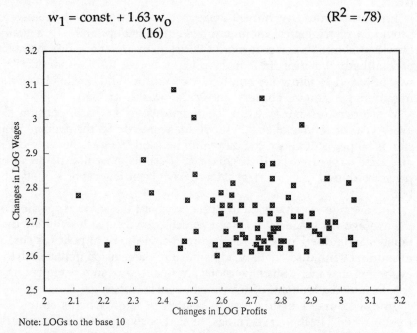

Note: LOGs to the base 10

Figure 7 Wage and profit change across regions (Jul 1992 relative to Jan 1991)

Surprisingly the change in wages is uncorrelated with either the change in retail prices or the change in recorded profits, as can be seen in Figure 7.

Conclusion

The main point we have established in this section is that wages in Russia are surprisingly flexible. In industries where employment has fallen, wages have risen very much less. Thus when aggregate employment falls far enough, there is every reason to expect that in Russia (as elsewhere) inflation will come down.

Social Safety Net

Pensioners

Those who have suffered most from the price rise have been the pensioners (see Table 2). The minimum pension has fallen from about 30 per cent of the average wage to around 25 per cent, where it was in 1985 and 1990. This was probably a necessary measure of expenditure control, but it caused great hardship to people so near the margin of subsistence.

In February the government developed a diet which was deemed to provide a physiological minimum level of consumption.[12] (It actually provided about 20 per cent more calories than are needed to maintain normal body weight.) In January prices this cost R475 a month. This was adjusted to allow for non-food expenditure and on this basis the minimum pension in February and March was set at R550.

Pensioners receive an extra 1 per cent above the basic pension for every year of service above 25 (or 20 for women). So the average pension is 30 per cent above the minimum pension.[13] Pensioners are often of course supported by their children. Despite some non-payment of pensions due to cash shortages, there have been few reports of starvation.

The average state pension in Russia is about the same proportion of the average net wage as in Britain, which is somewhat low by international standards. However for the time being the right policy is surely to continue with discretionary adjustment of the pension in line with the evolution of wages. Since pensions are financed from a wage tax, this has the added advantage of ensuring budget solvency.

In due course a state earnings-related pension scheme should be reestablished. In this the earnings- related portion should be calculated not on the basis of past nominal earnings but on the basis of past relative earnings (see Layard, 1992).

Children

Child support in Russia is fairly generous. Each child receives the following proportion[14] of the minimum wage (which generally equals the minimum pension):

Under 1.5	70%
1.5 - 6	55%
Over 6	38%

Children of single parents get more (details in Layard, 1992). There are well-known arguments in favour of means-testing children's allowances. At some stage this will be necessary, but it will take some time to sort out the administrative difficulties.

Unemployed people

The present system of unemployment benefit is relatively generous. For the first 3 months the employer pays the full wage. Then the worker gets the following proportion of his former wage (unindexed)

first 3 months	75%
next 3 months	60%
next 6 months	45%

subject to a minimum equal to the minimum wage. This is far too complex to administer and will inevitably lead to failures of payment when the numbers of unemployed people rise. For this reason and to save money, the government wishes to introduce a flat rate benefit close to the minimum wage, with an enhanced benefit of 125 per cent of the minimum wage for people in the first 6 months after lay-off. This should provide extra money for the active labour market policies which will be essential to prevent the growth of long-term unemployment. For each unemployed person, it will be necessary to spend on unemployment benefit plus active labour market policy an amount equal to roughly half of the average wage. This implies that the Employment Fund needs a wage tax equal to half the unemployment rate.

Conclusion

Russia has a quite effective social safety net (including also the schemes for the sick and disabled). And the process by which benefits have been adjusted has been quite skilful. The main problems have come from shortages of currency and failures of payment.

There are a few smallish gaps. For example 90,000 people of pensionable age are not now eligible for the minimum pension. These gaps should be plugged. But there is no need for any extra general means-tested safety net. The existing schemes can quite well handle each type of poverty, and a new means-tested benefit would be impossible to administer.

To see the real problems of social provision one can look at the social budget in the first quarter:

	% of GNP	
	Russia (1992 Q1)	Western Europe
Pensions	3.9	8
Children	1.2	1
Unemployed	0.3	2
Education	3.2	5
Health	2.2	6

Source: Ministry of Finance of the Russian Federation and OECD

The most striking feature is the low expenditure on education and health, which must surely be rectified. Cash transfers will also need to grow as unemployment rises, though there is room for saving on children.

Policy conclusions

We began with two questions and gave the following answers.

1. Prices have risen sharply relative to wages partly because of subsidy reductions and falls in productivity, but also because producers have deliberately chosen to accumulate stocks, anticipating higher future prices and costs. Excessive credit growth has also forced up prices faster than currency becomes available to pay wages.

2. Inflation is still rising due to credit emission, which is sustaining employment. When employment falls, wage pressure will be reduced. Our evidence shows that this is true in Russia, as everywhere else.

So is hardship going to get worse and what if anything can be done about it? It is inevitable that output will fall further. But how far it falls will depend on how quickly labour is redeployed from unproductive uses.

Consumption (as opposed to output) has already fallen so much that there is no obvious reason why it need fall further. We would suggest five main conclusions about how policy could influence the level of hardship.

Policy conclusions

Stabilisation could help alleviate hardship by reducing the tendency for prices to overshoot due to inflationary price expectations—leading to excessive stockbuilding. Controlled growth of credit would also help to alleviate cash crises, which limits wage payments and consumption. Efforts should be made to minimize future inflationary shocks. For example oil price rises could be adjusted on a monthly basis. These increases should consist in large measure of higher energy taxes which could be used to cut the VAT in an offsetting fashion. In this way relative prices could be changed without any major jump in average prices.

Privatisation would help by offsetting the tendency for workers to be kept on even when producing nothing, thus reducing their availability for productive redeployment.

Wage behaviour will be crucial in determining the employment-inflation trade-off. There is evidence that in Russia wages respond quite sharply to employment. But it is important to develop policies which restrain wages when unemployment is low. These include coordinated wage-bargaining (to prevent leap-frogging) and active labour market policy to prevent the growth of a pool of unskilled and unmotivated long-term unemployed (Layard and Philpott, 1991).

The social safety net has a few holes that need mending: for example, *all* old people should be entitled to the basic pension. In the medium term old people should be able to benefit again from an earnings-related pension, while children's allowances should be means-tested to make room for the cost of unemployment benefits.

Foreign aid is a thoroughly respectable way of alleviating hardship. Russia is potentially rich and should be able to borrow now to consume, anticipating higher production in future.

Annex

A Note on Statistics

The statistics used in this paper are official Goskomstat data. Most economic indicators of the Russian economy are published monthly by Goskomstat in *Ekonomicheskoe polozhenoe Rossiiskoi Federatsii* and its supplementary volume (*Dopolnitel'nye dannye*).

There has been virtually no change in the way that statistics are collected, defined and presented in the former Soviet Union. As such many of the former problems associated with Soviet statistics remain. Interested readers can refer to IMF, IBRD, OECD, and EBRD (1991), vol. 1, appendix II-2.

References

Government of the Russian Federation (1992), *Russian Economic Trends*, Vol 1, No. 1

IMF, IBRD, OECD, EBRD (1991), *A Study of the Soviet Economy*, Washington D.C.

R. Jackman, R. Layard and A. Scott (1992), "Unemployment in Eastern Europe", London School of Economics, mimeo.

R. Layard and J. Philpott (1991), *Stopping Unemployment*, Employment Institute.

R. Layard, S. Nickell, and R. Jackman (1991), *Unemployment, Macroeconomic Performance and the Labour Market*, Oxford.

R. Layard (1992), "The social safety net in Russia", mimeo.

OECD (1992), *Short Term Economic Statistics Central and Eastern Europe*

B. Popkin (1992), "Towards the Development of a Subsistence Income Level in the Russian Federation", Moscow, mimeo

Notes

1 We are extremely grateful to the following for all kinds of help: P. Boone, E. Gontmacher, A. Illarionov, R. Jackman, G. Kjällgren, I. Kolosnitsyn, V. Kosmarsky, J. Sachs, A. Shokhin, S. Shpilco, A. Stavnitsky, and Y. Testov.

2 Since the change in inflation depends on both the level and change in employment it is possible to hold inflation stable by increasing employment even when unemployment is still low.

3 Foreign aid can help to sustain real wages via an implicit subsidy.

4 There was of course, and still is, a flourishing secondary market at which households sell at higher prices goods they bought at lower prices in the state stores. The consumer price index is based on the state store prices. This may well be the best index for measuring the purchasing power of household income—though no index is adequate when goods are not freely available.

5 This is not a logical necessity since P is the consumer price index and a major devaluation would raise P relative to W. However it is not clear how enterprises priced imports during the period and the official NMP deflator actually

rose more than the retail price index—rather than less, as one would expect after a devaluation.

6 Consumption (thus measured) divided by retail sales was

1991				1992
Q1	Q2	Q3	Q4	Q1
1.25	1.13	1.11	1.14	1.19

This check is only valid provided there was no growth in the proportion of unrecorded income (including payment-in-kind).

7 The data on "stocks in wholesale and retail trade" do not record any accumulation of stocks there, and, as far as we know, there is no direct estimate of stock accumulation in enterprises. But from data on output and sales we can infer that they have accumulated greatly.

8 More frequent payments are now being encouraged.

9 Different coefficients apply to some industries.

10 Given this it is puzzling that inter-personal inequality did not increase. The Gini coefficient for the distribution of individuals according to income per head of family is 1991: 18.2; 1992 (Jan):19.2; 1992 (Mar):17.7. One possible explanation is more generous child benefits.

11 A similar coefficient of 1 to 2 was found in Poland (Jackman, Layard and Scott, 1992)

12 The monthly diet includes (kilograms) 8 bread, 6.7 potatoes, 10.1 vegetables, 2.3 sugar, 0.8 vegetable oil, 3.2 meat (products), 26 milk (products), 1.4 fish, 1 fruit, and 1.5 dozen eggs. This was influenced by Popkin (1992)

13 The value of the earnings-related portion of the pension has virtually disappeared.

14 Includes clothing allowance.

Part II
Government Strategies

4 Russia's Negotiations with the IMF

Alexei V. Mozhin

Introduction

The new Russian Government began cooperation with the IMF immediately after coming to office in November 1991. At that time, Russia had the status of associated member of the IMF, a status which had been granted to the USSR and its constituent republics in October 1991. From the very beginning the government was intent on applying for full membership for Russia. Moreover, it was decided that even before formal membership, Russia should begin serious discussions with the IMF on economic policy issues "as if we were members". These discussions eventually resulted in negotiations on the *Economic Policy Memorandum* which was signed by Deputy Prime Minister Yegor Gaidar and Central Bank Chairman Georgii Matyukhin and sent to the Fund in February 1992.

There were three main reasons for this strategy. It was expected that this memorandum would allow the Russian Government, first, to gain valuable experience in advance of formal negotiations with the Fund on its standard stand-by program; second, to gain international support for its economic policy; and third, on the basis of international support, to gain political support at home for its economic policy.

Russia applied for full membership in the Fund on January 3, 1992. The Resolution on Russian membership was approved by the Board of Governors of the IMF on April 24, 1992. The Russian Parliament ratified the Articles of Agreement of the Fund on May 22, 1992. Finally, on June 1, 1992, or less than five months after application, the Articles of Agreement were signed by the authorized representative of the Russian Government, and Russia became a full member of the IMF. Even before that the formal negotiations on the stand-by program had started. At this point it may be of some interest to examine the background of the Economic Policy Memorandum. This chapter will present a brief analysis of the memorandum negotiations, and present the commitments made and to what extent they have been implemented.

Pricing policy and inflation

Negotiation

The bulk of domestic prices in Russia were liberalized on January 2, 1992. However, prices of a number of basic consumer goods (bread, milk, vodka, etc.) remained regulated. There was little discussion about further price liberalization. The Russian side readily agreed to remove the remaining price controls on consumer goods in due time. The IMF side readily agreed that housing rents, public utilities, and public transportation fares should continue to be regulated for the time being.

The most intensive discussion concerned energy prices. Initially the IMF side did not insist on liberalizing energy prices. This idea was suggested by the Russian side. In response the IMF side suggested that energy prices be regulated with the use of export taxes that would capture the gap between domestic and world market prices, thus allowing the elimination of export quotas for energy products. Without offering any good explanation, the Russian side agreed to the export tax system but refused to eliminate quotas.

Commitments

The main commitments in this section are the following:
— all consumer prices remaining regulated should be liberalized by the end of March 1992 with the exception of housing rents, public utilities, and public transportation fares;
— by April 20, 1992 (supposedly the end of the heating season) energy prices would be liberalized and new export taxes for energy products should be introduced.

Implementation

All remaining consumer prices (except vodka prices) were liberalized by the Presidential Decree of March 7, 1992. The price of vodka was liberalized soon thereafter. However, the commitment to liberalize energy prices was not fulfilled. Instead oil price policy had become a very hot political issue in Russia. The influential enterprise lobby on the one hand demanded that domestic oil prices be kept low, and on the other hand that export taxes on oil should also be kept low. Such a system would entail a subsidization of unprofitable domestic sales of oil through highly profitable export sales.

Social safety net

Negotiations

There was no serious debate on social safety net. Perhaps the IMF side was too cautious to suggest cut-backs, trying to appear flexible in order to avoid the traditional criticism that they are insensitive to human hardship. They only insisted that the existing system of unemployment compensation was too generous and should be changed.

Commitments

The main commitments on social security measures are the following:
—housing rents, public utilities and public transportation fares should be increased in line with rising costs;
—the payment of pensions and social security benefits should be limited by the financial resources of the Pension Fund and Social Security Fund;
—a new system of unemployment compensation should be introduced by June 1, 1992.

Implementation

Between February and June 1992, housing rents and public utilities and public transportation fares were increased a number of times, more or less in line with increases in costs. In the first quarter of 1992, both the Pension Fund and the Social Security Fund showed surpluses. However, the new system of unemployment compensation has not been introduced. This has not yet entailed any serious problems, since unemployment is almost non-existent and not expected to increase before the fall.

Fiscal policy

Negotiations

During negotiations, much time was spent on discussing the conceptual issues of fiscal policy. The very notion of a budget on a commitment basis as opposed to a budget on a cash basis was a novelty to the Russian side. The idea of balancing the budget (presumably on a cash basis) by the end of 1992 was included upon the insistence of the Russian side. The IMF side was rather sceptical about both revenue and expenditure projections and predicted a budget deficit of about 14 percent of the GDP for the first quarter of 1992. At the same time it insisted on a number of revenue-increasing measures.

Commitments

The main commitments in this section are the following:
—the deficit of the consolidated budget in the first quarter of 1992 (on a cash basis) should be within 1 percent of the GDP;
—the full 28 percent VAT rates should be reimposed for all products in the budget for the second quarter;
—the number of tax concessions and exemptions should be reduced;
—additional taxation of energy production and consumption should be introduced together with the liberalization of the energy prices on April 20, 1992;
—imports should be made subject to the VAT and excise taxes by July 1, 1992.

Implementation

According to Russian data, the consolidated budget (on a cash basis) in the first quarter of 1992 showed a surplus mainly as a result of the policy of strict sequestering of expenditures not covered by revenues. Since Russia was not servicing either internal or external debt, the budget deficit on a commitment basis was estimated by the IMF side at the level of about 6-7 percent of the GDP. Fierce opposition in the Parliament prevented both the reimposition of the full VAT rates and the reduction of the number of tax concessions and exemptions. And while no liberalization of energy prices took place, increased taxation of energy production and consumption was introduced in April 1992.

Monetary policy

Negotiations

The main demand of the IMF side regarding monetary policy was that Russia should quickly move towards introducing positive real interest rates. Despite this very strong pressure, the leadership of the Central

Bank of Russia (CBR) refused to commit itself to any specific date. Another major topic of discussion was monetary cooperation in the ruble area. Since no progress was being made in negotiations between republican central banks, the CBR could agree only to a very vague declaration of intention to coordinate monetary policy with the other participants of the ruble area. Due to total uncertainty and confusion in the monetary sphere, no quantitative targets for the overall growth in money supply were discussed. However at the very last moment the leadership of the CBR decided to impose a limit on its lending to the government at the level of 2 percent of the GDP.

Commitments

The main commitments made in monetary policy are the following:
—the CBR should introduce positive real interest rates as soon as possible;
—the Government should introduce a more realistic interest rate on its internal debt by April 1, 1992;
—the ceiling for CBR lending to commercial banks in the first quarter of 1992 should be 15 percent;
—CBR lending to the government should be no more than 2 percent of the GDP.

Implementation

Despite the CBR's strong reluctance to make any commitments, the movement towards positive real interest rates was quite impressive. The CBR refinance rate was increased from 20 percent to 50 percent in April and to 80 percent in May. Since the budget in the first quarter showed a surplus, CBR lending to the government was not an issue. However CBR lending to commercial banks in the first quarter increased by more than 100 percent, instead of the agreed 15 percent. The government also failed to honour its commitment to raise the interest rate on its internal debt.

Incomes Policy

Negotiations

The IMF team was very insistent on the introduction of progressive taxation on excessive wage growth. The Russian team initially agreed but at the very last moment rejected the idea. There were three major reasons for its reluctance to commit itself to any tax-based incomes policy. First, in December 1991 the government had promised that price liberalization would be accompanied by wage liberalization. Second, the government did not want to freeze the existing wage structure since it was very distorted. Third, neither Russia's past experience with tax-based incomes policy put forward by the Deputy Prime Minister Leonid Abalkin, nor the Polish experience with the *popiwek* from the beginning of 1990 had been very encouraging.

External policy

Negotiations

Unification of the exchange rate for current account transactions had top priority on the IMF list. The Russian side readily agreed. However in February the Russian side had not yet been ready to reject the idea of a special investment rate. The major topic of discussion was a floating exchange rate regime versus a pegged exchange rate regime. The Russian side insisted on quick movement to a pegged exchange rate and demanded a clear statement about a stabilization fund. It also demanded a clear statement on other forms of external financial assistance including humanitarian aid, balance of payments support, and further debt-servicing relief. The IMF side finally had to agree.

Commitments

The main commitments regarding external policy are the following:
—the multiple exchange rate system should be abolished and a uniform exchange rate system should be introduced by April 20, 1992;
—a new law on foreign exchange regulation and control, providing for the development of the foreign exchange market, should be in effect by April 1, 1992;
—all export quotas except those on energy products should be eliminated by July 1, 1992.

Implementation

As a result of political struggle in April the Russian Government was unable to fulfil its commitments. The multiple exchange rate system is still in place. The new law on foreign exchange regulation and control has not been passed yet. The new plan is to introduce a uniform exchange rate system from July 1, 1992, and to simultaneously eliminate the export quotas.

Appendices to the memorandum

Initially it was expected that there would be three appendices to the Economic Policy Memorandum regarding the budget, balance of payments, and monetary targets. As mentioned above, it proved impossible to design monetary policy using quantitative terms because of the great uncertainty and confusion. For the same reasons it was agreed, with little difficulty, to discuss only the budget for the first quarter. The main battle was over the projections for the balance of payments. Since imports fell by almost 50 percent in 1991, the Russian side insisted on being allowed some recovery in imports. The difference between the Russian side's figure and the IMF figure for the financing gap was almost $20 bn. No agreement was possible at that time. Later, in March 1992, after a new round of negotiations in Washington, an agreement was reached.

Conclusions

Negotiations over the Economic Policy Memorandum allowed the Russian side to gain valuable experience which would be useful in the stand-by program negotiations that still lay ahead. The Memorandum also helped increase international support for the Russian Government's economic policy, which resulted in the international aid package to Russia announced in April. This international support also helped the Russian Government to strengthen its position at home and to survive a tough political battle in April. However, the credibility of the Russian Government may be damaged in the long run by its poor implementation of the proclaimed policies.

5 Economic Reform in Russia: Social, Political, and Institutional Aspects

Sergei A. Vasiliev

When analysing the course of economic reforms in Russia, observers often draw parallels with transformations in this field, in Eastern Europe and Latin America. However, they sometimes overlook a specific feature of Russia's transition period, namely that the transition in Russia involves more than a stabilisation and deregulation of the economy. It also constitutes a change of its basic elements, setting in motion a different mechanism.

In Russia, where communist ideology and practice evolved as a result of the country's own historical development, the model of the centrally planned economy has been rather firmly rooted. The economic transition has been much easier for Eastern Europe and the Baltic countries, since socialism was transplanted into these countries, and was always perceived as an alien system, kept alive by force. Accordingly, most people there were mentally prepared for a return to a market economy. Indeed, the swift transition to a market economy demonstrated by these countries is a result of concentrated efforts by both their governments and society.

Meanwhile, the countries where communism developed as an organic ideology (Yugoslavia, China, and Cuba) have to traverse a long and tortuous path to market economy and democracy. In 1989-1991, many analysts assumed that the people in Russia (the Soviet Union) would not accept radical reforms, with liberalised and rising prices as their first stage. Their assumption was that after price liberalisation, mass public protest would prompt the government to mount social expenditures to an extent that would soon lead to hyperinflation.

Reality proved to be different in practically every aspect. The multiple price rises following liberalisation in January 1992 did not provoke any upsurge in social protest either in the form of strikes or in any other action, whether organised or spontaneous. Yet, the process of change itself develops extremely slowly, which to a large degree is due to social inertia and institutional barriers to reforms. Thus, if we are to gain a clear view of the prospects for reforms, it is important identify the social, political and institutional factors that will aid or impede economic reforms in Russia.

Long-term social factors

Certain features of the Russian national character have commonly been regarded as serious impediments to increasing the role of the market in Russia. Indeed, traits such as the communal spirit (as opposed to individualism), contempt for commerce as an occupation, mistrust of the rich, especially of the newly-rich, and a grudge against prosperous neighbours have a long history. They impeded the development of capitalism in the 19th century and played a certain role in the socialist revolution. Naturally, they became even more emphasised in the post-revolutionary period.

No less important is the traditional Russian attitude of the individual towards power and law. For a Russian, power is always more authoritative than law. The lack of grass-roots initiative has been compensated by subordination to the initiative of the boss. Law was seen as just a nuisance in everyday life. While the boss's instructions or orders might occasionally be ignored, laws were never observed. Lodging a complaint with the powers-that-be, that is, the boss, the chief, or the superior administrator, was the most natural way of upholding one's rights in Russia. Turning to the court of law was condemned as petty solicitation.

The lack of respect for property rights and terms of contract arises from the same source. Over the centuries, the overwhelming majority of Russia's population had practically no property, and whatever it had could be removed any time by the arbitrary order of the authorities. Nor could contractual law develop, since the right of property is at its core.

For this reason the early Russian capitalist market was plagued by broken commitments. Business hinged on what we call common law and moral obligations, what playwright A.N. Ostrovsky termed as "the merchant's word of honour". Of course, this "word of honour" evaporated in the 70 years of socialism. And yet, the financial and industrial groups emerging today are very often based on kinship or friendship. Amid these vaguely defined patterns of property and contractual relations, bribes seem quite a natural instrument. They are still considered justified in pursuing private economic interests, but they also burden the economy, particularly the private sector, with additional non-productive costs.

On the other hand, there are also cultural and historical factors facilitating the implementation of economic reforms, for instance, the absence of xenophobia in business relations, and a public consciousness that treats Western businessmen as more experienced and practical than the local ones.

Achievements of socialism

These specific social features of Russia changed little over the socialist period, but there were some radical shifts in social structure, which most experts tend to overlook. These shifts, however, are highly important for Russia's readiness to accept a market economy today.

The transition to capitalism, to a market economy, in earlier times always occurred in the environment of the traditional stratification of society with a predominantly rural population. Social mobility was very low. The transition process and the development of market relations were accompanied by revolutionary changes in at least two spheres. Traditional societies were broken down and stratification barriers between estates collapsed. Second, the process of urbanisation swept the countries in transition, prompting huge masses of people to change their habitual way of life in the course of just one or two generations. Both these factors played a highly destabilising role in the transition period and set the stage for various extremist trends and deviations in the ensuing development.

Russia today is in an exceptionally favourable position in this respect. The urbanisation process is practically completed, society has achieved an advantageous homogeneity, and the geographical mobility of the population is high. Altogether, this creates favourable conditions for the development of a market economy, and contract-based relations between individuals.

Russian society is also much more homogeneous than the advanced Western societies, because its horizontal links are extremely slim and scanty. This is the heritage of the administrative command system under which all links in society were structured vertically and whatever horizontal links that spontaneously appeared were quickly suppressed. The abolition of the command mechanism has brought about the destruction of these traditional vertical structures. New horizontal structures are taking shape, albeit rather slowly. On the whole, this situation is highly favourable for market reforms.

Current social dynamics

Apart from the long-term factors that have a bearing on the course of economic reforms, recent changes have altered the dynamics of social forces and social expectations of the population in various ways. The process of polarisation of forces was nearing a peak in 1991, when the country was fraught with a destructive social outburst. Expectations grew that new conspiracies and coups would erupt and bring at least some clarity to the economic and political situation, stop the disintegration process, and break the vicious circle of populism, which had a strong impact on government policy both in the Union as a whole and in the Russian Federation. At the same time, it was evident that extremist actions could not solve the practical tasks facing the country, but only destabilise the situation, possibly giving rise to armed conflicts between various groups of the population.

For the economy, the political developments in 1991 contributed to an accelerated production slump and hyperinflation was set in motion. Various sociological surveys showed that pessimistic attitudes predominated among the public, and there was no serious hope for any real shifts in economic policy.

When the Russian president rejected his previous populist ideology he created a fundamentally new situation and resolutely turned towards real (however painful) socio-economic change, creating a fundamentally new situation. His turn offered a way out of the standard logic of revolutionary crisis, which usually entails a social explosion and dictatorship following the polarisation of social forces. Instead, a radical change of system in Russia could be implemented with smoother, peaceful political methods.

This, however, was in itself laden with socio-political dangers. To pursue economic stabilisation, and in particular a radical reform of a liberal type, amid a profound crisis, inevitably aggravates the social situation and entails considerable expenses for almost all strata of the population. The question that naturally arose was whether the people were prepared to go through such a reform despite the considerable cost, and thus whether the reform would work.

Historical experience and common sense indicate that economic stabilisation and subsequent reforms produce the best results in a society that has been recently hit by social upheavals, high unemployment, and hyperinflation. In these conditions, the people's expectations are lower, and the bulk of the population are prepared to pay a high price for the restoration of economic stability.

In this respect, the situation in the country in early 1992 was rather ambiguous. Although no explosive effect was evident, social attitudes were blunted by fatigue, the people were no longer responsive to slogans calling for violence, war, or confrontation of classes. The popularity of the president who led the government of unpopular reforms was still rather high. There were no indications of a "revolution of expectations". Hopes for an economic miracle were practically exhausted, and nearly two-thirds of the population did not believe the crisis could be overcome without declining standards of living. But the potential threat of mass discontent remains an essential element in the country's political life, and must be reckoned with in the economic stabilisation.

This threat has not materialised. Price liberalisation and the first stabilisation measures caused no open social conflict. On the contrary, the first stage of economic reforms were met with fairly high acceptance of the liberalisation and stabilisation policies. As indicated in Table 1, public opinion polls conducted regularly from November 1991 to March 1992 in four major cities recorded practically unchanging attitudes to free prices.

Table 1 Attitudes to free prices, 1991-1992

The table shows the share of respondents answering "yes" to the question:

"Will the introduction of free prices help overcome the economic crisis?"

City of poll	1991 November	1992 January	February	March
St Petersburg	32%	28%	35%	45%
Moscow	30%	30%	33%	29%
Kemerovo	—	—	23%	19%
Samara	—	—	—	19%

Table 2 Attitudes towards price liberalisation in St. Petersburg, 1991-1992

		1991	1992 January	February	March
% supporting price	Yes	32	28	35	45
liberalisation	No	25	33	22	16
% admitting respons-	Yes	19	17	20	27
ibility for their own	No	56	63	56	50
well-being					

In some places (e.g. St. Petersburg) the share of supporters of price liberalisation increased significantly in this period. In parallel, citizens grew more aware of their own responsibility for their own well-being, implying their acceptance of economic liberalisation.

At the same time, the next stage of reforms is likely to bring about a considerable realignment of socio-political forces. Certain conclusions can be drawn from the experience of both industrialised and developing countries. In a reform aiming at the stabilisation and deregulation of an economy, anti-inflationary measures face the least resistance. Indeed, inflation affects the interests of the entire society, while stabilisation may be tackled at the macro-economic level.

On the other hand deregulation measures, which forms the strategic continuation of the stabilisation programme, will encounter stiff resistance from various social groups, whose privileged status they undermine. Such privileges are all kinds of subsidies, credits on easy terms, and customs preferences. Each of these privileges incurs a certain cost on society as a whole, but the popular perception is that the cost in each particular case is insignificant compared with the lucrative benefits the group in question derives. A strong pressure group therefore tends to gather around each of the privileges to obstruct its repeal. During Russia's fast transition to a market economy, new pressure groups and corresponding political structures have not taken shape, while the old pressure groups are more or less demoralised at present.

Survey of political forces in Russia

Russia's political parties are small numerically and poorly organised. The parties' real political clout in an election will presumably depend on the strength of their candidates' appeal to the voters rather than on the party's organisational potential. The experience of the election campaigns in 1989 and 1990 indicates that so far it is the personality of the candidate, not the programme, that matters to voters in Russia. The introduction of proportional representation would accelerate the formation of parties, but it will not change the situation radically or swiftly.

Trade unions and associations of businessmen and industrialists are also only in their nascent stage. The traditional pro-communist trade unions, though retaining part of their property, financial resources and — formally — their members, are absolutely incapable of exerting any influence among the workers. Independent unions, though energetic and led by more intelligent people, are still small and locked in competition with one another. There is nothing similar to Poland's Solidarity in Russia as yet.

The situation is about the same in the entrepreneurial community. The proportion of businessmen who belong to associations is quite small, and their various organisations, as in the case of trade unions, compete in just about every sphere of activity. Many businessmen are merely formal members rather than active ones. This is not to to say that entrepreneurs exert no influence on the government, quite the contrary. However, entrepreneurs prefer to deal with the government on an individual basis, soliciting specific privileges for their enterprises. Of course, to a certain extent this devalues some reform measures, but poses no immediate threat to the principal course.

Considering the status of trade unions and business associations, the creation of a tripartite commission appears a mistake by the government, since in this commission the government has to interact with two other parties, the unions and business associations, which represent practically nobody. The government's obligations are real, while those of its partners are fictitious. In addition, since 90 per cent of Russia's economy is state-owned, employers and hired labour are in no conflict with each other, and consequently, the government does not have the role of moderator. In fact, it is the other way round — the unions and employers are in conflict with the government.

However weak the cohesion of workers and entrepreneurs, there are already indications that the situation is changing. The state employees who were hit hardest by the price liberalisation (medical workers, teachers and transport workers) staged well-organised strikes and managed to gain considerable wage increases. Thus, soon the government might no longer be able to ignore organised entrepreneurs and workers. Therefore it has to make the best of the time left to draft and enact rules and procedures for the interaction with the leading interest groups in society, in order to minimise the scope for non-constructive pressure.

Since parties, trade unions, and entrepreneurial interest groups are only loosely identified, we should instead look to the representative bodies of power elected three years ago, and to a lesser extent, to the presidency, as major possible sources of resistance to reform.

The power structure

The most essential element in Russia's political life today is the split of power structures, cutting society practically from top to bottom. The split is most pronounced in the upper echelons of power. The conflict between the executive branch and the legislature is certainly not of a personal nature and cannot be overcome by a mere reshuffling of posts.

The Congress of People's Deputies of Russia and the Supreme Soviet (Parliament) were formed on a non-party basis with candidates running as individuals. These bodies do not have close links with political parties, business associations, or trade unions. Deputies have poor ties to their electorate, since most of them stand no chance of being re-elected. The best organised groups in the Supreme Soviet, managers of collective farms and the old party cadres, are openly opposed to reforms.

In principle, the corps of deputies, connected as it is with the interests of pressure groups, cannot support harsh unpopular decisions. Given the absence of any clear stratification in post-Soviet society and the extreme weakness of political parties, parliamentary groups and individual deputies often come out as advocates of rather narrow interests that they purport are national concerns.

The government can interact with the Parliament through individual contacts with vacillating centrist deputies, who after all constitute a majority in Parliament, though their vacillation implies political instability. Another option would be to dissolve the Parliament and re-draft the Constitution; while this would provide for short-term stability, it would subvert the legitimacy of the government's further actions in pursuing economic reforms.

Before the presidential office was formed in Russia, the mechanism of parliamentary democracy itself (apart from the old communist structures) blocked any decisive economic transformations. The institution of the presidency arose as a new legitimate branch of power, it provided an alternative to the Parliament of equal legislative weight, and it is capable of pursuing a sufficiently independent political course. These constitutional measures opened the way for reforms, but they also provide a basis for inevitable political crises in the future. This is the political price that has to be paid for a democratic, non-violent path of economic reforms.

The Presidency exerts a rather contradictory influence on the course of reforms. On the one hand, the concentration of power in the hands of the president and the additional powers to implement economic reforms that have been granted to him by the Congress eliminate delays in the adoption of legislative acts. This accelerates the process of reform. On the other hand, this concentration of power makes the president's apparatus a very attractive place for sundry lobbyists, and the solution of various issues may be decided not only by the knowledge and experiences, but also by their biases and personal connections of presidential advisers. Such personal factors have led to the adoption of many decisions on specific privileges for certain enterprises and regions.

At the first stage of reforms, one distinction of the executive branch is the degree of ideological thrust in its policy, especially in matters of principle. This is a necessary condition, if profound reforms are to be implemented, while political pragmatism, which is normally justified, becomes extremely dangerous. But it has proved difficult to follow this principle. The list of compromises the reforms suffered in the first months of 1992 is sizeable, though it did not surpass the critical limits.

Another feature of the reform government was that it lacked both a political profile of its own and any visible and reliable social constituency. Since its measures were unpopular in all social strata, the government simply could not have such a base. Instead the reform team has to be prepared for continual political manoeuvring. Yet there is not much leeway for such manoeuvring for the reasons mentioned above.

At a practical level, the government has to choose all the time between alternative alliances with influential forces in order to achieve a constructive interaction and political stability, so that it can pursue its policies. This has been possible so far, because of a balance of powerful groups, support for the government and the support of the president. But the events during the 6th Congress of Russia in April 1992 demonstrated that the government has to turn into a political force in its own right, but this does not necessarily mean any orientation to a specific social group.

The relationship between politics and the economy

Political life today is characterized by a low degree of social and political activism among the population. We can see indications of this in the constantly declining turnout of voters in local elections, the lack of mass support for practically all political parties and movements, and the absence of mass actions on socio-political issues. Sociological surveys invariably demonstrate that rallies, both of democratic and communist orientation are dominated by pensioners and white-collar workers. Russian businessmen and industrialists are showing scant interest in political life. Exceptions to this rule are rare, and can be explained by personal traits.

The relationship between politics and the economy and their impact on the country has changed greatly since the reform government was formed in November 1991. Before, the economy was hostage to a political struggle, and it was used as a pawn in the fight for power. For instance, production slumps were provoked by strikes and local separatism, while duels over taxation and price between Russia and the USSR took place. The situation began to change in late 1991. Economic decline was getting out of control, assuming its own inertia and inner logic. Meanwhile, the depth of the crisis and the fall of living standards were brought out by the government's measures to liberalise the economy, to make inflation an overt process and to raise public awareness of the depression and prospects of unemployment. As a result, the population began to pay much more attention to the economic aspects of politics. Any government that wants to hold on to power must be able to convince the president and the people that it is best suited to grapple with the present economic problems. In short, the economy will become the field for decisive political battles in the foreseeable future.

If we look at the effect of social factors on the formation of reform policy, we can see that theorists and practitioners alike have suffered from a profound delusion. Their delusion has consisted of a belief that a correct policy must be based on a balance of the interests and demands of various social groups. Thus, a rational policy should emerge as a combination of the interests of all social groups, and the main objective of politicians should be to "expand the social basis for reforms". This approach may be justified in a stationary society or when the balance of various forces ensures a steady development of society. However, neither is applicable to a society in crisis. The present crisis of Russian society is of systematic nature. It was the "normal" functioning of social relations in the old system that led the country into steady decline; and it was the principle of political consensus of the Brezhnev era that was conserving the traditional system and slowly pushing the country into a crisis.

The reforms have not arisen out of the daily interests of any particular group of people, let alone social groups, but rather from society's awareness of being in an impasse. In fact the reform runs counter to the daily interests of most of the population, disrupting established patterns of production and consumption. This explains the unstable, contradictory position of reformist governments. A society vexed with crisis tends to entrust its destiny democratically to a charismatic leader and a group of reformers, because it believes in their programme and sees no other way.

Hence the government does not endeavour to maximise its popularity, but it is important that its active opponents are not too numerous at the critical political moments. In any case, public sentiment during a crisis cannot serve as an indicator of whether the course of reform is correct or not.

Social prospects of the reforms: The relationship between the executive and the legislative branches

The chance of the preservation of a strong legislative branch in Russia appears slim for the foreseeable future. The deterioration of the economic situation and the social hardships brought about by the economic reform have been accompanied by a reinforcement of authoritarian principles in the exercise of political power. The situation is compounded, first, by the absence of consensus in society and in Parliament, and second, by the need to bolster state authority so that important political decisions can be adopted quickly.

But concentration of power and strong state authority do not imply the centralisation of power, as power is concentrated in the hands of the leader and delegated down the entire administrative chain. How Russian state authority will be legitimized in the future will largely be clarified within a year. In the presence of two bearers of legitimate power, the Parliament and the president, there is a legal way to concentrate the entire authority in the hands of the president. The procedures for the formation of a government will be one of the crucial issues for the nature of a new political regime. In a democratic order, the weakening of Parliament and consolidation of strong state power will be accompanied by increasingly frequent messages from the head of state to the nation and regular referendums.

A simple dissolution of Parliament can hardly be expected. Parliament may stay put, turning in practice into a politically obedient body, sharply criticising executive power but supporting it in time of need. Then, the president will have a wider choice of means for exerting pressure on Parliament than if new elections were to be held on a multi-party basis. He can issue covert threats to organise a referendum, or to discuss the adoption of a new constitution in order to put pressure on Parliament. In such a situation, Parliament is likely to turn into a committee lobbying for the interests of rather small and socially unrepresentative pressure groups.

Direct dissolution of Parliament would be dangerous, since it might enhance political instability and undermine the legitimacy of presidential power in the eyes of part of the population, and especially in the regional administration.

The consolidation of presidential power, with the establishment of strong legitimate state authority, should be copied at local level: Local executive structures should grow more powerful, while regional councils should loose clout, regardless of their political colour.

But if strong state power fails to gain hold, with Parliament sticking to its guns and the president unable to get hold of the legislative structures, the result will not be the preservation of democracy and plurality. Instead the worsening economic crisis will increase the chances of illegitimate authoritarian rule being established.

Meanwhile, an aggravation of the economic crisis will be practically inevitable, as legislators will actively intervene politically in the functioning of the economy. At present, parliamentary groups do not adequately reflect the balance of forces in society. Therefore, a broad consensus in Parliament does not necessarily mean that a decision enjoys genuine majority support in society. The reason is that a considerable proportion of parliamentarians confuse their narrow factional interests with national and strategic aims. This is not strange, since industrial managers predominate among the legislators. As a result, their decisions tend to block radical reforms. All of this has the effect of discrediting those very institutes of democratic power, which makes the task of eliminating them so much easier for a "third force".

Social prospects of the reforms: Government and society

The strengthening of state power in the implementation of economic reforms would give a greater scope of action for the president in forming the government and its structures. The government would become more dependent on the president, while the constitutional system remains intact.

Undoubtedly, the political stability of the reform course depends on the consolidation of state power. However, as Parliament's role weakens, the president-government relationship may be endangered, if the head of state no longer considers himself bound by earlier obligations to the government. Therefore it will be critically important for the government's ability to implement reforms, but how the president will deal with well-organised pressure groups, such as the security and law and order agencies, while pressure from Parliament will be less significant, such pressure groups formed by traditional rivals, such as the military-industrial complex and the agricultural industries, or entrepreneurs and trade unions. In principle, the government does have the leverage to prevent the formation of such blocs, but these issues must constantly be kept in mind.

The government's effective tool here may be to differentiate the granting of credits, and later — tax privileges. A large number of unpredictable factors influence the prospects of the reform. One important issue is that the government develops a more definite and well established image. Essential features of the image of the present government should be: constant active moves, even if rather painful; a resolute rejection of any populist bent, and readiness to opt for unpopular measures, including allowing a growth of unemployment; a reduction of inflation; the saturation of the market, whatever the prices of the goods; and caution with regard to large-scale privatisation. A large part of the population is aware that considerable hardships are an inevitable cost of overcoming the crisis but they must be convinced that the measures are effective, so that they sense that they can see the light at the end of the tunnel.

As in January, in the middle of 1992, the question will again arise whether the effectiveness of the liberalisation policy should be measured by the amount of goods available in the shops. It is not only a question of inflation on the consumer market. First, the convertibility of the ruble and the liberalisation of foreign trade must be tackled. So far this has been a weak point in the reform programme, but now it is possible to take decisive reform steps in this sphere. Second, the harvest will have important consequences. Presumably deliveries of farm produce to the market will suffer from complications. Russian grain prices have moved closer to the world level and producers have reoriented themselves to free sales instead of the state, but because of inflationary expectations less grain will probably be available for sales. Meat supplies will be even more complicated, since production costs are increasing and production is declining. The situation will be worse if the Russian farm sector encounters foreign competition in the autumn of 1992. Imports of consumer goods will stimulate agricultural sales, while the influx of food will create dangerous competition on the home market.

However, the consumer market will probably become reasonably balanced in the course of 1992, which is highly important for the image and stability of the reform government. If the market receive first a certain minimum of goods thanks to the liberalisation of prices and at a second stage more goods because of the liberalisation of foreign trade, the main focus of social and political discontent will soon be the problems of stagnant production and unemployment. At present, the only plausible source of production growth is foreign investments. Therefore it will become an essential policy issue to attract foreign investment and make sure that they are used efficiently. However, before economic recovery starts, negative attitudes will grow among the population, causing a period of instability and unpredictability. If this period lasts for more than a few months, severe economic disruption is all too likely and it will pose a serious threat to the reform.

The regional dimension

The disintegration of the vertical power structures of the former Soviet Union prompted various regions of Russia to demand autonomy. Centralised authority within Russia has been greatly undermined. The traditional form of administration, which was based on the party's control and ultimately on fear and coercion, has disappeared, while a new, civilised interaction between power and society, based on the principle of law, has not yet taken shape. As a result, local government, which is located closer to the population has retained much more of its power than the central government.

Today Russia is often compared with the USSR, and many expect that

Russia will disintegrate into a number of independent states. Separatist trends do exist, but in themselves they present little threat even in the long term. There are several factors that influence interregional relations. One important factor is the deepening economic crisis. The struggle for survival amid the severe crisis brings people's primary values and links to the foreground, such as ethnic and territorial identities. Growing economies are usually more inclined towards integration. But it is yet to be proven that integration helps to overcome a profound crisis.

Second, this is a case of the disintegration of a huge unitary state which in its present form is poorly adjusted to a market economy. A search is under way for the most effective political and economic territorial structure for market economy and democracy. In the near future attention should be concentrated on the issues of administrative and territorial structures, on the one hand, and the improvement of the federal system of government, on the other.

Economic difficulties will soon cease to dominate as a cause of regional discord, if the reform policies continue. Economic stabilisation is impeding disintegration and promotes the formation of a national market. Neither ethnic nor political problems are so sharp that they will bring about a final disintegration of Russia. The dominating Russian nation does not suffer from any regional splits in its cultural roots or political links.

In order to curb the process of disintegration, a constitutional restructuring of Russia's territories would be advisable. No uniform federal pattern can be applied as current local developments are so varied. In contrast to the USSR, the present central government of Russia can conclude separate agreements with territorial governments concerning their scope of authority in its own right. The status of territories and ethnic formations may gradually change, eventually reaching a confederative level, which would not be very dramatic, if it is only caused by the geographic peculiarities of Russia.

Consequently, in order to ensure the success of the reforms as a whole, the central government will have to make significant concessions to regional elites. Deregulation of the economy means a shrinking of the sphere of political influence. In this regard the interests of the central and local governments diverge radically, as the local politicians want to retain power. The only way out is to transform local political elites into managerial personnel. This process has already gained speed: former party bosses are moving into recently founded commercial establishments, carrying parts of the state property with them.

This administrative privatisation should be treated with a measure of caution. What would be even more dangerous is the fusion of new commercial establishments with new bodies of power, through which these new businessmen could gain privileges, such as monopoly rights. The emerging regional monopolies are highly resilient: they use their extraordinary profits to retain their monopoly position by political pressure and bribery of officials. This kind of monopy presents one of the most grave threats to the reforms, since it blocks any local transformations.

Conclusion

This analysis indicates that while Russia's historical and cultural traditions are unfavourable for the development of a market economy, a number of prerequisites for market development, such as urbanisation and social homogeneity have appeared in recent times. The collapse of the vertical links that were characteristic of the communist society created an institutional vacuum in the wake of the transformation, but the weakness of democratic institutions makes the government vulnerable to pressure groups.

This contradictory state of affairs does not offer great hope for a speedy recuperation for Russia's crisis. Institutional changes will apparently go ahead, albeit slowly. At the same time, the stabilisation policy will come up against considerable difficulties. If democratic institutions are maintained, frequent changes of cabinets are inevitable, and at least some of them will opt for populist policies. In the near future, Russia's economy will probably face a sequence of stabilisation and periods of high inflation, while the depression will continue. Only gradually can successful privatisation and the development of the market infrastructure set the stage for long-term stabilisation as the basis for future non-inflationary economic growth.

Part III

Privatisation

6 Main Issues of Privatisation in Russia

Anatoly Chubais and Maria Vishnevskaya

Status of the privatisation process

The start of orderly privatisation in Russia can be dated to July 1991, when the Law on Privatisation of State and Municipal Enterprises in the RSFSR was adopted. Yet by the end of 1991 privatisation had been implemented on an extremely limited scale. This was for a number of reasons, ranging from the lack of a clear strategy for enforcing the new legislation to the absence of a clear division of state property rights. The legal framework for privatisation was clearly insufficient, and the institutional infrastructure was underdeveloped.

In the whole of 1991 the value of state property transferred to private and/or collective ownership equalled 2 billion rubles, while budget revenues resulting from privatisations amounted to less than 200 million rubles. By January 1992 only 70 enterprises had come under private ownership and 922 under collective ownership.

In practice, the privatisation process was launched only after adoption of the "Basic provisions for the privatisation of state and municipal enterprises in the Russian Federation in 1992". The legal basis for starting the organizational work came from the decree of the Supreme Soviet "On the division of state property into federal property, state property of the federation's constituent republics, krais, oblasts...", approved in January 1992 along with a set of normative documents governing the privatisation procedure.

State property management committees have been set up in almost all the 20 republics of the Russian Federation and in all its 86 okrugs, krais and oblasts. Such committees now function in all regional centres, as well as in many other cities. The establishment of property management committees at district (i.e., raion) level is soon to be completed. A massive sell-out of municipal property — primarily of shops and establishments providing consumer services — was launched in early 1992. By summer 1992 Russia was approaching the end of the first stage of the privatisation process, the purpose of which was:

- to elaborate the legal framework for privatisation;
- to create the organizational structure of privatisation at all-Russian and local levels, including provision of office facilities;
- and to move on to the substance of the process, i.e. to have local privatisation programmes adopted and implemented, leading to a sharp increase in the number of concluded privatisations, and of revenues obtained from them.

In this context mention should be made of the negative experience of small-scale privatisation in Moscow. It shows that the free transfer or preferential direct sale of shops and enterprises to labour collectives is a method of privatisation to be avoided. Clearly, no improvement was made to management in these businesses, and this threatens to discredit the very idea of privatisation among the population.

Fortunately, all segments of society now seem to approve of the notion of privatisation by vouchers. Growing support for this method represents a particularly welcome development, since it is the method preferred by the government in privatising large state enterprises and in bringing them under the control of responsible owners.

Yet, several critical issues remain to be tackled. One is the problem of sabotage of privatisation by local authorities and government employees. Another is the problem of "nomenklatura" privatisation. Of immediate concern has been the insufficient preparation for mass and large-scale privatisation, as in summer 1992 the commercialisation of large-scale industry was only beginning and distribution of vouchers was yet to start. Also, the legal system is in a state of flux, and various management bodies are engaged in conflicts over their respective powers in the process of privatisation.

Principles of state privatisation programme

The first main stage of privatisation in Russia is to implement the "State privatisation programme for the state and municipal enterprises in 1992", drawn up in March of that year. The guiding principles of the programme can be summed up in these points:

- to create effective owners;
- to quickly obtain and demonstrate the results of privatisation by transforming the major part of property immediately, and transferring it- for a charge or free – to Russian and foreign shareholders;
- to boost revenues from privatisation, as progress in privatisation closely depends on the extent of success in economic stabilization;
- to ensure priority of privatisation from above by means of mandatory targets laid down in the State privatisation programme, by means of strict control by the State Committee for State Property Management (Goskomimushchestvo - GKI) of the procedure of privatisation, and by means of assistance in the staging of pilot privatisations on request from below;
- to secure fairness, thus attracting broad popular and political support;
- to coordinate the interests of those who will participate in privatisation: workers, managers, public service employees, local authorities and federal government;
- and to make provision for the use of privatisation procedures that are simple and have low organizational costs, thereby avoiding complicated methods of asset valuation.

Russia must meet the challenge now confronting her. Our policy is to speed up the process of establishing a private sector and of swiftly finding effective management for the state enterprises. Unless we succeed in this, state enterprises will remain an easy prey to spontaneous privatisation by their old directors seizing the opportunity created by the present vacuum in enterprise management.

Entering the second stage of privatisation we intend:

- to implement "small-scale" privatisation;
- to create conditions for "large-scale" privatisation in 1993-1994; to convert all large enterprises into public joint stock companies;
- to distribute among the citizens of Russia a special means of payment in the form of vouchers;
- to set up a system of financial institutions (investment funds, holdings, stock exchanges, etc.), to facilitate capital movement, including vouchers;
- to provide for the wide participation of foreign investors in privatisation;
- and to organize effective management in the enterprises still under state ownership.

Small-scale enterprises up for sale

Eligible for small-scale privatisation are enterprises with assets valued at up to 1 million rubles and with up to 200 employees operating in whole-sale and retail trade, construction, agriculture, food industry and cargo transport.

The basic method of "small-scale" privatisation is through auctions, organized by local state property management committees (local GKI departments). The plan is to privatize 50-60 per cent of those enterprises by the end of 1992 and most of the rest in 1993. The revenues from privatisation will be distributed between local and central government with local authorities taking the major part (65 per cent).

Buyers of small-scale enterprises will help establish the foundation of a market economy. In many cases a local entrepreneur will be the buyer. In other cases, employees will get together to buy out their own enterprises. It will also be possible for enterprises to be bought by managers and employees together. As in auctions and tenders, the assets will go to the highest bidder. Thus, auctions will become an important means for local authorities to collect revenues. Moreover, auction sales of small-scale enterprises are likely to improve the quality of consumer services and to give privatisation a good image.

Mass privatisation of large-scale industry

In restructuring the economy, privatisation of large and medium-sized enterprises plays a key role. The Russian Programme sets the start of "large-scale" privatisation for autumn 1992, and plans to accelerate its implementation thereafter.

Obviously, this task would be impossible if privatisation were conducted by stages on the model of privatisation developed in Great Britain and in many developing countries of Asia and Latin America. Instead of this "classical" approach, mass privatisation will be used in Russia, with the exception of some enterprises and sectors that should be privatized in the "classical" way.

Mass privatisation refers to the distribution of shares of state enterprises among the population free of charge, or at minimum charge, as a rule through the medium of vouchers and privatisation accounts. The Russian programme lays down the various steps of mass privatisation and provides for the use of a wide spectrum of incentive schemes.

The first necessary step in the process of privatisation of large and medium-sized enterprises is to commercialize them, i.e. to transform them into public joint stock companies, allowing the free sale of shares.

This part should be completed by autumn 1992.

Some positive effects will make themselves felt in enterprises immediately upon commercialisation. First, they will have to introduce modern management structures, such as a board of directors. Second, using their preferential right to buy shares in the enterprise, managers will have an incentive to increase enterprise profits.

The privatisation programme provides for substantial advantages to managers and the workforce of an enterprise. In designing a privatisation plan enterprise managers, together with the workers, will have the option to choose one of three "privilege schemes":

Scheme 1. Employees are given a one-time gift of non-voting shares in the enterprise, equal to 25 per cent of the charter capital and up to a maximum of no more than twenty times the minimum monthly wage of each employee. They are also entitled to buy up to 10 per cent of the voting shares of the enterprise at a 30 per cent discount off the nominal value and with the right of deferred payment for up to 3 years (up to a maximum of no more than six times the monthly wage per employee). Enterprise officials and managers are, subject to contracts signed with them, given an option to acquire shares up to 5 per cent of the charter capital at its nominal value. Moreover, 10 per cent of revenues gained from the sale of shares is deposited into the personal privatisation accounts of the employees of the privatised enterprise.

Scheme 2. Enterprise employees are given the right to buy (by closed subscription) voting shares equal to 51 per cent of the charter capital. Note should be taken of the requirement that enterprise assets be evaluated according to GKI methods. In this case there is no free-of-charge transfer of shares, nor any sale of non-voting shares.

Scheme 3. By contract with the competent property management committee, a group of employees of an enterprise may assume responsibility for the improvement of the financial situation of the enterprise to be privatized, while also undertaking to maintain the competitiveness of enterprise products and keeping the number of jobs as defined by the privatisation plan. If the contract is signed with the consent of the workforce, and for a period of not less than two years, and if the terms of the contract are fulfilled on expiry of the contract, the members of such a group are entitled to acquire 20 per cent of the charter capital in the form of voting shares in the enterprise at its nominal value and with the right of deferred payment for 3 years. If the group fails to fulfil the clauses of the contract, this right (option) is not valid. The group enters a contract with the local GKI department, which stipulates the liabilities of its members, including material liabilities for the property in their private ownership (contributed on mortgage).

In scheme 3 all the enterprise employees (including group members) are subsequently given the right to acquire further shares up to the amount of 20 per cent of the charter capital, but for a sum of no more than 7000 rubles per employee at a 30 per cent discount off nominal value, and with deferred payment of 3 years. (As we have said, the amount of the initial contribution must not be more than 20 per cent of the nominal value of the shares.)

Thus, in the first stage of mass privatisation the government is seeking support primarily from workers and management, giving them unprecedented privileges and prompting them to corporatise enterprises and participate in privatisation. It should be noted that the basic position of the GKI is to not give the workforce voting shares free of charge, despite strong pressure to do so from enterprise management, workers' councils and trade unions. The point of privatisation in not to simply change owners, but to transfer property into the hands of the most effective owners. This will reinforce a new type of owner, who is able to act in a responsible and concerned way in order to increase his capital. It seems doubtful that this type of desired behaviour could be brought about through the free distribution of property. Moreover, the typical attitude of the workforce would not be to make investments in production, but to exploit existing capacities to squeeze out maximum profits with the help of price rises, especially when the enterprise has a monopoly position on the market. This would later lead to totally run-down machinery and equipment and to the shut-down of the enterprise.

Of course the subsequent sales and purchases of free-of-charge shares would eventually bring a change of owners. However, this process would take a long time, since far-sighted national or foreign investors tend not to invest in worker-managed enterprises.

Vouchers

The second phase of the mass privatisation, beginning from autumn 1992, involves introducing registered privatisation accounts (vouchers). In this way we can involve the majority of society, including groups working outside the sphere of material production — doctors, teachers, military personnel, etc — in the purchase of property.

The voucher project has a number of objectives:

- all Russian citizens should gain from privatisation, so that the process will be fair;
- society's support for the privatisation process should be gained;

- extra pressure should be placed on the administrative framework to make it speed up privatisation;
- the demand for property must be stimulated since, if the mass privatisation programme were not available, the savings of the population would be enough to buy only a small portion of state property (even at book value).

The voucher project contains five main provisions:

1. Every citizen of Russia gets a voucher (B) with a certain nominal value, if he pays a small fee to cover practical costs. The initial portion of B is offered in the fourth quarter of 1992 and extra portions will be available in 1993 and 1994. (The GKI estimate is that about 40-50 per cent of the property in Russia can be privatized by means of vouchers).
2. The voucher-holder may use his voucher together with money to buy shares of companies to be privatized. He may also exchange it for shares in investment funds or sell it for cash.
3. The federal government will get its proceeds from privatisation in the form of vouchers. All vouchers accruing to "property funds" (committees) from sales of shares will be transferred to the federal "property fund" and will be written off there.
4. The voucher project will cover all regional and federal companies (except those that are already leased). Every enterprise of this category converted into an open joint stock company will earmark a part of its shares for sale by vouchers.
5. The voucher will be valid during a limited period of time (the initial series of vouchers will be valid until the end of 1993, and the second one until the end of 1994).

The procedure for selling shares for vouchers will be described in the privatisation programme.

Problems with vouchers

The principal problem of the voucher project is the need to take the leading position in offering shares of companies to be privatized and in the conversion of many state-controlled enterprises into open joint stock companies, in order to prevent the invitation surge.

Moreover, additional problems can arise in the circulation of the vouchers due to: the simultaneous use of money and vouchers in the course of privatisation; possible attempts to issue special regional vouchers; possible sabotage of privatisation at the managerial level of enterprises; and the risk that the population would all want to sell their vouchers at the same time.

Investment funds will be badly needed to facilitate the voucher project. They will serve as intermediaries between households offering vouchers and money and companies offering shares. Moreover, investment funds help to protect the wealth of small-scale investors (i.e. the population) by spreading their assets over many enterprises. They should be established "from the bottom" and will be rather varying in size, and in industrial and regional affiliation. For a certain part of the population the investment funds will be the sole chance to make efficient use of their vouchers. Some investment funds can be established by privatisation authorities, i.e. property funds and committees for property management.

A wide system of holding companies will appear. By buying a large quantity of shares, holding companies and investment funds can considerably reduce the problem of ownership being spread among too many small shareholders during the issue of the vouchers. Vouchers can be used to modify the pension system. Pension funds will be advisable for this purpose.

The law stipulates several methods of privatisation for the medium- and large-scale companies. Almost all of them are competition-based schemes.

First, a company can be sold to the highest bidder by auction or by competitive tender (where company management will be subject to certain conditions in the future). Sale to the highest bidder will probably be used for selling medium-sized companies both as a whole, and for selling major blocks of shares in them. Second, very large companies can be sold through "investment biddings" (direct sales), where bids will be evaluated by a number of criteria. Here commitments on future investment and employment, ecological requirements, etc. will be considered along with price. If there is only one client at the auction, tender or investment bidding, direct sales will take place.

There are a number of advantages in using the competitive approach as the cornerstone of the Russian privatisation programme. This approach will facilitate the emergence of large-scale owners who possess enough shares to take actual control of the company and manage it in a proper way. Competition means that companies will go to the highest bidder, and as a rule this is a client who can maximize the company's profits and efficiency. The highest-bidder basis will give substantial government revenue. This approach will rule out corruption and bribery, and thus privatisation will be associated with open information and democratic methods.

In cases when less than 100 per cent of shares are offered at the auction, tender, or investment bidding and nobody gets a large block of shares, then the other shares will be offered at an auction or tender of small blocks of shares. These can be acquired for cash or vouchers. Such auctions are a key part of the programme, because all shares left under the control of the government will be transferred to the population or investment funds, thus completing the privatisation process. The privatisation profits will go to budgets on various levels and to state committees on privatisation, and will mainly be spent on social benefits for the population.

The basic reason for local authorities to participate in the privatisation process is their urgent need to improve their budgets and thus limit the inflation, which would otherwise imperil the reform effort, including privatisation.

Thus the program of mass privatisation in Russia will provide all potential "owners" (employees, managers, local authorities, private businessmen, households, etc.) with an economic incentive to support the privatisation policy. A major intention of the programme is to ensure a "balance of interests" for the different levels of society, and to let this be a guide in the process of economic reform.

Preparing for large-scale privatisation

During the second phase of the preparation for Russian privatisation (summer-autumn 1992) attention is focused on preparing and elaborating "large-scale privatisation", that is, the conversion en masse of state-controlled enterprises into public companies and the distribution of vouchers among the population, preparing pilot programmes for privatisation in all large companies, and on improving methods for attracting foreign investments. This is also the time when we begin to privatise insolvent companies controlled by the state.

It is planned to sell state property for a total value of 70-80 billion rubles and to give away (as gratis shares distributed among the employees) property valued at another 150-200 billion rubles. A certain part of property (the accurate figure is difficult to forecast) will be acquired by the population by means of transfer from the registered accounts (vouchers). The total amount of privatized property can reach 15-20 per cent of the value of fixed assets by the end of 1992.

In 1992 privatisation will cover the small-scale companies subject to compulsory selling to private owners. Most probably they will be sold by means of competitive and non-competitive tenders, and in some regions, for lack of demand, they will be sold directly to the only customer interested, namely the enterprise work force.

Resentment over the "fat cats" who bought up property at auctions should begin to decline when the real mass sell-out of shops starts, leading to substantial price decreases for trade and service properties, and after the distribution of vouchers among the population.

Survey data gives reason to suppose that the majority of employees (from one-half to two-thirds) will use their vouchers for acquiring shares in their companies. At the same time a considerable part of the society will have no desire to become owners and they will sell their free shares. Marketing surveys show that one-third of employees will not take part in the privatisation. In 1992 the most likely buyers of the privatised property will be its workers and representatives of new commercial groupings.

The third phase of the privatisation (roughly 1993-1994) will be devoted to selling shares of large industries and other spheres of the economy. This will be the main concern of the government, including regulation of the share sale, creation of conditions for free transfer of the capital including vouchers, issue of new portions of the vouchers and distribution of them among the population, regulation of the investment fund activities and holding companies' work, etc. Special attention will be paid to stimulating faster privatisation (including the distribution of Western aid as investment subsidies to privatized companies).

The final phase of privatisation will involve special procedures for privatising companies that have not yet been privatised, in particular, loss-making enterprises, and those whose functioning is harmful for the environment.

Foreign investment and privatisation

Particular attention should be paid to foreign investment, since this can be a decisive factor for the success of privatisation as a whole. Today the basic obstacle to foreign investment is the poor legal framework. Foreign investors very often cannot get an answer to very simple questions such as: Who are the partners? Who do we negotiate with? Who is the decision maker? And so on.

The government is supplementing the legal structure, know-how, and practical mechanisms for receiving foreign investments. The basic principle here is that local and foreign investors should be subject to similar conditions. In particular, the competitive approach and a lack of general restrictions should prevail (100 per cent of shares can be sold to a foreign investor). Nevertheless, there are a few distinct industries and services where restrictions and bans have to be imposed on foreign investment.

Privatisation in Russia is now entering a decisive phase. In the second

half of 1992 it will become the main focus of the economic reform programme. Based on the organisational, legal, and institutional work
already done, the government intends to widely extend small-scale privatisation, and to start to implement mass privatisation. The success of
privatisation will be decisive for the Russian reform programme.

7 The Voucher Program for Russia

Maxim Boycko and Andrei Shleifer[1]

Objectives of the voucher program

In accordance with the Decree of the President of the Russian Federation of April 2, 1992 vouchers will be introduced in Russia in the fourth quarter of 1992. By means of the voucher program, shares in privatized enterprises will be allocated to the citizens of Russia.

The voucher program is aimed at reaching a number of economic and political goals. Vouchers will generate demand for shares in privatized enterprises. The savings of the population are far too low to buy more than a fraction of all state-owned assets, even at residual value. The capacity of the nascent Russian private sector to acquire privatized enterprises is also limited, while the prospects of large-scale foreign participation in privatization remain unclear. Therefore, without vouchers, privatization may slow down soon because of low demand for state assets.

Vouchers will ensure fairness in privatization. All Russian citizens, and not just enterprise workers and managers, should benefit from privatization. Free transfer of privatized property through the voucher program will significantly increase political support for privatization and reform in general. All groups of the population without exception will take part in privatization. The voucher program is effectively the only really popular component of the whole economic reform pursued by the government.[2]

Voucher programs in Poland and Czechoslovakia

The voucher programs used in other reforming East European countries could not be easily transplanted into Russia. The cornerstone of the Polish scheme is a dozen government-sponsored mutual funds run by foreigners.[3] The scheme has a number of attractive features: it can greatly speed up privatization and provide reasonable corporate governance from the outset. However, we were concerned that because of the size of Russian industry a hundred mutual funds might be necessary in Russia. It is unlikely that foreign control on such a scale would be politically feasible. Also with so many funds the crucial transparency of the process might be lost. But our greatest concern was that the government would retain too much influence over the funds' managers, demanding social policies rather than maximization of the value of funds' shares. In return for soft policies, the funds might demand cheap credits from the government for the companies they run. In some sense, the principal aim of privatization — to separate the firms from the state — might be subverted.

In the Czechoslovak voucher program, a substantial part of the industry is to be sold in a single grand auction. Citizens and private mutual funds bid for shares of enterprises with vouchers denominated in points. The auction proceeds in several rounds, which are managed through a centralized computer system. Although we found many aspects of the Czechoslovak approach very appealing, we doubted that the Russian government had enough political power and implementation capacity to carry it out. Enterprise managers might resist the voucher program and it would be hard to fight them all at once. Also the sheer number of enterprises to be privatized in Russia, the size of the population, and the underdeveloped communication networks make a single computerized auction in Russia a logistical nightmare.

Key elements of the voucher scheme

A voucher program for Russia has to take into account the current political and economic situation in the country, and to fit into the overall privatization strategy of the government.[4] It has to emphasize speed and create reasonable governance structures for the newly privatized enterprises. But it should also be decentralized and minimize organizational costs.

The basic elements of the proposed scheme, developed with these objectives in mind, are:

1. Each citizen of the Russian Federation will receive a voucher that allows him to buy state assets in privatization. Vouchers would have a face value denominated in rubles. All citizens of Russia — regardless of age, residence, workplace, level of income — will receive a voucher of equal value.

2. Privatization agencies will accept vouchers as legal tender for state assets sold in the process of privatization. A voucher can be used to buy state assets only once: upon receipt by the seller, it shall be expired.

3. The voucher is a bearer document. The voucher holder may use his voucher in one of three ways: a) to buy shares of privatized enterprises in auctions or tenders; b) to exchange it for shares in a mutual fund; or c) to sell the voucher for cash.

4. The voucher program is a federal program. Vouchers will be accepted by sellers of state assets at an amount corresponding to the share of the federal budget in proceeds from privatization, namely 35 percent of the proceeds. Local and regional (oblast) budgets will receive their shares of proceeds from privatization in the form of cash. The federal budget will effectively relinquish its share of proceeds in favor of Russian citizens.[5]

5. The voucher program encompasses all regionally (oblast) and federally-owned enterprises subject to privatization (with the possible exception of leased enterprises with a buyout option). Each enterprise of this group, upon conversion into a joint-stock company, shall allocate 35 percent of its shares for sales in exchange for vouchers.

Circulation of vouchers

A controversial element of the program is whether vouchers should be tradable. The main pro-trade arguments are:

First, many people do not want to own property or securities. The philosophy of a market economy is that people should have freedom of choice. They should not be forced to become "capitalists".

Second, the right to sell vouchers is particularly important for the poorer groups of the population who do not have enough money to meet their immediate needs. Sellable vouchers will provide some safety net for the needy, especially for large families.

Third, people are likely to sell and buy vouchers, all bans notwithstanding. For example, they may use strawmen to purchase assets or simply bribe bureaucrats in charge of running auctions. Imposing a ban would only increase corruption and bribery in the privatization agencies.

Fourth, imposing a ban on the resale of vouchers is likely to produce a dispersed structure of share ownership. However, large shareholders are essential for effective corporate governance. Thus, a ban on trade in vouchers would compromise the fundamental goal of economic efficiency.

It is likely that extensive trade in vouchers will emerge immediately after the issue of the first tranche of vouchers, thereby establishing a market price for vouchers. We think that the government should encourage the development of a liquid voucher market. If the market is unorganized, prices of vouchers will be much lower, reflecting a discount for illiquidity, and this will create public discontent. Poor people will try to sell their vouchers, and get lower prices and worse deals. There will be more corruption and rip-offs. Similarly, illiquid markets will reduce the demand for vouchers by investors who might want to use them to buy privatized assets, since they will have to pay large transaction costs to assemble significant blocks of vouchers.

Therefore we believe that it will be far better if the markets for vouchers are liquid and efficient, and that whoever wants to sell or buy vouchers can do so easily. Here are a number of measures to reach this goal:

— Vouchers should be legally tradable at organized exchanges.
— Commercial banks (and some other intermediaries) should be allowed to accept vouchers as deposits in order to facilitate transactions with large blocks of vouchers.
— An extensive information campaign should be launched, explaining that vouchers are worth more than their market value if used directly for privatization.
— The use of vouchers should be permitted in various types of sales of privatized assets, not only in special voucher auctions. In particular, workers and managers should be allowed to use vouchers in buyouts and in purchases of shares at preferential terms; strategic investors should be allowed (with certain limitations) to use vouchers for purchases of controlling blocks of shares (see below, under mutual funds).
— Strong support should be offered to private mutual funds that take vouchers.
—.Most importantly, there should be a rapid and significant supply of shares for vouchers, so that market participants indeed believe that vouchers have a value in privatization. The government should

organize the massive sale of privatized enterprises' shares for vouchers in the fourth quarter of 1992 and in 1993. A significant amount of vouchers should be sold as early as the first half of 1993, i.e., well before the vouchers expire. Nothing would help more to generate the demand for vouchers than rapid privatization.

Inflationary effects of vouchers

A major concern about vouchers is that they are inflationary. There are three independent channels through which vouchers may generate inflation.

The monetization effect

Vouchers might come to be used as money in transactions, particularly for large purchases. For example, consumers might use vouchers to buy furniture, appliances, or other durables. In this case, vouchers will become just like bills of large denominations. Large bills tend to have a lower velocity than smaller bills, but still the effect would be very inflationary, because the effective money supply would then include vouchers.

To reduce the monetization effect, the following steps should be taken:

— Vouchers should be made unacceptable as a means of payment to state enterprises.
— Vouchers should come in large denominations, again to reduce their value in transactions. Indeed, the actual face value of the Russian voucher is 10,000 rubles.
— A final expiration date should be set for vouchers — one year after the date a particular tranche was issued. In Russia, this date was December 31, 1993.
— The demand for vouchers as a means of payment in privatization transactions must be reinforced. This is the most potent weapon against their becoming currency. In part to accomplish this goal, the Russian government increased the supply of assets to be sold for vouchers in October, 1992.

The wealth effect

The voucher program enhances the perceived wealth of all citizens, and hence raises the demand for current consumption. This can have the effect of raising the price level. However, relative to wages, vouchers are not that significant, and therefore this effect is likely to be small. For example, a person who gets 10,000 rubles in vouchers might want to spend an extra 500 rubles of that on current consumption, which is fairly small relative to the flow of wages in the economy.

The liquidity effect

For the poorer groups of the population, vouchers entail significant benefit. These people would have liked to borrow money before to increase their consumption, but could not. They are likely to sell their vouchers immediately and to increase their consumption substantially. This liquidity effect is probably much more significant than the wealth effect, since a poor person is likely to spend all of the vouchers he gets on current consumption rather than just a fraction. The main consequence of this effect, however, is that the prices of goods consumed by the poor, such as food and clothing, will rise relative to the prices of goods consumed by the rich. It is hard to appraise the magnitude of this effect, but if the government manages to convince the poor people to participate in privatization, it can probably be significantly reduced.

One important aspect of the liquidity effect is that any redistribution of wealth to the poor — whether in the form of vouchers, cash, or property — will increase their liquidity as long as assets given to them can be sold. There is nothing special about vouchers. Unless the government decides to exclude the poor people from the privatization process — a highly undesirable strategy — the poor people will try to convert the assets they get into consumption which will increase inflation. This inflationary effect is not enormous and is worth living with. To fight it by making trade in vouchers illegal would be a bad strategy, since this would alienate the poor people, and make them worse off.

To summarize, there are several inflationary effects of vouchers of which by far the most dangerous is the monetization effect. Other effects are clearly second-order. They may add a few percentage points to the price level (but not to long-term inflation), and they are likely to be drowned in the background inflation due to the printing of money.

Mutual funds

We expect that very few people would be willing to buy shares in privatized enterprises directly — in most cases such investments will prove too risky. Many will invest in private mutual funds that will hold diversified portfolios of enterprise shares.

The government should encourage private mutual funds, for example, by granting them tax (or other) benefits. At the same time, their operations should be strictly regulated to avoid misuse of funds.

Parallel use of cash and vouchers for purchasing privatized assets

Using vouchers along with cash in privatization transactions poses a serious problem. Obviously, if the market price of the voucher is below its face value, and both cash and vouchers are accepted without any limitations as a means of payment at an auction, no buyer will ever pay in cash. At the same time, it is essential that local and regional governments and privatization agencies receive their respective shares of proceeds from privatization in the form of cash. Otherwise they will have little incentive to privatize and the process will grind to a halt.

We suggest that this problem be dealt with at the level of an individual enterprise. The privatization plan will define specific rules for making payments in vouchers for the enterprise in question or for its shares. The following general principles should be followed:[6]

1. Thirty-five percent of each enterprise's assets shall be offered for vouchers. This percentage corresponds to the share of the federal budget in the proceeds from privatization, as stipulated by the privatization program.
2. If an enterprise is to be sold at an auction or tender as a single entity, the investor shall have the right to pay up to 35 percent of the price in vouchers.
3. Specific rules for the sale of shares for vouchers in each joint-stock company will depend on how its shares are to be sold in principle (i.e. whether the buyout option is exercised, what the size of the controlling block of shares offered for sale is, etc.) The general rules for the sale of enterprises' shares for vouchers provide that:
    3.1 The total number of shares offered for sale by all methods combined in exchange for vouchers shall be 35 percent of the total.
    3.2 If employees choose to receive benefits under Option 1 provided for in the State Privatization Program, they may pay fully in vouchers for the shares they get at preferential terms, namely, 10 percent of shares at a 30 percent discount off the face value offered to workers, and 5 percent of shares at face value offered to managers.
    3.3 If employees choose the buyout option (Option 2 in the privatization program), they may tender up to 50 percent of their payment in vouchers.

3.4 In any case, at least 10 percent of the shares of every enterprise shall be sold for vouchers at a tender for small investors. This tender would be for vouchers only, cash would not be accepted.

3.5 When the controlling block of share is sold (at an investment tender or at an auction) a portion of the price may also be paid in vouchers. The ceiling for the use of vouchers would be determined by requirements 3.1, 3.2, and 3.4.

4. With the exception of the tender described in 3.4 above, whenever payment in vouchers is allowed, the investor may pay in cash too. If the payment was made in cash instead of vouchers, for a specified period of time (say, one month) the investor will have the right to turn in the vouchers and get his cash back.

Rules 4 and 3.4 merit additional discussion. On the one hand, we want to give investors sufficient flexibility in using cash instead of vouchers when vouchers are accepted. Otherwise, if the market for vouchers is not liquid enough, some auctions might fail simply because investors would be unable to accumulate vouchers in the amounts required. On the other hand, allocating some assets for sales *for vouchers only* would provide voucher holders with an automatic protection against (high) inflation, which is likely to continue in Russia. In fact, vouchers may then even start trading at a premium and may turn out to be an attractive means of saving as compared to available alternatives.[7] We believe that the combination of rules 4 and 3.4 provides a reasonable compromise between the two conflicting aims described above, although other solutions may be possible as well.

Upon privatization of an enterprise, the seller will prepare a report on the sale of the enterprise's shares. The report will show which shares were offered for vouchers, the actual amount of vouchers, and the amount of cash received for the shares. The proceeds both in cash and in vouchers will be split between the federal, regional, and local budgets, and privatization authorities in accordance with the rules established by the State Privatization Program. All vouchers received shall be transferred to the federal budget and then extinguished.[8]

Determining the face value of a voucher

Determining the face value of a voucher is an extremely important and difficult political decision. If the government suggests too low a value, popular expectations may be disappointed and the whole program may be bungled. A value that is too high may bring about inflation or, more likely, a steep fall in the vouchers' market value.

Nevertheless, it seems that in determining the value of the first-tranche vouchers it would be advisable to exercise restraint and caution, promising to issue further tranches of greater denominations. In this case, the expected average monthly wage and average family savings by the end of this year may be used as a basis for establishing the lower limit of the face value.

Regional aspects of the program

The risk that oblasts, regions or autonomous republics within the Russian Federation might independently issue vouchers poses a serious danger to the voucher program. This would destabilize money circulation in the country and create unpredictable regional distortions in the privatization process.

The government and the Parliament of the Russian Federation should make it clear that it is forbidden to issue local vouchers. Local privatization authorities should not be allowed to accept any vouchers other than federal ones. Regions that issue their own vouchers should be excluded from the Western technical assistance program.

Conclusion

During the summer of 1992, it became clear that the voucher program is the most popular and most promising part of the government reform program. This paper has outlined several technical issues connected with the voucher program. We must stress in conclusion that some elements of the program are still in a state of flux and are being adjusted. Nonetheless, assuming some continuity of government, voucher privatization is almost certain to actually begin in 1993.

References

Blanchard, O.J., R. Dornbusch, P. R. Krugman, R. Lazard, and L. H. Summers (1991) *Reform in Eastern Europe*, Cambridge, MA: MIT Press.

Lipton, D. and J. D. Sachs (1990) "Creating the Market Economy in Eastern Europe: The Case of Poland," *Brookings Papers on Economic Activity* 1.

Shleifer, Andrei and Robert W. Vishny (1992), "Privatization in Russia: First Steps", *National Bureau of Economic Research*, forthcoming.

Notes

1 The authors benefited from many discussions with Jonathan Hay, Dmitrii Vasiliev, and members of the World Bank Mass Privatization Team, headed by Ira Lieberman

2 For a general discussion of mass privatization, see O.J. Blanchard, et al. (1991)

3 For a discussion of the Polish scheme, see Lipton and Sachs (1990)

4 See Shleifer and Vishny (1992) for an exposition.

5 In October 1992, it appears that the number of shares sold for vouchers will be increased.

6 The arguments in this subsection apply even if the amount of shares sold for vouchers is increased.

7 The rich might then shift out of dollars and into vouchers, which will reduce the price of dollars in terms of rubles and be extremely beneficial to the stabilization policy.

8 See Appendix for a couple of examples of how cash and vouchers might be combined in purchases of shares of a particular enterprise.

Appendix to Chapter 7: The Voucher Program for Russia

Here we consider two examples of how vouchers and cash can be combined for purchasing shares of an enterprise.

Example 1: Selling shares of enterprise X for cash and vouchers

1. Enterprise X has been converted to an open-end joint-stock company and has issued 100 shares. The employees of X decided to go for option 1, of receiving benefits whereby they were to receive 25 percent of shares for no consideration, plus 10 percent of shares at a 30 percent discount of the face value, plus 5 percent of shares to be sold at face value to the enterprise's managers.
2. The privatization plan provides for the sale of the controlling block of shares as a whole — 50 shares — at an auction to a strategic investor. The balance of 10 shares shall be sold in the market to small investors.

   Allocation of shares:

To employees for no consideration	25
To employees at a 30 percent discount	10
To executive officers at face value	5
The controlling block	50
To small investors	10
Total	100

3. The privatization plan shall provide that 35 shares be offered for vouchers, including:

   3.1 Ten shares shall be offered to the employees at a 30 percent discount off face value, 5 percent to X's managers at face value. Each employee or manager can pay up to 100 percent of the price in vouchers;
   3.2 Ten shares shall be offered for sale as part of the controlling block of 50 shares. Thus each bidder at an auction for the controlling block can pay in vouchers up to 20 percent of the price (10/50);
   3.3 Ten shares shall be sold at a tender for small investors. Each investor has to pay 100 percent of the price in vouchers.

4. A local fund shall prepare a report for the federal fund on the sale of

the enterprise's shares. The report will show the amount of vouchers and the amount of cash received from the sale of shares in cases 3.1, 3.2, and 3.3. In cases 3.1 and 3.3, all proceeds (cash and vouchers) shall be remitted to the federal fund, as compared to 20 percent of the proceeds, including all vouchers, in case 3.2.

Example 2: selling shares of enterprise Y for cash and vouchers

1. Enterprise Y has been converted to an open-end joint-stock company and issued 100 shares. Y's employees opted for a buyout (chose to receive benefits under Option 2).
2. The enterprise's privatization plan provides for the sale of the controlling block of shares — 50 — through a closed subscription to the employees. The balance of 50 shares shall be offered to small investors, including 10 shares offered for vouchers only.

   Allocation of shares:

Closed subscription	50
Sale for cash to small investors	40
Sale for vouchers to small investors	10
Total	100

3. The privatization plan shall provide that 35 shares are to be offered for vouchers, including:

   3.1 Twenty-five shares shall be offered to employees for vouch ers under closed subscription. (The balance of 25 shares will be sold for cash.) The procedure of such a closed subscription shall be as follows: each employee can pay up to 50 percent of the price in vouchers;

   3.2 Ten shares shall be sold to small investors. Each investor has to pay 100 percent of the price in vouchers.

4. A local fund will prepare a report for the federal fund on the sale of the enterprise's shares. The report will show the amount of vouchers and the amount of cash received from the sale of shares in cases 3.1 and 3.2.

In case 3.2, all proceeds (cash and vouchers) received shall be remitted to the federal fund, as compared to 50 percent, including all vouchers, in case 3.1.

8 Privatisation with Foreign Participation

Boris G. Fedorov

This paper addresses various practical issues and problems involved in privatisation and foreign investment in Russia. It is based on experiences gained while implementing various privatisation projects in the St. Petersburg area.

A few concrete privatisation projects

Up until now, little attention has been devoted to the role of foreign participation in the privatisation process in Russia. In fact, Russian officials are often excessively cautious, if not outright hostile, towards foreign investment. This is evident for example in the restrictions on foreign investors, and the incessant talk about the danger of foreigners buying everything too cheaply. This reluctance existed long before the start of the current reforms and must be tackled as an unavoidable reality.

In view of this, it is not surprising that very little foreign or even domestic investment has been actually made in the acquisition of enterprises in Russia. Nor is it surprising that privatisation and foreign investment have been taken on as separate issues, and to a large degree, mismanaged. Far too many Western businessmen, after a single visit to Russia, vow to stay away until the the situation becomes stabilized. Russia is missing out on the foreign capital that could and should play a major role in privatisation.

Despite a multitude of legislative acts (such as the Foreign Investment Law of 1991) foreign companies still have serious reservations about investing in Russia. This indicates that the biggest problem is not a lack of legislation. I would say that far more important is the lack of understanding on the part of government bodies, the nearly total inaction in attracting foreign investment, and the inability or unwillingness to make decisions.

Most investment has been in the form of joint ventures, that is, new corporate structures created with the participation of local partners. Since fully-owned foreign entities have been allowed for some time now, this can be seen as a means of minimizing risk. What is even more significant is that many of these ventures are in intermediation or the retail trade and service industry, while relatively few are in manufacturing or other productive industries.

The caution of Western firms is understandable given the ever-changing legal framework, political instability, and the increase in crime. Curiously, the authorities are doing little to dispel these justified fears nor do they seem interested in foreign capital. No meaningful strategy for attracting foreign capital has emerged, in particular for the process of privatisation. In privatisation programmes and legislative acts, foreign investors are mentioned in passing and mainly for political reasons.

Red tape, sleepyness, and inaction are common traits of the authorities throughout Russia. The fraud and corruption of various officials are scaring off serious Western businessmen while attracting a lot of small-time crooks. This paralysis of power means even the smallest things can take ages unless the bureaucrat can be offered personal advantages. Inefficient government procedures seem to be inbred in the Russian people, and only a real reform from above can start the wheels of change. So far, an alteration of bureaucratic style seems unlikely and the administrative system is practically the same as in the past.

Finally, many potential investors are still debating the fundamental issue: whether acquisitions or greenfield investments are best. And unless procedures for foreign participation in privatisation are significantly simplified, it looks as if many companies will opt for the greenfield approach since it is least costly. From the authorities' point of view it would have been logical to try to attract as much foreign capital as possible into the existing enterprises in order to modernise them, save jobs, etc.

The hesitation of the foreign investors has several causes. First, the whole process of privatisation is slow in taking off. Second, foreign investment is not officially appreciated or encouraged. Third, aside from organisational or political obstacles, many fundamental factors continue to hinder the inflow of foreign capital to Russia.

Interaction between privatisation and foreign investment

At present, many people do not seem to understand that real privatisation is not over as soon as a mechanical transfer of title has been made, even if politically this is considered to be the primary task. Transfer of title is only the initial and largely superficial stage of the privatisation; the new entities must also be restructured to run more efficiently, and enjoy the benefits of corporate governance. This is why practically nothing will change if the populists have their way and allow property to be given away for free, e.g., to workers lacking the necessary capital and management skills to develop the enterprise. Unfortunately many Western advisers are urging for a "political privatisation" in Russia and the other CIS states and thus are endangering the whole process of economic and political reform.

The whole process of privatisation hinges on making the right decisions on several key aspects. These are: the speed or pace of the privatisation process; the stages of the privatisation; the use of capital for further investment in privatised enterprises; and the integration into the world economy as a means of increasing competitiveness and efficiency, and acquiring technological and managerial know-how.

Speed is clearly a political issue, since political survival depends on demonstrating results and avoiding public criticism. But if rapid privatisation becomes a target *per se* it could bring disaster, scandals, or the absence of real change, which would seriously threaten the success of privatisation efforts. Voucher schemes, for example, seem to have highly unpredictable consequences. Speed is, however, justified if it does not compromise the quality and fairness of the process. No less important is setting the right priorities — deciding what is to be converted first, where, and using what techniques. Unless the strategy and stages of the whole process are properly defined, it can easily turn into a mess.

In my opinion the crucial factor is capital. The best-suited owners are those who can bring in new funds to restructure and modernise their newly-acquired property. It stands to reason that there is a shortage of such capital in the domestic market; the capital that does exist often comes from unknown and suspect sources. It is inherently wrong and dangerous to push workers into buying their enterprises or even taking them over for free. Workers simply do not have adequate capital to handle e.g. rapidly depreciating assets, not to mention their lack of management skills.

At the same time there is a lot of capital in the world, but this capital will not be placed in Russia *en masse* unless the environment there is attractive. This does not necessarily imply that new tax breaks or special privileges are needed. Normal conditions assuring a sufficiently high rate of return would be good enough. If oil production is overtaxed nobody will invest in the ailing oil industry and production will continue to fall. If foreign nationals have to pay a 60 per cent income tax on all incomes above $4000 per year (as the original draft proposed) many firms will think twice about operating in Russia. Even though the rate today is 40 per cent, the ceiling for untaxed income is still ridiculously low.

Foreign capital will not only substantially speed up the process of privatisation. It will also benefit the transforming economy in several important ways. It will facilitate the transfer of better technology, know-how, management skills, and business culture; allow penetration into foreign markets on a more competitive basis; and it will help enterprises to find strategic partners who can give them better chances of survival in a more liberal and competitive environment.

It is quite clear that Russian authorities must adopt a special strategy for foreign investment in the enterprises undergoing conversion, simplifying procedures and assisting investors whenever possible. This means that for instance the State Property Committee (GKI) and Committee for Foreign Investment must work very closely on a day-to-day basis. Eventually they could be merged. Each potential investor should have easy access to all privatisation legislation and rules, information on what is being offered and where, whom to appeal to, and what legal protection he or she enjoys in Russia.

Problems of foreign investment in privatisation

A properly-defined strategy for foreign investment in the Russian privatisation must fully address all the existing problems affecting the actual flow of capital, as well as those which may arise in the near future.

The biggest problem of foreign investment in privatisation is that no authority really cares about the results. Even though the government is clearly in need of the money that foreign investment could bring, they have curiously not encouraged it. The government and local authorities are still mostly pushing small-scale privatisation, auctions, and voucher privatisation. No special procedures or incentives exist for foreign investors aside from a number of restrictions. The current crash programme for the transformation of state enterprises into joint-stock companies is a good example of this.

A number of industries, selected rather arbitrarily, are subject to prohibitions against, or limitations on, privatisation with the participation of foreigners, or in general. Quite often privatisation requires a special decision or authorisation from the government. In other cases restrictions may come in the form of licensing (although this can apply to any enterprise) or be placed on the size of the investment.

While most restrictions make some kind of sense, some are obviously not well-founded. An example of this is the privatisation programme enacted by the presidential decree of 29 December 1991, which required the permission of the GKI for foreign participation in auctions. It also required government permission for foreign participation in the privatisation of enterprises with a book value of the fixed capital of more than 200 mn. rubles (about $1.5 mn.) or with more than 10 workers. Moreover, it prohibited foreign purchases of insurance or securities companies. Finally, it required a special agreement of the Foreign Investment Committee if investments exceeded $10 mn., or 50 mn. rubles (in later documents changed to $100 mn.), or 50 per cent of shares. Aside from the obvious discrepancies between the different types of restrictions, it was interesting to learn that the government wishes to stimulate foreign participation in the privatisation of loss-making enterprises.[1] How can that be justified?

The other problem is that the organizational framework of privatisation that was created under current law is not very efficient. Two types of authorities coexist: *privatisation committees* (under executive power) and *privatisation funds* (under legislative power). Given the shortage of qualified staff, it was unwise to create a framework like this. It often results in confrontations (especially at the local level), and delays decisions. Since the functions of the two institutions are very close, it would have been more expedient to have only one.

However, the State Property Committee did quickly accomplish quite a bit in terms of creating an organisational and legal framework for privatisation. In fact, this was the only institution that actually produced the necessary regulations, and that managed to develop its network and to make reasonably efficient use of foreign advisers.

Yet an efficient system for attracting foreign capital is still lacking. Publicity and advertising are hardly used. There is no proper documentation about how a potential foreign investor is to proceed — where can he go to obtain the proper application materials, documentation, instructions on procedures, or just advice? In addition, it is high time to establish the privatisation bank that has been proposed. If it lives up to our expectations, it could certainly help to attract capital.

At the same time the legislation does not show enough stability. An inexperienced investor can easily become discouraged. He spends time carefully studying the existing laws, but he can learn the next day from the newspapers that new procedures have been established, Alternatively, his Russian partners may be stalling for time because they have heard a rumour that new regulations are being drafted in Moscow. Or some provisos of the legislation may be so vague that they can be interpreted quite differently by different people.

A second problem is that many Western companies seem incapable of integrating themselves into the Russian environment and availing themselves of the business opportunities that do exist. Many discouraged investors never tried innovative or alternative ways of working in the Russian markets; they did not bother with using local experts, familiarizing themselves with the laws, or getting to know the right people. In many cases the start-up costs for foreign investors could have been considerably less if they had identified the right partners. The same goes for difficulties with personnel, supplies, the bureaucracy, and the like. Their slogan should be: 'when in Russia, do as the Russians'.

A third important issue is the insufficient convertibility of the ruble. Convertibility is always cited as one the major problems for foreign investment in Russia. Naturally, export-oriented projects with hard currency revenues can be targeted but this cannot be the only or the main trend. The more logical attitude is to have at least a medium-term view and target the potentially huge domestic market.[2]

There are various degrees of convertibility. In practical terms the investor just wants to be able to convert his ruble revenues into his own currency at an exchange rate that safeguards a certain rate of return. This is necessary, for example, to service debts incurred in starting the project, to purchase components, and to repatriate dividends. The obvious solution is to develop the foreign exchange market to a degree where liquidity is sufficient to guarantee relatively stable exchange rates and the easy acquisition of currency, at least for the three purposes mentioned above.[3]

Unfortunately practically nothing is being done in this direction. Instead, some officials are giving people false hope. Of course a certain convertibility of the ruble can be achieved through barter and other commodity operations, but most investors are not prepared to engage in such activities. So, in their strategies for acquisition of real assets in Russia, the majority of foreign investors will have to assume that it will take several years before a working convertibility will be introduced.

An important issue for foreign investors is an insurance at least against political risks. Recently some types of such insurance seem to have become available but this is not enough. If foreign investment is to be expected in significant amounts then a wide range of possibilities are needed. For example, national agencies, private companies, and special funds with the participation of the Russian government could be envisaged. The Russian government is currently unwilling to extend any sovereign guarantees. Yet without these, many investments will not take place. This means that a proper mechanism must be put in place with clear-cut rules, lists of authorised guarantors, and clearly specified official priorities.

The more general question of protecting foreign investment should be properly addressed. Guarantees contained in the law are not adequate because they are vague and difficult to apply. Bilateral protection schemes are being set up, and this process should be speeded up. Perhaps it would be possible to work out some less traditional schemes for the protection of foreign investment with the participation of international financial institutions and big commercial insurers.

The next obvious step could be to redefine the functions of the Foreign Investment Committee or the newly created Agency for International Cooperation so that they would facilitate investment instead of hampering it.[4] We need increased promotion, publicity, information, advice to investors, and decreased powers to stop or delay projects. The Committee could act as an implementation agency vis-a-vis certain privatisation projects, fulfilling some of the usual functions of an investment bank. A much more commercial and project-oriented approach is urgently needed.

This leads us to the question of who can actually help foreign investors in their attempts to exploit the opportunities for privatisation in Russia. So far, aside from a few technical assistance projects initiated and paid for by international financial institutions, little has happened and few privatisation specialists are available. The reasons are that there are virtually no Western bankers with the right experience in Russia, nor are there very many people in Russia who would be willing to pay their fees. In addition, there is no tradition of investment banking in Russia, and few competent Russian advisers are available.

In the meantime a new approach must be developed to combine international and local skills. Joint ventures have the best chances of achieving this, since depending on circumstances, they can present either a Russian or a Western face, and deal with the local environment, while having a firm base and reputation outside Russia. Otherwise, unnecessary expenses are incurred and the Russian customers get irritated by the legions of Western consultants who are roaming around, consuming technical assistance and other funds, only to produce mountains of worthless paper.

The St. Petersburg project

In late 1991, the European Bank for Reconstruction and Development (EBRD) initiated several privatisation projects in St.Petersburg: The Nevsky cosmetics factory, the Samoilova sweets factory, the DLT department store chain, and several buildings slated for refurbishing. The main idea was to advise the city authorities on privatisation by means of a few concrete pilot projects using Western expertise.

The first two enterprises are relatively small (about 500 employees each). They were originally leased by the state, who exercised the legal option of a staff buy-out. It is relatively easy to deal with them. In one case the management is quite strong and industrious and can be a useful partner to a buyer, while in the other the management is relatively weak and perhaps willing to be bought out. DLT is a superb department store in the very centre of the city with 24 affiliates. For over a year it has had the status of a joint-stock company with a majority municipal stake, meaning that the city is selling its shares. The buildings are in practice empty shells in the centre of the city, crying out for development and proper management.

The idea of the St. Petersburg project was that before giving any recommendations to the city authorities, practical, hands-on experience had to be gained through several pilot transactions. Criteria that were used for selecting these enterprises included their potential interest to foreign investors, the quality of their Russian management, the homogeneity of the enterprise, uncomplicated legal status (if that is possible in Russia), relatively small size, and lack of any serious handicaps.

With a good team of auditors, investment bankers, and lawyers, the EBRD staff has carefully analysed numerous enterprises and produced analytical offering memoranda to be distributed among possible investors. These memoranda included factual data, an analysis of the positive and negative sides of the enterprises, and potential benefits to all partners in the transaction.

After that, groups of potential investors were contacted and sent a brief description of these enterprises and a query whether they would like to get full information. After perusal of documents, those who were still interested were invited to visit to the enterprises. Such visits are still being organised and the hope is to get several foreign investors to submit offers, and then to proceed with negotiations.

Several important findings have emerged from this experience. First, the usual evaluation techniques are not very efficient in the current environment. Instead one has to rely more on comparisons and actual negotiations. The basic approach is to start by estimating the minimum capital requirement for putting an enterprise into shape. The amount of equity commensurate with this capital is a negotiable issue and depends on the strategy of the foreign investor. In most cases foreign investors want a majority stake but some actually prefer a 50:50 approach or a minority stake, or a gradual increase of their participation if the Russian partners agree to follow their business development strategy.

Second, in the case of enterprises in the hands of workers and management, we must ascertain that capital increases go into real investment and not into their pockets. In certain cases this applies also to purchases from the state.

Third, the cooperation of the management is crucial, but one should never forget the interests of the staff. It is wise to invest in people and not only in hardware. When the company is partly owned by the state (as in the case of DLT), it is important to know whether there are conflicts of interests between it and the management of the enterprise, and how these conflicts can be resolved. One viable strategy is for the Western partner to give financial assistance to the management in order to acquire control over the enterprise through the privatisation procedures. That means financing a management buy-out in order to get a mutually profitable deal on the equity. Of course the state will be the loser, but the privatisation process will be facilitated and privatised enterprises stand a better chance of survival. This is perfectly legal and in fact huge opportunities for investors have been opened by new regulations that allow the workforce to make a bid at preferential terms for 51 per cent of equity.[5]

Fourth, all interests involved in the project, including central and local authorities should always be evaluated and taken into account. Some authorities or individual officials may be indifferent or even belligerent to the project for reasons that defy logic.

Fifth, it is absolutely crucial for investors to be diligent and double-check all documents and facts. More often than not Russian and Western partners do not exactly understand each other and misunderstandings often occur.

Sixth, delays, changes in opinions and unanswered faxes are to be expected. A meeting with a Russian official does not necessarily guarantee anything; surprises abound. Even after a careful selection of a pilot investment an investor can encounter unpleasant facts and unexpected twists of events.

Clearly, it has been very difficult to obtain relevant information. Some of the investors have been around for years but have failed to identify the best possibilities. A good interpreter can avoid a lot of misunderstandings and often plays a much more important role than a shipload of Western executives, who arrive more or less as tourists, knowing little of the local customs.

The EBRD real estate project, where we tried to create a joint-stock company to develop several buildings, demonstrated that nobody really has a feeling for the real prices, or is willing to take responsibility for naming one. At the same time, Russians often have a distorted idea of markets and seriously fear an investor who is applying to buy palaces or historical landmarks. They tend to overvalue properties and try to lobby for certain foreign companies looking for easy profits. Many seem to have difficulty understanding the simple financial aspects of the project, such as the principle of the present value of an asset. That is why auctions are looked upon as a cure-all and as a way to avoid personal responsibility for the outcome.

Despite all the problems, St Petersburg seems to be a much better place for investors to do business than Moscow or Kiev. The unavoidable delays in the EBRD projects were mostly caused by the institutional red tape and the need to educate the EBRD team (including outside experts) about the local environment, laws, and ordinances. There is a reasonable chance that the projects described will be very fruitful.

A few practical recommendations

There are currently thousands of privatisation opportunities in Russia which are potentially very lucrative from a commercial point of view. The question is where to go and how to arrange deals. What is essential is to make a proper assessment of risk, and in the current Russian environment, this is very difficult.

Few rules directly apply in this situation, but some principles can be outlined. The simplest and perhaps the most important is to avoid getting involved in any political conflicts, claims, or counterclaims. The first thing to do is to ascertain who is the owner and whether there is a chance that somebody else will be proclaimed the owner next month and annul all the previous decisions. For example both in Moscow and in St. Petersburg, a number of decisions made by the Mayor's office are currently being disputed by the local councils. In this sense it is better to target a locally-owned enterprise, rather than federal property, for instance, on the territory of a certain autonomous region.

In times of economic transformation and political upheaval investments should be relatively short-term, with a time horizon of up to 3–5 years. It is simply too difficult to assess risks for longer periods. At the same time, the cost of entering the market is still low and many firms are willing to take risks if they believe there is a reasonable chance that things will be better within a few years. In Russia investors should not participate in privatisation in the hope of quick returns — they must come to stay. The investor must take a long-term view on investments, while trying to minimise the short-term risks.

Another criterion is that most, if not all, solid projects in Russia at the moment have to generate enough hard currency so that they are currency self-sufficient. Dealings in rubles are possible, but they are unfamiliar terrain for most Western companies. However, one cannot entirely count on hard currency in privatisation, and most firms do not need additional products for existing foreign markets. Therefore investors should select a company mostly for its domestic potential, but a certain capacity to export could help a lot. It is interesting that there are already cases registered where foreign companies have participated in privatisation by paying rubles.

In today's situation it is still often better to deal with an existing enterprise, restructuring and boosting its efficiency, than to start from scratch (i.e., greenfield investments). In this way, most people are solving the dilemma; acquisitions are more common than greenfield investments. Rather inexpensive techniques do exist for increasing the output of functioning enterprises. Even more important is that they give an investor people, connections, and roots. Investors should get to know the track record of companies and people with whom they are dealing, and even in Russia checks can be done on a counterpart.

Relations with management are extremely important. A hostile management (which usually also makes the staff hostile) can ruin everything, even if the investor has first-class assets, the support of the authorities, and a clear-cut legal case. There are several ways to take into account the interests of the management, staff, and local authorities. In many cases, a special deal should be struck with the management, for example in the form of job guarantees or golden handshakes. Assurances on employment or benefits should also be provided to the staff in order to avoid trouble.

The projects that have the best prospects for success today are relatively small and self-sufficient projects that are not dependent on too many factors, rather than the jumbo deals of the stagnation years. A solid project in Russia will typically entail the participation of serious companies on both sides, strong commitment of the partners, and clear-cut risk sharing, with a high degree of control over implementation exercised by the Western partner. For example, opening a quality hotel near the Red Square is a relatively fool-proof project, whereas restructuring a disputed enterprise might be a dangerous venture.

The types and forms of foreign investment in Russia are not different from any other country. There are thousands of joint ventures; it is possible to have enterprises that are 100 per cent foreign-owned; joint ventures themselves may become borrowers and lenders; and some initial signs of real estate investments are visible. Because the market is in its formative stage, equity participations are potentially more profitable, as well as more risky, compared with traditional greenfield joint ventures.

Regarding the sectoral breakdown of inward investments in privatisation, I would imagine that Russia's traditional specialisation in the extraction of mineral and other resources will remain a priority, since they already have a competitive edge. However, the authorities will not be encouraging any privatisation in this sector (such as oil and gas). And any privatisation that does occur will probably be covered by special legislation.

Simultaneously, a search for new areas of specialisation should proceed. I am quite sure that careful analysis of pros and cons of the Russian environment will bring to light immense and unimagined opportunities. Russia's specific features, such as cheap labour, high standards of education, an abundance of natural resources, and a deep domestic market spell out a potential bonanza. For example areas such as light industry (garments, textile), various consumer goods, food processing, health care, retail trade, and some machinery enterprises stand a very good chance of attracting foreign investment, if the current obstacles are removed.

The EBRD's work in St. Petersburg has shown that staff-owned enterprises (staff buy-outs) are the best first targets for foreign investment, since the investor is not obliged to deal with authorities or follow complex legal procedures. The next obvious target is state-owned joint-stock companies, since there it is much clearer who owns what and what is actually sold. In cases of a state enterprise on the verge of privatisation, it is crucial to check first whether the staff is getting what it wants and whether the privatisation authorities support the process.

Conclusions

Unlike in the rest of the former Soviet Union, privatisation in Russia is gaining pace, albeit slowly. Foreign investors will be more and more extensively involved in the privatisation, providing that certain criteria are met:

First, government support (legal and political) of foreign participation must be genuine and whole-hearted.

Second, the economic and political situation in the country must radically improve, which would enhance the credibility of the authorities.

Third, more pilot transactions should be initiated with official intergovernmental support, and information about their outcome should be widely shared. One very successful public relations campaign is the IFC involvement in small-scale privatisation in Nizhniy Novgorod.

Fourth, Western investors must try to integrate themselves into the Russian environment and adjust their practices to meet the Russian reality.

Fifth, more investment guarantees, insurance, and co-financing funds should be made available to support the privatisation and foreign investment. For example, the Privatisation Bank that was recently announced could be an important part of this process.

Notes

1 *Vse o privatizatsii*, Moscow, 1992, pp. 132-133.
2 At the moment there are two trading sessions per week with the average volume of transactions concluded of about $30 million.
3 The current policy of the Russian government on the convertibility of the ruble remains very contradictory: intermediate targets are not met, the Central Bank publicly declares its doubts, and there is no consensus within the government itself.
4 After the first of November 1992, the Foreign Investment Committee has ceased to exist, and its functions have been taken over by the Agency.
5 "Polozhenie o zakrytoi podpiske na aktsii pri privatizatsii gosudarstvennykhi munitsipalnykh predpriyatii 27 07.1992" Kommersant, 27 July - 3 August 1992, p.21.

Part IV
Money and Foreign Trade

9 Remaining Steps to a Market-BasedMonetary System in Russia[1]

Jeffrey Sachs and David Lipton

Introduction

The monetary problems facing Russia are perhaps the most complex in world history. At the beginning of 1992, the fifteen newly independent states of the former Soviet Union each had central banks issuing ruble credits without coordination. Recently, Estonia and Latvia have successfully introduced new currencies and others are sure to follow. Russia faces the challenge of coordinating monetary policies throughout the ruble area. At present, it remains difficult to make payments and settlements in a banking system that was designed for central planning. The enormous and mounting inter-enterprise arrears require urgent attention. And Russia must also develop payments mechanisms for its trade with countries leaving the ruble area.

Russia began its economic reforms lacking the basic monetary arrangements necessary for a market economy. It is essential to undertake fundamental monetary changes in several areas. The areas of greatest importance are:

1) establishing clear and unified control over monetary policy in the ruble area,
2) establishing mechanisms for market–based trade with states that leave the ruble area,
3) unifying the ruble exchange rate,
4) improving the payments mechanism of the banking system, to eliminate delays which now threaten the economy,
5) overcoming the cash crisis, and unifying the cash ruble (*nalichnyi*) and non-cash ruble (*beznalichnyi*) markets,
6) establishing central bank independence, and
7) managing the huge build up of inter-enterprise arrears.

This paper outlines the basic issues in each of the areas. Most of what is presented is straightforward and well known. Perhaps the less-well-known areas include: the mechanisms for trade with countries that leave the ruble area; improvement of the payments mechanism of the banking system; and unification of the cash and non-cash ruble markets. In any event, the goal of the paper is to pull together suggestions for the key remaining actions in one document.[2]

The ruble area: rules and sharing procedures

For monetary policy to be effective and for the stabilization effort to succeed, there must be a single monetary authority with adequate control over the instruments of monetary policy. To make this possible, the states that use the ruble must adopt a common set of rules and procedures for the management of the ruble monetary area (see Appendix A for an outline of a charter). Most importantly, *the Russian central bank should become the sole bank of issue of the ruble.* There are several important principles that should be followed in establishing the rules and procedures of the ruble area, and these are outlined below.

In the event that another central bank refuses to agree to Russian control over the ruble issue, the country should politely be invited out of the ruble area. In effect, Russia must nationalize the ruble, but in a fair and transparent way, that is equitable among the states that remain in the ruble area.

Earlier this year, the IMF proposed that each of the central banks in the ruble area retain the right to issue rubles, and that credit policies be coordinated by negotiation among the members of the ruble area. In our view, there is no realistic possibility of controlling credit in a system in which several independent central banks each have the independent authority to issue credit. The reason is simple. There is an overwhelming pressure in each of the states to "free ride" by issuing ruble credits at the expense of the rest of the system. Even IMF conditionality will not be strong enough to make friendly agreements stick.[3]

Monetary economists take it as a nearly self-evident proposition that a single currency area should have a single bank of issue:

> The key feature of a unified currency area is that it has at most one central bank with the power to create money — "at most" because no central bank is needed with a pure commodity currency. The U.S. Federal Reserve System has twelve regional banks, but there is only one central authority (the Open Market Investment Committee) that can create money. Scotland and Wales do not have central banks.[4]

Our recommendations for rules and sharing procedures within the ruble area are as follows:

One authority over monetary policy. There should be one institution, which could be called the Ruble Monetary Authority, with the sole jurisdiction over monetary policy. This Authority should include representation from all states using the ruble, but voting should be based on membership quotas calculated to reflect the economic size of the participating states. In other words, Russia should have 55 percent or more of the votes and should unilaterally control the decisions of the Authority, subject to the safeguards spelled out below.

One bank of issue. The Charter of the Ruble Area should establish that the Central Bank of Russia will be the sole bank of issue for rubles. What this must mean is that only the Central Bank of Russia will extend credits either in the form of currency emission or in the form of bank reserves. Centralizing control over credit creation is necessary, because it is the best way to prevent an abusive creation of credit by other states, a process that would be fatal to the effort to establish price stability.

Fair treatment of member states. To make these terms for membership in the Monetary Authority (and the continued use of the ruble as legal tender) acceptable to other states, the Articles of Agreement of the Authority should set out clear procedures that establish fair treatment of member states. The fair treatment procedures should be changeable only by a super-majority (e.g. 66.6 or 80 percent).

First, the gains from the creation of ruble cash money (seignorage) must be distributed fairly among member states. In other words, the cash issue should be distributed routinely to the governments of member states according to an equitable distribution formula.

Second, credit creation by the Central Bank of Russia must be apportioned fairly among the member states. There must be an agreement on a sharing formula for the allowable amount of credit to member state governments to finance budget deficits. If there are to be refinancing credits to commercial banks, there must be a sharing formula for the allowable amount of refinancing credits so that banks in each of the member states have access to their fair share. Under a credit sharing arrangement, the central banks of member states would serve as the conduits for refinancing credits from the Central Bank of Russia to commercial banks, but would issue no net credit themselves.

Third, the Monetary Authority must also take responsibility to coordinate foreign exchange market intervention throughout all member states, so as to guarantee equal access to foreign exchange and a unified exchange rate in all member states.

With these procedures, potential member states should be attracted to join the Monetary Authority for main two reasons. First, each member is protected from the abusive behavior of other members by the fact that Russia has strong control over the Authority and that there are rules to prevent member states from abusive credit creation. And second, the system will be administered in a way that is fair to all members. Monitoring by the International Monetary Fund will help to assure all members that other states are not abusing the procedures of the system to their own advantage.

Freedom to join or leave. All of the states using rubles at present should be given the choice to join the Ruble Monetary Authority, or to leave the ruble area by introducing their own currencies. There should be no active dissuasion of any state that wishes to have its own currency. When a state leaves the ruble area, it would do so under rules of behavior that will protect the remaining members of the ruble area (as described below). In particular, Russia would insist that any state introducing its own currency should do so via a currency exchange that withdraws the cash rubles circulating in the state, and that converts the bank balances into the new national currency. Rubles withdrawn from circulation should be returned to the Ruble Monetary Authority. Russia should request that the International Monetary Fund help enforce the ruble withdrawal requirement as part of its conditionality.

Ruble Monetary Authority. Once established, the Ruble Monetary Authority should take responsibility for the conduct of monetary policy. The Authority would set interest rates on credits of the Central Bank of Russia (mainly refinance credits to the commercial banks). The Authority would also establish reserve requirements (and the interest rates for remuneration on reserves) that would obtain for commercial banks in all member states. The Board would also manage exchange rate policy, either pegging the exchange rate (and devoting foreign exchange reserves to the defense of the pegged rate) or declaring a floating or managed exchange rate system.

Member states' central banks. As a consequence of membership in the Ruble Monetary Authority, the central banks of member states would cease to be independent monetary authorities. These central banks would not create credit, would not emit currency, and would not make monetary policy. They would serve a coordinating role in the monetary system, and would operate in cooperation with the Ruble Monetary Authority. They would retain an important role in the supervision of commercial banks in their state and would be involved in inter-republican settlements.

National currencies. It will be possible to accommodate other states in a symbolic way by allowing a distinct national cash money to circulate on a rigid one-for-one basis with the ruble (akin to Scottish pounds or banknotes of the Federal Reserve Bank of Boston). In effect, the money in circulation would be redenominated, and replaced with new currency notes (e.g. the Belarus ruble), but the republican central bank would have no monetary authority except to change Belarus currency into Russian rubles, and vice versa, on a one-to-one basis. In effect, the republican central bank would become a strict currency board, attached to the Russian Central Bank.

Reorganizing balance sheets. There are important issues of transition to a centralized Ruble Monetary Area. The balance sheets of the member central banks must be reorganized in line with the principle goal of establishing a single bank of credit issue. The details for reorganizing the balance sheets in an effective and equitable manner are outlined in Appendix B.

Trade and payments with the non-ruble area

Estonia introduced its own currency, the kroon, in June, becoming the first state of the former Soviet Union to introduce a new currency.[5] Latvia followed in July, introducing the lat. In the coming months, Ukraine will probably introduce its own currency as well. In each case, the new currencies will be the sole legal tender for transactions within these states. There are a number of technical issues that must be resolved for those states that elect to leave the ruble area, and we shall discuss these issues using Estonia as an example (the same principles should apply to Ukraine and other countries introducing new currencies). These issues include the return of rubles circulating in Estonia, the nature of the exchange regime between the ruble and the kroon, and the features of the settlements mechanism between the Russian and Estonian banking systems.

Return of the cash rubles

Estonia agreed to return to Russia the ruble cash in circulation. This measure has prevented Estonia from incurring a trade deficit with Russia by purchasing goods in Russia with the outstanding ruble cash, and thereby adding to the money supply in Russia (this issue obviously is much more important in the case of Ukraine). To accomplish this, the Russian and Estonian central banks agreed that there would be an exchange of kroon for ruble cash in circulation over a short and limited period of time.

The Estonian central bank and commercial banks have also swapped rubles for kroon in bank balances (and in the denomination of contracts). There are some technical issues to be resolved in converting ruble bank balances to kroon. It would have been irregular for Estonia to insist that deposits of non-residents (e.g. Russian enterprises holding accounts in Tallinn banks) should be converted involuntarily. The possibility of allowing Russian enterprises to maintain ruble balances in Estonian banks could be taken up in connection with discussions about the payments mechanism to be adopted for trade between Russian and Estonian enterprises.

The ruble-kroon exchange rate

In order absorb the ruble cash in circulation, Estonia converted ten rubles into one kroon. Once the exchange was complete, both Estonia and Russia agreed to allow the exchange rate to float. Estonia was uninterested in maintaining a peg to the ruble, as it is trying to escape from the tight link to Russian monetary policy. For Russia, a commitment to support the kroon at a stable rate in the foreign exchange market would be tantamount to supplying an open credit line of rubles to Estonia. Of course, it was precisely this obligation that Russia wanted to avoid.

Estonia decided to peg to the deutschemark. Note that if Russia, in time, decides to peg to a convertible currency, the cross-rate of the kroon and ruble will also in effect be pegged. But in this case, Russia will have no obligation to support the kroon, and Estonia will have no obligation to support the ruble. Foreign exchange interventions in each country will be against convertible currencies, not against each other.

Settlement of trade transactions

Once the former republics have their own currencies, it will be important to have a settlements mechanism that allows trade to operate without long payments delays or cumbersome procedures. One possibility, to conduct trade in hard currency settlements, would require a large holding of foreign exchange reserves, and is therefore too expensive. More realistically, trade should continue to be settled in rubles, *but strictly on a market basis.* For ruble trade to continue, however, a new settlements mechanism must be put in place.

This could be done through a series of correspondent banking accounts, held by republican banks in Russian banks. To see how this would work, consider how Russia now trades with Germany (or any other hard-currency country). Enterprises are not supposed to own German bank balances directly (although of course some do). Instead, they own bank accounts in Russian banks, while the Russian banks hold bank accounts of the same amount in German banks. Thus, when an enterprise owns a deutschemark (DM) bank balance in Moscow, it is really holding an account in a Moscow bank that is backed by the bank's ownership of the same amount of DM in a German bank. The bank accounts of Russian banks held in German banks are correspondent bank accounts.

When an enterprise without DMs wants to make an import from Germany, it purchases a DM-account on the inter-bank auction market. In effect, it becomes the (indirect) owner of the bank account in Germany, by owning a DM claim on a Russian bank which is backed by the Russian bank's ownership of the DM claim on the German bank. When a Russian enterprise makes an export to Germany, the German buyer deposits its DMs with the German correspondent bank of the Russian exporter's bank. The Russian bank increases its correspondent account with the German bank (or at least is supposed to do so !).

In principle, Estonia will now trade with Russia in exactly the same manner as Russia trades with Germany. Trade will (mostly) be denominated in rubles (though some trade will naturally be denominated in hard currency as the ruble is not yet stabilized), with Estonian banks holding correspondent accounts in Russian banks. When an Estonian exporter to Russia earns rubles, the correspondent account will rise. When an Estonian importer wants to make an import from Russia, the correspondent account will fall. Also, the ruble accounts will trade freely against kroon in an auction market in Tallinn or Leningrad.

In the past, the Central Bank of Russia has opposed a system of direct correspondent accounts between commercial banks on the grounds that "(it) would no longer have the necessary information on flows between the two countries". This view was a relic of the old "control mania," when money flows were used to track the planning process rather than to facilitate market based trade. However, there are no crucial facts that can be learned under this system that could not be gathered by customs houses and direct reporting by banks and enterprises on cross-border shipments. (In any event, the Central Bank has been completely overwhelmed administratively, and has not even been able to process in a timely way the inter-republican transfers through its correspondent accounts).

Therefore, a system of correspondent accounts should be established between Russia and each republic's commercial banks.[6] This will require a change of Russian Central Bank procedures to allow republic banks to hold ruble accounts directly with commercial banks in Moscow.

Moreover, to make the new trading system function well, banks will have to acquire and maintain adequate ruble balances in their mutual correspondent accounts. There is a simple way to accomplish this. The major commercial banks in each country and Moscow should arrange to swap correspondent accounts. For example, Russian banks would receive a ruble account in Tallinn, which could be used by their customers to make import purchases from Estonia, while Estonian banks would receive ruble accounts of the same amount, in order to facilitate imports from Russia. The central banks in each country should take care to make sure that these correspondent accounts are set up before the central bank correspondent accounts are discontinued.

To the extent that the major banks are illiquid, there may be a role for a one-time central bank loan in each country to their respective banks for the purpose of establishing the correspondent accounts. These central bank loans would take place at the refinance interest rate.

Unification of the exchange rate

In preparation for the stabilization of the ruble, the foreign exchange market should be simplified and the multiplicity of exchange rates should be unified so there is a single exchange rate for all current account transactions. At present there are several exchange rates, because of regulations that segment the exchange market and reserve special rates for certain current account transactions.[7]

Our recommendations for the unification of the exchange rate are as follows:

a. The commercial exchange rate, currently set at half of the central bank's quasi-market exchange rate, should be eliminated. This rate is used solely for exchange surrender of 40 percent of the proceeds of energy and raw materials exports that take place at the commercial rate. When the commercial rate is eliminated, an explicit export tax on these products could raise an amount of revenues for the budget equivalent to the penalty involved in surrender at a sub-market rate.

b. The special budget rate used for centralized imports and external debt service should also be eliminated. Purchasers of centralized imports should pay the full market exchange rate, and receive explicit budget subsidies if necessary for distribution of the goods to the final customer (e.g. in the case of medicine). Budget accounting should use true, market exchange rates so that the economic cost of transactions undertaken by the government is reflected accurately in the budget. The use of accounting exchange rates distorts budget accounting and provides a misleading impression of budget outcomes.

c. The official exchange rate set by the central bank should be set routinely and frequently to reflect the outcome of transactions in the auction market for foreign exchange. The present system of setting a quasi-market rate with only a loose connection to market outcomes should be replaced by an automatic process (based on averages of the most recent auctions from around the country). The period of adjustment should be shortened, and the exchange rate should be adjusted every few days to reflect the result of the auctions. To make it possible to have a market-based official exchange rate, the auction market for foreign exchange must be broadened to permit greater access for buyers and sellers.

d. This will be made easier if the value of the ruble is strengthened. There are two instruments of policy that can make this occur. First, the central bank will have to limit the creation of credit and raise interest rates to positive real levels. Eliminating the abundance of deposit money held by enterprises will heighten the demand for rubles and strengthen the exchange rate. Second, the central bank should sell foreign exchange in the auction market in much larger quantities as soon as it is feasible to do so.

e. There should be 100 percent repatriation of foreign exchange earnings, but no surrender requirement. This means that the dollar earnings would have to be returned to Russia in the form of a bank balance held in a Russian bank. However, the Russian bank account could remain in dollars, rather than being converted to rubles. The Russian commercial bank would then be required to hold an equivalent amount of foreign exchange in its correspondent accounts with foreign banks. In effect, there would be a 100 percent reserve requirement on the foreign currency deposits.

f. To the extent that the Russian government requires dollars, it should either take them from revenues (e.g. export taxes paid in hard currency), or purchase them for rubles, on the auction market.

Banking system reform: managing bank liquidity in a market system

The Stalinist payments system in Russia has not yet adjusted to the new market system. The old division between cash money and non-cash money remains the law, and even the practice, for most state enterprises. Cash is used for retail purchases and wages, while non-cash money must be used between enterprises. The banking system does not serve the most basic function that it does in a market economy: allowing the depositor to withdraw deposits in the form of cash.[8] Nor does cash serve its most basic function, as legal tender for all transactions in the economy.

The commercial banking system is completely unreliable, so the present arrangements have very high costs. When an enterprise makes a cash deposit, there is no sure (or even legal) way to get the deposit out in cash again, except in the form of wage payments (and even for wages, the access to cash has become unreliable). Therefore, private enterprises find it difficult, or impossible, to rely on the banking system, and they tend to rely on cash instead, despite the high transactions costs of using cash. Moreover, since the legal circulation of cash is completely regulated, there is little innovation by commercial banks and enterprises in the efficiency of cash utilization. At the same time, as cash is drawn into the private trading system, the central bank has become unable to guarantee that cash circulates within the official channels to be available to state enterprises for wage payments.[9]

It also appears that the division of cash and non-cash markets causes serious problems for macroeconomic control. Consider what happens if bank credit is expanded while the supply of cash in circulation is left unchanged. The credit expansion leads to a rise in producer prices, and these higher producer prices are passed along to retail prices. Since the supply of cash remains unchanged, however, nominal demand in the retail sector remains unchanged. With higher prices, and constant nominal demand, real demand by households actually falls. The result is that the expansion of enterprise credit leads to inflation and a fall of consumer purchases. Presumably, arrears increase as well, as retailers are unable to repay their suppliers out of sales.

The huge arrears buildup in the first half of 1992 probably resulted, in part, from the discrepancy of cash and non-cash money (there were other causes as well, which are discussed below). Most observers agree that: enterprise credit conditions were more expansionary than cash conditions during 1991; that, upon price liberalization, enterprise prices thereby increased by more than could be absorbed in the retail market; that retailers therefore were unable to sell their goods; and that this has contributed to the rise of arrears. Interestingly, a 1977 description of the classical Soviet payments mechanism similarly pointed to shortfalls in retail sales as the main reason for arrears buildups:

Delays in settling for goods occur mainly when consumer goods reaching retail outlets are selling slowly or not at all. This is the point in the deposit transfer circuit where the greatest "unplanned" use is made of short-term bank credit. It takes the form of an automatic (but not unlimited) extension of loans, either to the seller to bridge the settlement gap, or to the purchaser to enable him to make payment on the date due.[10]

Note that an expansion of credit to primary producers in the current environment could actually *worsen* the arrears problem, rather than improve it. Production would continue, and producer prices would remain high, but the goods would still not be sold at the retail level.

In view of the end of the planning system, and the introduction of a market-based economy, it is necessary to recreate the payments system on a normal basis, in which bank depositors can convert their sight deposits into cash upon demand. In order to do this, there are four major changes that must be made:

1) the supply of cash money relative to the supply of non-cash money must be increased, by printing more cash and restricting the issuance of non-cash credits.
2) the attractiveness of non-cash money should be enhanced by raising interest rates on bank deposits, especially on Sberbank deposits (Sberbank is the household savings bank).
3) the legal distinctions governing the use of cash and non-cash money should be eliminated. Both cash and bank deposits should be legal tender for all debts, public and private. All enterprises should be free to use cash or non-cash money in any transactions, and to hold cash or non-cash money balances.
4) the Russian Central Bank should stand behind the reserves in the banking system, in the sense of providing cash *upon demand* to commercial banks that seek to draw down their reserves held at the Central Bank.

To back up these changes:

1) credit expansion should be low;
2) foreign exchange should be sold into the non-cash market auctions, in order to absorb liquidity (this should also be done to strengthen the exchange rate);
3) cash money should be printed in large amounts, including very high denomination notes.
4) households should be encouraged to shift out of cash money and into savings deposits, by raising interest rates on Sberbank deposits.

Sberbank interest rates and the cash crisis

One key way to ease the cash crisis is by encouraging households and enterprises to economize on cash. Many enterprises, for example, already pay wages directly into Sberbank accounts of their workers, rather than in cash payments at the workplace. This practice is typically resisted, however, since workers prefer the convenience of receiving cash, especially during a period of high inflation. Sberbank deposits can, and should, be made more attractive to workers, to encourage the practice of economizing on cash payments.

This can be done in several ways. First, and perhaps most important, the Central Bank should ensure that Sberbank itself remains liquid, so that deposits are readily available in cash. It will be much easier to guarantee the liquidity of Sberbank than of tens of thousands of workplaces at which wages are now paid. Second, special attention should now be given to creating a Sberbank checking account system. Third, interest rates on Sberbank deposits should be raised significantly, in order to protect the real value of deposits. The Government has already declared that it will pay 80 percent nominal interest rates on delays in wage payments owing to cash insufficiency. The Government should encourage a similar interest rate on savings deposit accounts.

The balance sheet of the Sberbank is essentially as follows. There are liabilities, in the form of household savings accounts. These liabilities are matched by Sberbank claims on the Treasury, in the form of Treasury bonds (there are also some claims on the non-budgetary sphere, including loans to enterprises). The Finance Ministry has insisted that its interest payments on Treasury bonds held by Sberbank should remain very low, in order to avoid strains on the budget. As a result, the Sberbank has also insisted on maintaining low interest rates on household deposits, in order to maintain its own solvency. [11]

The Government has so far resisted a rise in interest rates on Sberbank deposits, on the grounds that this would substantially increase the budget deficit. This is a mistaken position, as the increased deficit arising from higher interest rates could readily be financed in a non-inflationary way, if the government were to issue Treasury bonds to Sberbank in order to pay the interest due to the bank. Moreover, the real (inflation-adjusted) value of those bonds would not increase rapidly as long as the real interest rate on deposits remains low. In fact, since interest rates (even after a substantial increase) may well remain below inflation rates, the real value of the government's debt could actually decline.

Consider an illustration. Suppose that the Sberbank begins with exactly 200 billion rubles of household deposits, matched by 200 billion rubles of claims on the Treasury. The nominal interest rate on the Treasury debt and on the deposits are set at 20 percent per annum, at a time when the annual inflation rate is 100 percent. At the end of one year, the nominal value of household savings accounts will have risen to 240 billion rubles (200 x 1.2), while the real value will have fallen to 120 rubles measured at beginning-of-year prices. Similarly, the public debt to Sberbank will have risen to 240 billion rubles (presuming that interest payments are redeposited in new Treasury bills, an assumption we return to momentarily), but the real value will have fallen to 120 billion rubles.

According to standard definitions, the interest payments to Sberbank would contribute to budget expenditures of 40 billion, which would increase the deficit if these are not financed by tax revenues. In real terms, by contrast, the budget would record a budget surplus of 80 billion rubles, reflecting the fall in the real value of the public debt from 240 rubles to 120 rubles. In essence, the Treasury is paying a negative real interest rate so that the real budgetary burden of the debt to Sberbank is negative not positive.

Now let us consider what would happen if interest rates were raised to 100 percent per year, to match the inflation rate. Clearly, household deposits would rise to 400 billion by the end of the year, as would the public debt. Measured in real prices, there would be no change in the value of deposits or Treasury debts to Sberbank. The budget burden of the debt would show 200 billion of interest payments, which would be matched by an equivalent budget deficit (assuming no other sources of revenue). In economic terms, however, the budget deficit would be zero, since the real value of the public sector's indebtedness would remain unchanged. There is no risk to the public finances in raising the interest rates to Sberbank, since the real value of the debt (and its burden on the budget) would not increase.

One important problem could arise, of course. If the Treasury had to pay the interest in cash, rather than new bonds, the interest payments would still generate inflation (even though the real value of the debt to Sberbank would be falling). Thus, it is important that Sberbank should accept payment from the Treasury in the form of new Treasury bonds, rather than in cash. It will be in a position to do this under two conditions: (1) that households are not attempting to liquidate their accounts at Sberbank, but rather are prepared to maintain their value in real terms; and (2) that the Treasury bonds are tradeable (if only to the Central Bank), in the emergency event that Sberbank faces a sudden and large withdrawal. To provide further protection to the budget and the Central Bank, the highest interest rates should apply only to time deposits, with a significant penalty in the form of early withdrawals.

To summarize, the Government should encourage a rise of interest rates on Sberbank deposits. To do this, it should be prepared to raise the interest rates that it is prepared to pay to Sberbank on the bank's Treasury bonds. Interest payments should be in the form of new bonds issued to Sberbank. The bank should be required to accept these bonds, perhaps with the understanding that they will be repurchased in part by the Central Bank in the event of a run on Sberbank deposits. In this way, the higher "deficit" of the Treasury would be financed by bonds, rather than by money printing (except in the event that the Central Bank had to repurchase the bonds).

It is thus important that the measure of the budget deficit should be adjusted to reflect the real value of the interest payments on the debt, instead of the nominal value of interest payments.

Bank reform: payments mechanisms

There is an urgent need to simplify the system for payments transfers between banks. When an enterprise with a deposit in one bank wants to pay an enterprise with a deposit in another bank, the process of transferring accounts can take *several days* if the two banks are within Moscow; *two weeks* if one of the banks is outside Moscow; and up to *two months* if one of the banks is in another republic. By simplifying the payments mechanism, most of these delays could be eliminated, and the majority of settlements could be done in a day or two.

The payments delays are wreaking havoc with the economy. They are one of the major factors causing the inter-enterprise arrears: enterprise B cannot pay enterprise C because it has not yet received payment from enterprise A.

These delays will occur as long as the Central Bank tries to monitor every transaction that takes place in the economy, and to maintain a paper document for every transaction. This is a relic of the old planning system, in which the settlements process was used as a control mechanism to make sure that plans were being implemented. The result, of course, is that the whole system is breaking down, and the Central Bank actually controls nothing: it has no time (or reason) to analyze the millions of paper documents being generated in the payments system.

Consider just one example of the perversity of this system. If an enterprise with a deposit in one branch of a Moscow bank wants to make a payment to an enterprise with a deposit at another branch of the same bank, each branch bank must maintain a separate correspondent account at the Central Bank. A payment order must be sent from one branch of the bank to the Central Bank, which then sends the payment order to the other branch of the bank. The central bank then credits the account of one of the banks and debits the account of the other bank.

In a normal market economy, such a transaction has nothing to do with the central bank! The bank, including all its branches, maintains just one account at the central bank. This account is used only when there are settlements between the bank and a completely different bank. For settlements between two branches of the same bank, however, transfers are left to the internal accounting of the bank, which has nothing to do with the bank's account at the central bank. It is crucial that each bank consolidate its accounts at the central bank into one correspondent account so that intra-bank settlements (i.e. transfers between branches of the same bank), would not involve the central bank at all.

Banks should also open correspondent accounts directly with other banks so that transfers between banks linked by correspondent accounts will not require Central Bank settlements. Consider the following example. Suppose a depositor at Moscow Business Bank wants to make a payment to a depositor at Menatep Bank. Instead of sending the payments order from the Moscow Business Bank to the Central Bank and then to Menatep Bank, Moscow Business Bank would hold its own account directly at Menatep Bank. To make the transfer, Business Bank would debit the account of its depositor; Menatep bank would debit the account of Business Bank; and Menatep Bank would credit the account of its depositor (the enterprise receiving the payment). In this way, there would be no change in the correspondent account balances of either bank held at the Central Bank, and the Central Bank would not have to be involved in the transaction.

A group of banks on a voluntary basis should also be allowed to organize a clearing-house for payments orders, outside of the Central Bank. Suppose that there are three banks (A, B, and C). Each is ordered (by depositors) to make transfers to other banks. A is to transfer 50 rubles to B; B is to transfer 75 rubles to C; and C is to transfer 40 rubles to A. In the current system, all three transactions must be processed separately by the Central Bank. In a clearing system, the banks would get together (once a day in Moscow, and without the involvement of the Central Bank) and they would establish net positions. A's net position for the day is -10 (40 receipt less 50 payment); B's net position is -25; and C's net position is +35. Obviously, the net positions add to zero.

After the banks agree on the net clearing, they would report just three numbers to the Central Bank (in a document signed by all of the banks): A, -10; B, -25; C, +35. The Central Bank would then debit or credit the central bank correspondent accounts of each bank by the requisite amount (e.g. A's reserves at the Central Bank would be reduced by 10 rubles). There would be no paper flows to and from the Central Bank, except the one sheet recording the changes in the net positions.

Central bank independence

History clearly shows that the legal arrangements surrounding a central bank play a critical role in determining central bank policies. The independence of the German Bundesbank from direct political interference, for example, has been a central reason why the deutschemark has consistently been a stable currency. Independence should have the following features:

Chairman (Governor) of bank appointed for several years, fixed term;

Board of Directors appointed for several years, fixed term;

no requirement for government approval of monetary policy;

no requirement for Parliamentary approval of monetary policy;

statutory requirement that the Central Bank should pursue the aim of monetary stability;

legal protection of Central Bank in conflicts with government and Parliament;

no automatic financing of budget deficit;

deficit financing at market rate of interest;

ceiling on total government borrowing from Central Bank; and

discount rate set by Central Bank, not Parliament or government;

Even with central bank independence, both the Government and the Parliament would retain some prerogatives. The Parliament would continue to monitor monetary policy, in committee hearings and debate, but not through explicit directives to the Bank. The Government (or President) would make appointments of the Chairman, and the Board of Directors, that must be confirmed by the Parliament. Neither the Government, the President, nor the Parliament, would have the power to remove the Chairman of the Bank, nor the Board of Directors, except for malfeasance in office. Terms of the Chairman and the Board would be confirmed for several years, independent of the Government and the Parliament.

It may seem naive to expect that the assignment of political responsibilities could be worked out now, in view of the feuding between the

Parliament and the Government. But perhaps there is a way to make progress on central bank independence, by having both the Government and the Parliament simultaneously renounce operational control over the Central Bank of Russia, in favor of a properly independent central bank.

We recommend that the Government and the Parliament would reach an agreement on the overall organization of the Russian Central Bank. A Board of Directors of the Bank would govern general policy, and the day-to-day management would be under the direction of the Governor of the Bank. Members would be nominated by the President of the Russian Federation, and approved by the Parliament. There would be a fixed term, say of three years, for the first board. Similarly, the Governor of the Central Bank would be nominated by the President and approved by the Parliament.

The Central Bank should also have an establishing charter. The goals of the Central Bank would be clearly stated, in order of priority: (1) to guarantee a stable value of the ruble, on domestic markets and in international exchanges; (2) to organize an efficient payments system in conformity with the needs of a market economy; (3) to guarantee the international convertibility of the currency; and (4) to maintain credit conditions conducive to overall macroeconomic stability, as a basis for long-term economic development. The Charter would clearly state that the Central Bank is to undertake monetary policies conducive to these goals, and is proscribed from financial operations that would be detrimental to these goals.

The Central Bank should be obligated to make timely reports on monetary conditions and monetary policy to the Parliament, and to hear recommendations of the Parliament and Government on the conduct of policy. Parliament and the Government, however, would be explicitly barred from interfering in the operation of monetary policy.

The Central Bank would be proscribed by its Charter from making subsidized loans in the economy, except as provided explicitly by the budget.

Managing inter-enterprise arrears

It is now well understood that there is no single explanation for inter-enterprise arrears. There are, in fact, many important contributing factors. Final demand has fallen more than production. The cash shortage has contributed to a squeeze of final goods purchases, while producers have continued to produce at old levels. As mentioned earlier, there has been a breakdown of bank payments mechanisms. Because of the archaic methods used to clear payments between banks, there are large delays in receiving payments. Enterprises therefore lack the money to pay their suppliers because they have not yet received payments from their own customers. This is exacerbated by the breakdown of payments between republics. There has been a particularly sharp breakdown in the clearing of settlements between Russian and non-Russian enterprises. Settlements can sometimes take up to two months.

At the same time, military industrial enterprises continue to produce. Despite the cutback in budgetary spending, the military sector has maintained production even where there is no demand from the government budget. These enterprises are not paid, and therefore they cannot pay their own suppliers.

The microeconomic incentives governing shipments and payments are also deficient. There is an absence of incentives to clear arrears. Enterprises in arrears are still able to pay wages, and even to raise wages. In addition, interest charges on arrears are negligible, so that there is a strong incentive to delay payments. Moreover, there is a lack of clear sales-verification mechanisms. There is not yet a system of bills of exchange, letters of credit, bank checks, and so forth, to allow shippers to guarantee that they will be paid by suppliers. Finally, there is a lack of bankruptcy provisions. Since there are no legal bankruptcy mechanisms in place, there are very limited means for enforcing debt contracts.

These problems have several clear implications. Increased credit is dangerous. Credit might allow some production to continue, but it will not raise final demand of consumers. For that reason, it is crucial to overcome the cash shortage, which can only be done by raising the amount of cash relative to the amount of bank credit. Therefore, more credit will simply lead to inflation, higher inventories, and even higher arrears because of unsold goods. An improvement in the payments mechanism is crucial. There will be no way to prevent a further growth in arrears unless there are reliable ways to make payments between customers and between banks. And, incentives are needed to encourage firms to pay their bills. Incentives should include higher interest rate charges on arrears; legal mechanisms for creditors to seize assets of debtors; restrictions on wage increases to enterprises in arrears; and finally, a bankruptcy law.

A strategy for solving the arrears problem should aim at three things:

Postponing the repayment of arrears. These should be postponed for a period of several months, perhaps one year. The goal of this step is to prevent the old arrears from destroying future production. Many firms lack the liquidity needed both to pay off their arrears and to buy inputs for future production. By postponing the repayment of arrears, firms are given the opportunity to continue current production.

Stopping the accumulation of new arrears. Steps should be taken in several ways. We urge the immediate improvement of the payments system between enterprises, and between banks, according to specific suggestions. Penalties should be levied on enterprises in arrears (including wage limitations and high interest rates on the arrears). Bankruptcy proceedings should be imposed on enterprises that cannot pay off the old arrears and that continue to generate new arrears.

Providing a way to settle past arrears. A clearing system should be established for the old arrears, by netting them out, and then providing a new schedule for repayments. To give incentives for the eventual repayment of these arrears, we recommend that enterprises with arrears be subjected to strict wage limitations until the arrears are cleared.

Managing the old arrears

A date should be chosen to separate old arrears from new arrears. All arrears between Russian enterprises that are bona fide (e.g. registered in *Kartoteka dva*) would be registered with a payments agent. These debts would be converted into [one-year] loans, with [one-third] of the debts due in each [four-month] period. The loans would carry an interest rate [equal to] the Central Bank discount rate. (Obviously, a different maturity and interest rate of the debt could be selected. We are merely aiming to provide a specific illustration here.)

At this point, after the conversion of the arrears into securities, there are two possible variants.

Variant 1. The debts remain in the form of inter-enterprise claims, between specific enterprises. These claims would be marketable, so that the creditor enterprise could sell its claims to other enterprises, or even to the debtor firm, at a discount. At the end of the period, when the claims come due, failure to honor the debt could lead to the initiation of bankruptcy proceedings (under new procedures being established by the State Property Committee).

Variant 2. The debts would be converted from bilateral obligations between particular enterprises, into obligations to and from a central Clearing House (CH). The purpose of establishing the CH would be to permit the multilateral netting of claims and debts. For example, if Enterprise A owes 50 million rubles to Enterprise B, and 70 billion to

Enterprise C, while at the same time it is owed 60 million from Enterprise B, and 20 million from Enterprise C, the CH would establish a net claim on Enterprise A of 40 billion rubles (50+70-60-20). Since the CH would lead to a significant netting out of claims, thereby reducing the stock of gross arrears into a much smaller stock of net debt either owed to, or owed by the CH.

In both variants, additional sanctions would be imposed on enterprises in arrears, as the terms for winning a debt workout, and as a disincentive to any further increases of arrears. For example, such enterprises would be subjected to strict wage limitations. Also, if the enterprise does not pay off the debt on the new [one-year] schedule, the enterprise would be subjected to bankruptcy proceedings. In particular, the management and workers in the enterprise would stand to lose their equity claims in the enterprise.

Clearing house mechanics

If variant 2 is selected, the precise CH mechanism might work as follows. All arrears owed by an enterprise to other enterprises would be converted into debts owed by the enterprise to the CH. All claims by an enterprise on other enterprises would be converted into claims by the enterprise on the CH. The CH would then cancel out offsetting arrears and claims of each firm, and calculate a net debtor or creditor position for each firm with the CH. Thereafter, enterprises would pay their debts into the CH (managed by the Central Bank), and enterprises would receive their payments from the CH. This system obviously applies only to the old arrears, before June 1.

Consider the following illustration.

Arrears	Owed to		
Owed by	Enterprise 1	Enterprise 2	Enterprise 3
Enterprise 1	—	50	70
Enterprise 2	60	—	40
Enterprise 3	20	45	—

Note that Enterprise 1 has total arrears of 120, and total payments due of 80 from the other firms. Therefore, Enterprise 1 has a net position of 40 in arrears (i.e. a net debt of 40). Enterprise 2 has total arrears of 100, and total payments due of 95 (net arrears 5). Enterprise 3 has total arrears of 65, and total payments due of 110 (net arrears are -45, i.e. a net credit position).

Total arrears are 285 (=120+100+65). These arrears are converted into net claims to or from the Clearing House, as follows:

		Debt to CH
Enterprise 1		40
Enterprise 2		5
Enterprise 3	(i.e., net credit)	-45
Total		0

Now, if we add up the net debt of the debtor enterprises, the outstanding balances have been reduced to 45 (= 40 + 5). By construction, the CH has a net worth identically equal to zero.

Payments made to the CH by debtor firms would simply be passed along to the creditor firms, on a *pro rata* basis. Thus, if Enterprise 1 and 2 each pay half of their respective debts (20 from Enterprise 1, and 2.5 from enterprise 2), that amount would be passed along to enterprise 3. The Clearing House would, by construction, never run a surplus or a deficit on a cash-flow basis. It would simply pay out what it takes in from debtor firms. If the debtor firms default (in part or in whole) on their payments, the creditor firms would receive only a fraction of what is owed to them.

In general, the CH would have the responsibility of trying to enforce the debt claims. Firms that owe money to the CH will be under a wage freeze, and with the threat of closure and bankruptcy if the debts are not paid on time to the CH. The CH could also try to sell its claims on specific enterprises into the capital market (at a discount on face value), and let the new creditors that purchase the debt try to collect.

Since the arrears are being turned into one-year debt, the CH would have several months to start up operations. For example, the arrears recorded at the commercial banks (in the *Kartoteka dva*) could be registered in 60 days, and netting could take place in the next 30 days. Firms would then be notified of the payments falling due, and would have another 30 days to come up with the first payment. Therefore, many of the administrative problems could be resolved *after* the CH is set up.

Two further comments are in order. First, the debts would probably be eroded by inflation, as long as the real interest rate is negative. Second, there would no doubt be political pressures on the CH to make payments to the creditor enterprises even when they fail to receive payments from the debtor enterprises. It would be essential to resist these pressures.

Each variant has its advantages and disadvantages. Variant 1 has the following advantages. First, it is administratively straightforward, since no new CH must be set up. Second, it preserves the legal status of creditors and debtors, and thus does not set a precedent that debts might be cancelled or taken over by some other entity. Third, it allows a decentralized approach for working off the debt, since creditors and debtors can bargain amongst themselves for debt reduction, debt buybacks, etc.

Variant 2 solves one problem, which may be enormous and worth solving: the complex web of claims in which enterprises are both creditors and debtors. The CH allows for a rapid netting out process, which can simplify matters immensely *if the gross arrearages are much larger than the net debts*. For example, if most enterprises are both creditors and debtors on inter-enterprise arrears, than netting could be hugely advantageous. If most enterprises are either creditors or debtors, but not both, then the clearing house would not be advisable, and smaller amounts of netting could take place on a decentralized basis. Remember that the CH alternative has the serious disadvantage of making it much harder to reach decentralized, bilateral settlements, and that disadvantage must be weighed against the possible benefits of netting.

Once the Government has investigated the extent of the gains from a netting operation; it will better be able to decide between variant 1 and variant 2. All claims arising from arrearages before the chosen date would be transformed into one-year claims. An international investment firm could assist the Central Bank of Russia in analyzing the extent to which a clearing house would reduce the overall amount of debt. If the total arrears (on the order of 3.0 trillion rubles at end-June 1992) would be reduced to, say, 1 trillion in net claims, by the CH operation, then establishment of a CH probably makes sense. If the net claims were to remain above 1.5 trillion rubles, on the other hand, then leaving the debts in bilateral hands probably makes sense.

Preventing future arrears

It would be extremely important to prevent a new buildup of arrears after the conversion of the old arrears into one-year debt. Enterprises should be warned to make shipments only to enterprises with the money available to make the purchase. Banks should issue letters of credit or other conditional payment instruments to guarantee the suppliers of the capacity to pay before shipments are made. Work on improving the settlements system should proceed more rapidly. There are many easy things to do, such as allowing banks to consolidate all of their branches into one account at the Central Bank; allowing the major banks to do their own clearing among themselves; and allowing banks to set up correspondent accounts with other banks. Interest rates on new arrears should be at a punitive rate of interest, even higher than the refinance rate.

Firms in arrears (whether old or new) should be subject to a wage freeze, and ultimately to bankruptcy procedures.

Conclusion

The steps we have outlined toward achieving a market-based monetary system in Russia are aimed at creating monetary institutions that will restore the usefulness of the ruble as a money, support price and exchange rate stability, and depoliticize monetary policy. Russia must abandon the structures and practices held over from the Stalinist economic system and perpetuated by the mentality of central control over monetary matters. In its place, Russia must build a monetary system that places the key instruments of money and credit policy firmly in the hands of a single, independent monetary authority. Not only must the Central Bank of Russia be made independent, but the independent states must quickly decide whether to remain in the ruble area (and join a monetary authority) or introduce new currencies (and take full responsibility for domestic stability).

With the instruments of monetary control firmly in independent hands, the ruble must be made a real, usable currency. The distinction between cash and non-cash money, which exists nowhere else in the world, must be eliminated. The multiplicity of exchange rates must be eliminated, so that international trade and finance can develop naturally. And, the commercial banks should be freed to conduct their domestic and international banking business without undue interference from the monetary authority.

The actions we have outlined are the most urgent. Further banking-sector reforms will be needed over the years to come. These should include: enhanced banking sector supervision, including capital adequacy and portfolio diversification requirements on the vast proliferation of banks that have opened in the past two years; securities trading and disclosure laws; and efficient bankruptcy procedures, including mechanisms for converting debt into equity of existing state enterprises.

Appendix A: Illustrative Charter of the Ruble Monetary Area

I. ESTABLISHMENT OF THE RUBLE AREA

I.1. This Charter establishes the Ruble Area (RA), and describes the rules and operations for participating nations. The RA is a voluntary association of nations. Countries may join the RA or may withdraw from the RA under the terms of this Charter.

I.2. The Governing body of the Ruble Area is the Ruble Monetary Authority (RMA), which is composed of the Governors of the participating central banks. Voting is on a weighted basis, according to the terms of Section VII of this Charter.

I.3. The aim of the RMA is to guarantee stable monetary conditions of the participating countries, including a stable domestic price level, convertibility of the ruble on the foreign exchanges, non-discrimination among participating countries, an efficient settlements system, and open trading relations among participating members, and between the RA and other nations.

II. BASIC GUIDELINES FOR MONETARY POLICY

II.1. All transactions between residents of the ruble area shall be settled in rubles, subject to guidelines agreed to by the RMA. Ruble banknotes and bank reserves held at the Russian Central Bank will be the legal tender for transactions between residents of the ruble area.

II.2. The Russian Central Bank (CBR) is the sole bank of issue of ruble base money (currency and commercial bank reserves). In particular, ruble reserves of commercial banks in all republics are the direct liability of the CBR.

II.3. Initial balance sheets of member central banks will be established and approved by the RMA by October 1, 1992, following an international audit of the participating central banks. Procedures for allocating initial assets and liabilities are described in the appendix, and will be elaborated by the RMA.

II.4. The CBR will extend credit to the non-Russian central banks (NRCBs) by crediting the correspondent accounts of the NRCBs at the CBR. In turn, the NRCBs may relend these ruble reserves to commercial banks or to their respective Treasuries. The guidelines for credit expansion within the Ruble Area are described in Section III.

II.5. The RMA will prepare an annual monetary program that will describe the guidelines for credit expansion during the year. These guidelines will be the basis for monthly credit targets, which will be established by the RMA for each month, at the end of the preceding month. A review of the annual guidelines will be completed each quarter, and revised annual targets will be established, which in turn will be the basis for revisions of the monthly credit targets.

II.6 Within the RA, there will be uniform conditions of management of foreign exchange, interest rates on refinance credits, and commercial bank reserve requirements.

II.7. The RMA will be responsible for harmonization of settlements and payments systems within the ruble area.

II.8. The RMA will issue monthly public reports on monetary conditions in the RA and on its own activities.

III. PRINCIPLES GOVERNING DOMESTIC CREDIT EXPANSION

III.1. Domestic credit (which means within the RA) will be extended on a *pro rata* basis among the participating states. Each state will be assigned a participation share (PS) within the RA. This participation share will determine the *pro rata* allocation of every extension of domestic credit. The Russian share of domestic credit will be extended directly by the CBR to Russian commercial banks and the Russian Treasury. The non-Russian share of domestic credit will be extended by the CBR to the NRCBs in the form of interest-free loans, without fixed maturity, deposited in the correspondent accounts of the NCBRs at the CBR. These loans may not be called, except in the case that the country departs from the Ruble area. Procedures for separation from the ruble area are outlined in Section V. (An illustration of the principle of *pro rata* credit allocation is provided for in the Appendix.)

III.2. The RMA will certify that domestic credit is being allocated according to the conditions of this Charter, and according to the aims of monetary policy, and in particular, according to the agreed-upon participation shares. The RMA will retain an internationally recognized accounting firm to audit the RMA on a regular basis to guarantee conformity with the agreed credit policy.

III.3. Domestic credit expansion is defined to include the following operations of a participating central bank: refinance credits to commercial banks; purchases of government bonds; and rediscounting of eligible commercial paper. Guidelines for the division of domestic credit within a republic among these various categories will be determined by the respective central banks and governments, though the RMA may agree on a unanimous basis to guidelines for the division of domestic credit.

III.4. Refinance credits to commercial banks will be at a uniform interest rate within the RA. There will be no interest subsidies granted by the Ruble Monetary Authority, or by participating central banks.

IV. PRINCIPLES GOVERNING PAYMENTS AND SETTLEMENTS WITHIN THE RUBLE AREA

IV.1. The CBR is obligated to redeem all reserves held at the CBR in ruble banknotes upon demand.

IV.2. During a brief transition period, in which a cash-note shortage still prevails, the CBR will deliver cash notes to all republics on a *pro rata* basis.

IV.3. A NRCB may introduce its own ruble banknote for circulation within its own state, subject to the following guidelines:

a) the RMA is notified of the intention to introduce the state's banknote;
b) all issue of the banknote is debited against the NRCB account at the CBR on a one-for-one basis, and is within the limits of overall credit emission prescribed by the RMA;
c) the banknote is denominated in rubles, and is strictly interchangeable with rubles in all settlements. The ruble banknotes issued by the CBR remain legal tender in the state.
d) the NRCB stands prepared to exchange the state's banknote for a ruble banknote on a one-for-one basis.

IV.4. The Central Bank of Russia, together with the NRCBs and the commercial banks, will endeavour to speed settlements through the adoption of the following principles: establishment of correspondent accounts directly between commercial banks; multilateral clearing houses of commercial banks in major cities; intra-bank clearing of settlements among branches of the same bank; trucation of paper payments orders in the settlements process; use of wire transfer procedures; penalties paid by the Russian Central Bank for delays in transfers.

V. ORGANIZATION OF THE BANKING SYSTEM

V.1. All participating states in the RA are committed to the operation of a two-tiered banking structure. The central bank will be responsible for the overall management of monetary policy and banking supervision. Commercial operations and direct operations with non-financial enterprises will be the sole purview of commercial banks and specially designated state banks independent of the central bank.

V.2. There will be a uniform set of reserve requirements for all commercial banks operating within the ruble area. All domestic reserves of commercial banks within the ruble area will be liabilities of the Russian Central Bank.

VI. PRINCIPLES GOVERNING FOREIGN EXCHANGE MANAGEMENT

VI.1. The ruble shall be convertible for current account purposes at a unified exchange rate. All residents in the ruble area are eligible to purchase foreign exchange for current account purposes at the market exchange rate.

VI.2. The RMA is responsible for setting general guidelines for exchange rate management. The Central Bank of Russia has operational responsibility for foreign exchange market intervention. The CBR is also obligated to sell foreign exchange to other central banks at the market exchange rate.

VI.3. The CBR will maintain an intervention account (IA) for foreign exchange market intervention. The net foreign asset position in the IA will be owned jointly by participating central banks, with *pro rata* shares. The initial net foreign asset position of the IA will be established by a pooling of foreign exchange assets now held by the participating central banks.

VI.4. Increases in the net foreign asset position of the intervention account will lead to a simultaneous debiting of the net foreign asset (NFA) positions of the NRCBs and a crediting of the NRCBs' accounts at the CBR. Similarly, a decrease in the net foreign asset position of the intervention account will lead to a simultaneous crediting of the NFA position of the NRCBs and a debiting of the NRCBs' account at the CBR.

VI.4. Central banks may maintain net foreign asset positions of their own, independent of the intervention account.

VI.5. Participating central banks may lend gross reserves to the IA (for example, out of IMF credits). In this case, the net foreign asset position of the IA remains unchanged, though gross reserves increase.

VI.6. In the event that a country leaves the ruble area, the country is entitled to receipt of its share of the net foreign assets of the IA.

VII. PRINCIPLES GOVERNING VOLUNTARY SEPARATION FROM THE RUBLE AREA

VII.1. In the event that a member country decides to separate from the Ruble Area, it should agree to give 60 days notice, or to seek special permission for withdrawal in less than 60 days.

VII.2. Upon separation, the following actions will be taken:

  a) all ruble banknotes in circulation will be withdrawn through conversion with the banknotes of the new currency. The ruble banknotes will be returned to the CBR;
  b) all commercial bank reserves at the CBR are transferred to the NRCB;
  c) the correspondent account of the NRCB at the CBR is *credited* by the sum of cash rubles (a) plus commercial bank reserves (b).

VII.3. After separation, the correspondent account of the NRCB is converted into an interest-bearing account, with the interest rate equal to the basic refinance rate.

VII.4. The CBR and the NRCB will prepare modalities for payments and settlements on a market basis after currency replacement.

VIII. ORGANIZATION OF THE RUBLE MONETARY AUTHORITY

VIII.1. The RMA will be composed of the Governors of the participating central banks. Each central bank will also designate alternative executive directors.

VIII.2. The RMA will be chaired by the Governor of the Central Bank of Russia.

VIII.3. Voting rights will be on a weighted basis, according to quota rights within the RMA. Initial quota allocation will be on the basis of [...].

VIII.4. Decisions on the instruments of monetary policy (credit limits, interest rates, reserve requirements) will be on the basis of simple majority voting. Changes to the Charter will require a vote of not less than [75] percent.

Appendix B: Establishment of Initial Balance Sheets and the Mechanics of Credit Expansion

I. THE ESTABLISHMENT OF INITIAL BALANCE SHEETS

In order to implement the terms of the Charter, the CBR must assume the reserve liabilities of the ruble area, and adjust the correspondent accounts of the NRCBs accordingly. For this purpose, the following steps are taken.

1. CBR assumes as a liability the sum of ruble cash in circulation in the non-Russian states, plus all ruble reserves of the commercial banks resident in the states.
2. CBR debits the correspondent account of the NRCBs by the amount of the liability assumed in (1).

The balance sheet of the Russian Central Bank (CBR) will be as follows:

Assets	Liabilities
Net foreign assets	Currency (notes and coin) in Russia in Non-Russia
Net domestic assets	
(credit to Russian government)	Bank reserves
(credit to Russian banks)	Russian banks
(credit to NRCBs)	Non-resident banks
(other assets, net)	

The balance sheet of a Non-Russian Central Bank (NRCB) will be as follows:

Assets	Liabilities
Net foreign assets	Net liabilities to CBR
Net domestic assets	
(credit to NR government)	
(credit to NR banks)	
(other assets, net)	

II. AN ILLUSTRATION OF CREDIT EXPANSION TARGETS

Suppose that reserve requirements are 25 percent, and the desired cash-deposit ratio is 50 percent. Notice that each 1 ruble of base money will be held as 67 kopeks of cash, and 33 kopeks of reserves, which in turn supports 1.33 rubles of bank deposits. (This division of high-powered money into cash and reserves guarantees a cash-deposit ratio of 50 percent.)

For purposes of illustration, assume that Russia (R) is twice the size of Non-Russia (NR), and that the participation coefficient of Russia is 0.67, and of non-Russia is 0.33. This means that for every ruble of credit expansion in the RA, 67 kopeks goes to credit expansion by the RCB, and 33 kopeks goes to credit expansion by the NRCB.

Suppose that the starting monetary position is as shown in Table 1. Notice the difference in central bank balance sheets. The RCB has the liabilities for currency and bank reserves. The NRCB does not have such liabilities. The CBR has a (non-interest-bearing) asset in the form of a claim on the NRCB, while the NRCB has, of course, a corresponding liability to the CBR.

Note that the money supply (M2) in Russia is 300 (cash plus deposits in Russia). The money supply in non-Russia is 150. High-powered money in Russia is 150 (cash plus reserves); high-powered money in non-Russia is 75. Total high-powered money of the Ruble Area is 225.

Now suppose that the RMA decides on an overall inflation target of 20 percent, matched by an equivalent increase in the money supply. High-powered money should increase by 20 percent, or by 45 rubles. According to the participation coefficients, 66.6 percent of this increase is domestic credit of CBR, and 33.3 percent is credit expansion by the NRCB. Thus, CBR credit goes up by 30 rubles, and NRCB credit goes up by 15 rubles. The NRCB credit is added to the correspondent account of the NRCB (liabilities to CBR are increased). Initially, CBR extends finance credits to Russian commercial banks in the amount of 30 rubles, while the NRCB extends finance credits equal to 15 rubles. The first-round results are shown in Table 2.

Because of cash demands, some of these refinance credits are subsequently withdrawn from the banking system in the form of cash holdings by the public, which must (ultimately) be supplied by the CBR. Under our assumptions of currency-deposit ratios, the end-position balance sheets are as shown in Table 3. Of the overall 45 ruble increase in high-powered money, 30 rubles ends up as an increase in cash, while 15 ends up as an increase in bank reserves at the CBR (which, in turn, supports a 60 ruble increase in total deposits).

Table 1 Illustration of Monetary Survey of Ruble Area

Russian Central Bank

Assets		Liabilities	
Credit to banks	100	**Currency**	150
Credit to Gov	50	in Russia	100
		in Non-Russia	50
Credit to NRCB	75		
		Reserves	75
		Russian banks	50
		Non-Russian	25
Total	225	Total	225

Russian Commercial Banks

Reserves	50	Deposits	200
Loans	250	CBR credit	100
Total	300	Total	300

Non-Russian Central Bank

Assets		Liabilities	
Credit to banks	50	Credit from CBR	75
Credit to Gov	25		
Total	75	Total	75

Non-Russian Commercial Banks

Reserves	25	Deposits	100
Loans	125	NCRB credit	50
Total	150	Total	200

Table 2 Initial Change in Balance Sheets

Russian Central Bank

Assets		Liabilities	
Credit to banks	30	**Currency**	0
Credit to Gov		in Russia 0	
		in Non-Russia 0	
Credit to NRCB	15	**Reserves**	45
		Russian banks 30	
		Non-Russian 15	
Total	45	Total	45

Russian Commercial Banks

Reserves	30	Deposits	120
Loans	120	CBR credit	30
Total	150	Total	150

Non-Russian Central Bank

Assets		Liabilities	
Credit to banks	15	Credit from CBR	15
Credit to Gov	0		
Total	15	Total	15

Non-Russian Commercial Banks

Reserves	15	Deposits	60
Loans	60	NRCB credit	15
Total	75	Total	75

Table 3 Final Change in Balance Sheets

Russian Central Bank			
Assets		Liabilities	
Credit to banks	30	**Currency**	30
Credit to Gov		in Russia 20	
		in Non-Russia 10	
Credit to NRCB	15	**Reserves**	15
		Russian banks 10	
		Non-Russian 5	
Total	45	Total	45

Russian Commercial Banks			
Reserves	10	Deposits	40
Loans	60	CBR credit	30
Total	70	Total	70

Non-Russian Central Bank			
Assets		Liabilities	
Credit to banks	15	Credit from CBR	15
Credit to Gov	0		
Total	15	Total	15

Non-Russian Commercial Banks			
Reserves	5	Deposits	20
Loans	30	NRCB credit	15
Total	35	Total	35

References

Freidman, Milton (1992) *Money Mischief: Episodes in Monetary History*, New York: Harcourt, Brave and Jovanovich.

Garvy, George (1977) *Money, Financial Flows, and Credit in the Soviet Union*, Cambridge, Massachusetts: National Bureau of Economic Research.

Hansson, Ardo and Jeffrey Sachs (Sept, 1992) "Estonia's Monetary Independence". World Bank *Transition*, forthcoming September.

International Monetary Fund (April, 1992) *Economic Review: Russian Federation*, Washington.

International Monetary Fund (April, 1992) *Economic Review: The Economy of the Former U.S.S.R. in 1991*, Washington.

International Monetary Fund et al. (1991) *A Study of the Soviet Economy Vol. 1*, Feb, 1991.

Moody, Stephan S. March (1992) "Eastern Approaches: Rubles, Western Aid and Ruble Stabilization". *Perspectives on Change*, Vol. 1, no. 2.

Sundarajan V. March, 1992. "Central Banking Reforms in Formerly Planned Economies". *Finance and Development*, Vol. 29 (no. 1) pp. 10-13.

Notes

1 The authors would like to thank Stanley Fischer for many discussions, and for collaboration on an earlier version of the discussion of inter-enterprise arrears.

2 These actions are the most urgent. The next round of banking-sector reforms should include: enhanced banking sector supervision, including capital adequacy and portfolio diversification requirements on the vast proliferation of banks that have opened in the past two years; securities trading and disclosure laws; efficient bankruptcy procedures, including mechanisms for converting debt into equity of existing state enterprises.

3 The problem has been acutely underscored by Ukraine's announcement on June 12, 1992, of its intention to proceed — unilaterally and without consultation — on an enormous credit expansion (between 300 and 600 billion rubles), in order to settle inter-enterprise arrears. This massive amount of credit issue threatens to re-ignite explosive inflation in Russia unless the currencies of Ukraine and Russia are quickly separated. Ironically, there are far superior ways to address the inter-enterprise arrears in any case, as we document later in the paper.

4 Milton Friedman (1992, p. 242).

5 The introduction of the kroon took place over the weekend of June 20-21, 1992. This paper was prepared in the weeks leading up to this event. The following discussion of the mechanisms being adopted reflects our understanding of how the new system will function.

6 It would be possible, in theory, to maintain the existing system. Up until the introduction of the kroon, Estonian commercial banks have held correspondent accounts only with the Estonian Central Bank, which holds a correspondent account with the Russian Central Bank, which in turn holds correspondent

accounts with Russian commercial banks. Under the new system, it is conceivable that every time that an Estonian enterprise wants to make a purchase in Russia, it would debit its account at its bank; its bank would debit its account at the Estonian Central Bank; the Estonian Central Bank would debit its account at the Russian Central Bank; and the Russian Central Bank would credit the correspondent account of the exporter's bank. But this cumbersome procedure, through long delays in settlements, has already contributed to a collapse of inter-republican trade.

7 Some of the changes recommended here were adopted by the Central Bank of Russia on July 1, 1992. The exchange rate system was unified and the CBR began to set the official exchange rate at the level prevailing in the interbank foreign exchange auction.

8 The convertibility of bank money into currency and vice versa is considered such a central role of a banking system that it is rarely even questioned. Deposit banks in operating the payments mechanism play the role of converting notes and coin into bank money and bank money into notes and coin.

9 In the classic central planning system, households spend cash in retail markets. Retail shops deposit the cash in the Central Bank. The Central Bank then allocates the cash among the "commercial" banks (where state enterprises maintain deposits) to allow enterprises to withdraw their wage payments in cash. Under present circumstances, a smaller proportion of cash is being redeposited in the central bank, so that the central bank is unable to the banks the cash that the enterprises need to make wage payments.

10 Garry (1977).

11 It has been able to do this, in part, because the new commercial banks have not attempted to lure away household deposits by offering higher interest rates on household deposits. The new commercial banks argue, by and large, that they lack the facilities, branch offices, and technical capacity to service small household depositors.

10 The Trouble with the Ruble: Monetary Reform in the Former Soviet Union[1]

Ardo H. Hansson

Introduction

Few persons can claim to have predicted the extent to which the failure of the August 1991 coup would be a death blow to all things Soviet. Formally gone are the USSR, its ruling Communist Party, and the unified central planning of its economy. Going is the Red Army, to be replaced by defence forces of the individual successor states. Even the new CIS seems to waver between a talkshop and a divorce court, with most members being unenthusiastic and some likely to withdraw.

It this setting, it would be surprising if another pillar of the Soviet state—the unified ruble zone—were to survive, even in a modified fashion.[2] The imminence of its shrinkage or demise is seen in the many proposals or actions in the ex-Soviet states, including Russia, which aim to introduce forms of national currencies.

An outside observer of ruble zone monetary reform developments is presented with a confusing picture. Some states announce the imminent introduction of their own currency, but take little action. Others make monetary reform a longer-run goal, while a few Central Asian states seem little interested. Lithuania and Ukraine, among others, have emitted their own notes, but stated that 'monetary reform' still lies in the future. Only two countries, Estonia and Latvia, have undertaken comprehensive monetary reforms.[3]

Until recently, calls for republican currencies met stiff resistance from Moscow and puzzlement from the West. Soviet authorities and others viewing the ex-Union as a unitary state saw such monies as near-treasonous. The fear of Union government reprisals explains much of the delay in translating monetary reform proposals into actions.

The political evolution of the USSR into independent states, and the economic pressures arising from a still unworkable union, have led Russian leaders to increasingly accept the introduction of national monies, and even to encourage this if done in a proper way (*Financial Times*, 31 July 1992, p. 2).

In many respects, the greatest enthusiasm for the ruble zone is now found in the West. The formal independence of the new states has removed one psychological barrier to Western acceptance of separate currencies. Yet, some American and European federalists, having moved or now moving in the opposite direction, remain puzzled by the underlying motives. The IMF, while recognizing the desire for national monies, continues to favour delaying most currency reforms, and appears to encourage the reconstruction of a smaller ruble zone on a new foundation (*Baltic Independent*, 15 May 1992, p. 7).

Even if some ex-Soviet states choose to maintain a common currency, many (possibly including Russia) will choose monetary independence. As the resulting monetary reforms will have strong repercussions both within and outside the current ruble zone, it is important to better understand the processes at work. Why is there an interest in national currencies? What major choices must be made in preparing and carrying out a monetary reform? What can be learned from the way in which Estonia, the first country to complete monetary reform, did this and began operating an independent monetary system?

In answering these and other questions, we proceed in several stages. After first describing the political and economic reasons for monetary independence, we distinguish the different forms of note issue which have taken or will take place in these countries. Next, we describe the main issues in transition from the ruble to the new currency, and in the use of the new currency to guide the macroeconomy. Finally, we present a brief overview of the Estonian programme, followed by some concluding remarks.

Reasons for a move to national currencies

Three broad categories of factors lie behind the desire to establish independent currencies in the ex-Soviet states; enhancement of national sovereignty, economic stabilization and the promotion of structural adjustment.

Enhancement of national sovereignty

National independence has both symbolic and real dimensions. Symbols of sovereignty include flags, state airlines and border posts. Among the most powerful is a national currency. While it is not uncommon for groups of countries to share a currency, e.g. the future European

Monetary Union (EMU), several currencies rarely circulate within the same state.[4] Put differently, states are rarely larger than the zone in which a currency circulates.

Before August 1991, and particularly during the early years of perestroika, calls for economic sovereignty were used as a 'Trojan horse' of political independence in the Baltic States and Ukraine.[5] Advocating economic sovereignty was then politically less risky than calling for outright independence. A central part of these proposals – separate currencies – could be claimed to be a technical economic measure, while in fact carrying a powerful political message.

While such strategic factors have disappeared with the achievement of international recognition, the establishment of national currencies is still viewed by the domestic public as a step in consolidating independence.

Yet, the case for monetary sovereignty goes beyond mere symbolism. As national monetary and exchange rate policies are ruled out in the ruble zone, monetary independence would enhance the economic sovereignty of the new states. They would gain the macroeconomic policy instruments which most governments normally use to direct their economies.

At first, monetary independence appears to go against a recent current in economic thinking which opposes active monetary policy. This argues that as there is no long-run 'Phillips curve', or positive link between inflation and economic activity, any attempts to stimulate the economy through monetary policy will only produce high inflation, with little if any real impact. Access to discretionary monetary instruments might only encourage harmful actions by governments pursuing short-run goals.

The perception that the cost of giving up monetary sovereignty is low explains some of the present willingness of EC countries to devolve monetary policy to a common central bank. However, starting in a common currency zone where high inflation has become the norm, and where monetary independence is thus a near-precondition for disinflation, this argument is reversed and the case for a national currency merely strengthened.

Three other politico-economic factors favour monetary sovereignty. First, the ruble zone countries vary greatly in their initial conditions and desired speed of economic reforms. Estonia, the first ex-Soviet republic to implement serious reforms, may feel encumbered by the pace of Latvia, not to mention Uzbekistan. Others may find the Estonian or Russian pace too rapid. Monetary independence would allow each state to better choose an ideal speed of reform.

Second, after 50-70 years of enforced dependence under Soviet rule, the notion of international cooperation is as compromised as that of 'socialism', even though its new forms may have little in common with earlier ones. Proposals for political, economic or monetary union generate little enthusiasm. In the trade sphere, such principles may find grudging acceptance only because the alternative of broken linkages is clearly worse. As monetary sovereignty should carry lower costs than trade autarky, most arguments about the benefits of a common currency will initially fall on deaf ears. In the coming years, the new currencies will be republican ones.

Finally, one aspect of greater sovereignty is achieving control over the local tax base. While overt taxes have now been devolved to the new states, Russia as the issuer of the ruble has the potential to capture most of the seignorage, or the 'tax' accruing to the issuer of a fiat currency. In a unified or federal state, one could argue that seignorage revenues are implicitly redistributed to all regions through a transfer system. With the collapse of the Union and its institutions, Russia has been distributing some seignorage through ad hoc 'gifts' of new rubles to the various republics, but an independent currency would be the only guarantee that the distribution of seignorage is fair.

Economic stabilization

The three primary functions of money are as a store of value, a medium of exchange, and a unit of account. Were the ruble adequately fulfilling these functions, some ruble zone members might sacrifice the greater sovereignty of their own money for the benefits of being in a common currency area.[6]

Relative to the end of 1991, the ruble is now an improved currency. With lower inflation and higher interest rates, it is a modestly better store of value. With the improvement of market balance through extensive price liberalization, it is an improved means of exchange. With the gradual unification of the exchange rate, it is now both a better unit of account and more convertible.

Yet, these successes are tenuous and far from what could be achieved. Russia's bold stabilization effort has encountered strong opposition from conservative members of its parliament. New ministers who are less committed to stabilization have been added to the cabinet (*The Economist*, 11 July 1992, p. 26). The Central Bank of Russia has been accused of running a cripplingly tight monetary policy, even though its discount rates are highly negative in real terms (*Financial Times*, 2 June 1992, p. 2).

The reforms have also been difficult to consolidate.[7] Advances one week have given way to major retreats the next. If Russia's ability to continue on its path of stabilization is in doubt, the other ex-Soviet states may seek to ensure against a negative outcome by acquiring their own monies and other macroeconomic policy instruments.

Even if reforms were to find strong political support within Russia, ruble stabilization would still be impaired by the lack of enthusiasm for the CIS and other new inter-state arrangements. Viewing its options in isolation, each member-country of a common currency area has an incentive to run large fiscal deficits and loose monetary policies, as the benefits accrue domestically while the costs in terms of higher inflation are spread across all members. Therefore, a stable common currency requires the establishment and following of a clear set of rules to guarantee fiscal responsibility by member states.

If a workable arrangement for burden-sharing cannot be found, it is probably better to go the route of separate currencies. Countries that continue to run loose policies will simply experience currency depreciation, while a floating exchange rate between the new monies would allow responsible states to insulate themselves from the negative inflationary effects.

From the end of 1991, a 'cash shortage' has impaired the ruble's role as a medium of exchange, even when goods are in plentiful supply.[8] This has also been reflected in a varying premium on cash over account rubles of up to 100 percent. Since these monies are formally of equal value, there is a desire to make all payments in account rubles but to be paid in cash. The resulting excess supply of account money and excess demand for cash has crippled payments in the ruble zone. Yet, if local reforms are possible in areas such as privatisation and price policy, one can scarcely 'repair' the ruble at a regional level. If this situation is expected to continue, the only opportunity for an ex-Soviet state to solve the 'cash shortage' is to escape the ruble zone.

Finally, stabilization also involves the achievement of a sustainable balance of payments. In most former socialist countries, this has been strongly influenced by terms-of-trade shocks. With the move to market prices, producers of previously underpriced raw materials (primarily Russia) have benefitted, while makers of overpriced manufactured goods (esp. Central Europe and the Baltic States) have lost.

The magnitude of terms-of-trade shocks varies greatly across ruble zone countries, depending upon their production structure. The primary vehicle for adjusting to such shocks (as in Finland in 1991) is devaluation, the ideal degree of which will differ with the magnitude of the shock. As differentiated exchange rate adjustment requires independent currencies, recent terms-of-trade shocks have been another source of pressure for national monies.

Promotion of structural adjustment

The former Soviet republics have a more daunting agenda of structural adjustment than do the countries of Central and Eastern Europe. They must both move from rigid central planning to a market system, and restructure their provincial economies to ones befitting independent states newly opened to markets in neighbouring countries.[9]

A national currency can speed restructuring in at least three ways. First, while large countries might survive inconvertibility, small open economies such as the Baltic states cannot. Currency convertibility must be a cornerstone of their economic policy. The resulting close integration with the world economy will enhance competition in the domestic market, introduce correct relative price signals about their comparative abilities, and induce the restructuring needed to exploit these abilities.

If Russia's declared intention to make the ruble convertible were certain to succeed, other countries could achieve this goal within the ruble zone.[10] But as the timing and final success of this move remains in doubt, national currencies may better guarantee eventual convertibility.

Second, real restructuring has been hampered by the slow pace of privatisation. While this tempo has been common to all former CPEs, the existence of a poorly functioning common currency has created further obstacles in the ex-Soviet states.

In Estonia, for example, the unwillingness to sell state assets for 'worthless rubles' has been a key barrier to privatisation. The main constraint is probably not that rubles are 'worthless', as persons trying to dump them will offer sums which command substantial real resources in other ex-Soviet markets.

The real barrier is the common currency nature of the ruble, and the negative political effect of the ownership structure likely to emerge from uncontrolled sale for rubles. As in almost all countries, the governments of the new states will wish to grant preferences to local residents, at least in the initial rounds of some types of privatisation. When each state is securing its real sovereignty, a process which could spread ownership claims over the whole ruble zone will find little favour, even if these assets are acquired at fair value. National currencies would allow the registration or screening of capital movements, providing a barrier to such acquisitions.

Privatisation in the ruble zone has also been hampered by the difficulty of asset valuation under hyperinflation. If the new currencies are more stable than the ruble, which is far from guaranteed, they could also lower this barrier to the sale of state assets.

Finally, an integral part of the transformation to a market system is the establishment of a modern financial and banking sector. The poor regulation, frequent illiquidity and probable insolvency of many ruble zone commercial banks hinders a rational development of this sector. If the pace of banking and financial reform in the whole ruble zone is too slow, some ex-Soviet states may opt for a separate currency to allow accelerated progress in this area.

Forms of national currencies in the ruble zone

In the cases where the declared intent to establish a national money has somehow been implemented, this has taken three forms; coupons, ruble substitutes and bona fide currencies.

Coupons

The first notes to be issued by Soviet republics were the so-called coupons introduced in Lithuania and Ukraine. Until late-1991, the ruble zone suffered from excess demand at the prevailing level of largely fixed prices. This resulted from the combined effect of a 'monetary overhang' of accumulated savings arising from past shortages, and the heightened demand resulting from very expansionary macroeconomic policies.[11]

The result was a severe and growing shortage of most goods. Lacking their own currencies, and in the absence of a contractionary Soviet policy, the republican governments could try to restore balance in one of two ways; through quantitive rationing and controls at the prevailing price level, or via price increases or liberalization to reduce demand through market means.

All republics, fearful of the consequences of free prices, initially opted for the first solution. This included the erection of inter-republican borders to stem 'exports', and the rationing of basic consumer goods.

Over time, the deepening of suppressed inflation made this policy increasingly repressive, stimulating the search for alternatives. The Baltic states were the first to adopt the second strategy, trying to outrun Soviet inflation and to balance trade via market means.[12] This policy was adopted throughout most of the ruble zone in January 1992.

The coupon scheme was an attempt to introduce a local 'monetary policy', while not risking the political wrath of the central authorities which a full-fledged currency might bring. It was hoped that this quasi-money would allow freer prices without extreme inflation. Under the scheme, workers would in addition to their ruble wage, receive a lower parallel wage in coupons. In turn, many consumer purchases would require the payment of matching numbers of rubles and coupons.

The intended effect was that of a contractionary macroeconomic policy, as the smaller sum of coupons would act as a real wage cut. At the same time, it contained a 'beggar-thy-neigbour' feature which made it unpopular in adjacent regions. Rubles paid out in Lithuania, but without coupon coverage, could presumably be spent in neighbouring areas, adding to inflationary pressure there. In fact, persons who were able to spend most of their wage in other republics might feel little real wage reduction.

These schemes had a similar life-cycle of brief success followed by collapse. At introduction, they appeared to improve the local supply situation, and were popular among the public. Coupons traded at a strong premium to the ruble. Over time, however, the positive effect dwindled, the market price at which coupons traded fell, and they were finally abandoned (*Times of London*, 15 January 1992).

The coupon scheme had several weaknesses. It was cumbersome to administer, as it was necessary to specify the spheres in which coupons would be required, and the rules by which they would be paid and could be purchased. There also appeared to be no coherent 'monetary policy' programme for ensuring their stability. In relations with other republics, they tended to impair trade, although not necessarily by more than the physical barriers which they were meant to replace.

Ruble substitutes

Being a response to the 'monetary overhang', coupons became irrelevant once extensive price liberalization had restored broad aggregate balance and reduced the real money supply. The problem of 'too many rubles' quickly gave way to the 'cash shortage'.[13] As during the Soviet hyperinflation of the 1920s, this created pressure to try to ease the shortage by issuing surrogate currencies to circulate alongside the Soviet currency.[14]

Most republics lay the blame for the 'cash shortage' on Russia, arguing that it comes from Russia's refusal to provide them with adequate banknotes. While this is part of the story, the fact that the shortage exists throughout the ruble zone (albeit differing in intensity by region) means that other factors must also be at play.

While we are unaware of an accepted theoretical model of the 'cash shortage', as opposed to the general drop in real money demand in response to hyperinflationary expectations, the frequent appearance of this phenomenon during times of extreme inflation suggests that surrogate currencies could merely exacerbate the situation.[15] A greater supply of cash could fuel the very inflation which is at the root of the problem, especially by validating the provision of ruble credits by republican central banks. This is one case where restricting supply, i.e. tight monetary policy, may be the best remedy for a shortage.

Ruble substitutes were introduced in May 1992 in Latvia and Lithuania, states where a full fledged currency was not yet prepared, but where the pressure to solve the 'cash shortage' could no longer be resisted. The 'Latvian ruble' was introduced as a parallel currency meant to circulate at par with the Russian ruble, to extensively replace it in domestic trade, and to become the sole currency for salary payments.

Lithuania began gradually reintroducing the coupons it withdrew from circulation, but now as full substitute currencies. Forty percent of salary payments were to be in coupons.

In Estonia, a proposal by the Prime Minister to introduce the one- kroon note as a 500 ruble substitute before the actual currency reform was not accepted by the Monetary Reform Committee. However, the second largest city, Tartu, issued its own local ruble substitute, withdrawing it a few weeks later in response to political pressure.[16]

The emission of surrogate currencies may also reflect a desire to capture some of the seignorage now going to Russia. This is both a matter of principle (greater sovereignty) and an attempt to cover incipient government budget deficits via inflationary finance.[17]

The initial experiences with surrogate currencies show both successes and failures, but are uniformly dominated by uncertainty. In the Latvian experiment, official foreign exchange traders appear to have maintained the parity to the Russian ruble, while in the parallel market, the Latvian ruble traded at a slight discount. As the Latvian authorities threatened to punish traders that did not maintain the parity (*Baltic Independent*, 29 May 1992, p. 5), it is unclear how much this reflected market developments and how much the fear of sanctions.

From the perspective of consumers, the ability to use the Latvian ruble was also uncertain. It was most difficult to use the larger denominations (as change might have to be given in more desired Russian rubles), and to purchase from private and non-Latvian traders (*Baltic Independent*, 15 May 1992, p. 2).

Over time, the ruble substitute schemes could unravel because they contain inconsistent monetary and exchange rate regimes. Without strong capital controls, a central bank issuing a parallel ruble can maintain a fixed exchange rate with the Russian ruble only by standing ready to buy and sell Russian rubles at that rate, so as to accommodate all shifts in the demand for its currency. Put differently, a fixed exchange rate requires an endogenous money supply.

In reality, most parallel currencies are emitted by quite different rules, for example as a fixed fraction of monthly salary payments. These make the stock of money relatively exogenous. If the emission of the parallel currency is not restricted, which is likely when its introduction is in response to pressures to ease the cash shortage, the Russian ruble reserves of the issuing bank may be quickly depleted. The result will be either inconvertibility at the fixed parity or the forced floating of the parallel currency at a depreciated rate.

Bona fide currencies

Both coupons and ruble substitutes have a stop-gap nature. Countries adopting them continue to speak of a future 'monetary reform'. The *bona fide* currency emerging from this reform would neither complement nor supplement the ruble, but replace it. Its subsequent emission would be determined by an explicit monetary policy. At least in the longrun, it would be meant to become the sole legal tender in its country of issue.

Estonia was the first ruble zone state to introduce a *bona fide* currency, doing so in one step in June 1992. Latvia accomplished this in two steps, turning the parallel Latvian ruble introduced in May 1992 into the sole domestic currency in July 1992.

Introduction of the currency

A new currency can be introduced in one of two ways. Conversion involves the exchange of most cash rubles for the new currency and the comprehensive redenomination of loans, deposits and other contracts into the new money. This standard monetary reform strategy was used in western Germany in 1948, eastern Germany in 1990, and Slovenia in 1991, among others.

The alternative is incremental emission, where the ruble is left in circulation while some or all subsequent government payments are made in the new currency. This implies a period of transition in which several legal tenders circulate simultaneously, with the ruble finally eliminated either by its own gradual disappearance or by a subsequent conversion. Incremental emission was used in the case of the chervonets or 'gold ruble' of Soviet Russia in the early 1920s, and in the coupon and ruble substitute schemes noted above.[18]

There are strong economic and political reasons for pursuing a conversion strategy. First, the benefits from rapidly achieving a single medium of exchange in each state can be huge. The ex-Soviet economies are now crippled by the confusion arising from numerous monies circulating in parallel. After introducing its new currency, Latvia reached the extreme situation where Latvian rubles, Russian cash rubles, account rubles and hard currencies all circulated together, with a complex set of rules determining which money could be used in which cases.[19] Monetary reform is an opportunity to eliminate this awkward situation in one step.

Political factors also argue for conversion to at least be attempted. As in the coupon scheme, extensive issue of a new currency without collecting old rubles has a beggar-thy-neighbour element. Russia's nightmare is the introduction in such a fashion of a Ukrainian currency, as the rubles which become worthless in the hands of 52 million Ukrainians could flood the remaining ruble zone.

At the same time, Russia's unilateral seizure of some other republics' ruble assets in the former Soviet Savings Bank (*Sberbank*) and of hard currency assets at the Vneshekonombank (*Baltic Independent*, 28 February 1992, p. 4), was itself a beggar-thy-neighbour move. This has created bad feelings and made it more difficult for the other states to justify 'good behaviour' towards Russia to their own residents.

There are two possible outcomes; deterioration into a series of retaliatory actions, or an amicable resolution. The potential gains from the second outcome are large. Ex-Soviet republics exhibit a much greater interdependence in trade than do the Central European countries or Finland. The collapse of trade which could follow a disruption of payments would be even more harmful than the severe negative effects observed in these other cases.

An amicable agreement on treatment of existing claims is likely to be a prerequisite for a trade finance arrangement which would preserve some of this commerce. One possible resolution, with an act of goodwill on both sides, would combine a Russian commitment to unfreeze deposits which it unilaterally seized, with a pledge by the reforming state to collect as many rubles as possible from circulation.

The removal of rubles from circulation can be paired with many rules to fix the volume of new currency given in return. There are three general options to choose from:

a) Proportional exchange – all assets, liabilities, wages and prices are converted at the same rate. Whether this involves a change in units, e.g. a 10:1 diminution of all values, is a matter of convenience rather than economic significance.
b) Partial confiscation – some or all assets and liabilities are exchanged at a less favourable rate than wages and prices. This will change the relative size of the flows of incomes and payments, and of the stocks of wealth.
c) Partial freezing – this will notionally change all values at the same rate, but then leave some assets and/or liabilities frozen. Freezing could be indefinite, or involve the changing of short-term into longer-term contracts, e.g. into 10-year bonds.

As a result of hyperinflation, one can hardly speak of a remaining monetary overhang. While macroeconomic factors no longer argue for confiscation or freezing, such steps could be motivated by three other factors:

1) Expectation of a currency reform may induce inflows of rubles if the implicit conversion rate into a hard currency is expected to be favourable. In this case, a stipulation that converters of large sums must first explain the source of these monies (which requires temporary freezing and possible confiscation) could be implemented.
2) Similarly, the authorities may wish to use the occasion of monetary reform to liquidate wealth acquired through illegal means. A required explanation of large sums can equally serve this purpose.
3) If some inflationary pressures remain, the option of converting some liquid balances into privatisation vouchers or long-term bonds could be an additional tool of stabilization, and could facilitate the financing of privatisation.

Post-conversion monetary and exchange rate policy

Monetary reform is not an end in itself, and goes beyond the simple introduction of a new currency on 'Day X'. From that moment onwards, the authorities must also have a workable plan for using their new monetary and exchange rate instruments in the pursuit of macroeconomic stability.

World experience offers a diverse menu of options for setting or managing the money stock, interest rates and the exchange rate. The ideal choice from among these will depend on the specific initial conditions in the reforming country. Of all features of an ideal post-reform policy regime in the ex-Soviet context, three stand out.

First, the policies must be simple to implement. There is now little need to fine-tune the macroeconomy, as even rough stabilization would improve on the high and varying inflation and exchange rate fluctuations of the past year.

Simplicity is also dictated by the lack of experience in using such instruments. Under central planning, money was a passive unit of account rather than active determinant of resource allocation, making Soviet 'monetary policy' quite different from that required in a market setting.[20] Russia is the only ex-Soviet republic with (most likely irrelevant) experience in running any monetary policy. Yet, the monetary policy conducted by Western central banks is a subtle art learned through much practice. Placing a full arsenal of policy instruments in the hands of inexperienced persons would make little sense.

Thus, one should not be ambitious at first, but should start with simple, easily learned, and relatively fail-safe policy rules. Only after experience is gained in operating these, should more sophisticated strategies be developed and finer tuning of the economy attempted.

Second, as most ruble zone countries are suffering from inflationary pressure and balance of payments difficulties, the new policies should be restrictive. The worst possible outcome would be an inflationary, non-convertible currency, as this would have all of the ills of the ruble while further crippling international trade.[21]

In Estonia, there has been a debate between those arguing that a strong economy is a prerequisite for a well-functioning currency, and those arguing the opposite. Here, the lessons from historical cases in which initial conditions resembled those of the present ruble zone clearly support the latter view that stabilization must be the anchor of the reform programme.[22]

Third, an ideal scheme would contain explicit guarantees that a government setting out to stabilize its economy will likely be able to stay the course. A technically sound stabilization programme is worth little if political pressures will soon cause it to be abandoned.

The historical record and recent experience in Central and Eastern Europe show that the political pressure will be intense. Two years into its transformation, Poland's new government responded to public pressure and began a strategy of reflation (*The Economist*, 9 May 1992, p. 32). The newly elected Slovak government appears to favour a similar strategy after 1.5 years of tight policies (*The Economist*, 13 June 1992, p. 31).

With the dual task of marketisation and creating an independent economy, the pressure in ex-Soviet states will be even greater. Russian monetary authorities are already under intense pressure from state enterprises to ease credit policy, even though real interest rates are already highly negative (*Financial Times*, 5 August 1992, p. 10). The pressure to introduce ruble substitutes in the Baltic states also included an element of desired reflation.

Therefore, the new institutions should include firewalls to protect the monetary authority from political pressure. These can be unilateral, such as laws governing the maximum permissible budget deficit or laws prohibiting all but temporary, seasonal central bank financing of the government.

More fail-safe but politically less palatable solutions include external monitoring or supervision of macroeconomic policy. Examples include IMF supervision of a conditional stand-by agreement, or the granting of some decision-making power to foreign citizens or governments.[23]

The Estonian model

Among the former Soviet republics, Estonia was the first to introduce a *bona fide* currency, doing so on 20 June 1992. As the initial experience has generally been successful, this represents a possible model for other states wishing to leave the ruble zone. At the same time, some unique features of the Estonian case may reduce its transferability. This section provides a brief outline of the Estonian monetary reform.

Motivations

Most of the above-noted motivations were present in Estonia. The symbolic element of a separate currency contributed to the strong public support for monetary reform and to the lack of interest in a common Baltic currency. The relatively fast desired pace of economic reform, the need of a small economy to achieve currency convertibility, and a severe terms-of-trade shock were key economic sources of interest (*Baltic Independent*, 26 June 1992, p. 1). The pressure to resolve two particularly acute problems—the cash shortage and the slow pace of privatisation — heightened interest in quickly introducing the *kroon* (or 'crown') in the spring of 1992.

Method of introduction

As the kroon was to immediately become the sole legal means of payment, and as negotiations with Russia had proceeded smoothly, the new currency was introduced through conversion.[24] Each registered resident was allowed to convert up to 1500 rubles at a rate of 10:1, the same rate used to convert most prices, wages, assets and liabilities. The remaining rubles could later be exchanged at 50:1. As most residents would redistribute excess rubles to those with less than the maximum amount, and since the quantity of cash collected was close to the estimated cash in circulation, the cash conversion was close to proportional.

The conversion of bank deposits was also done at a 10:1 rate, with the exception of very large transfers which were subject to control of origin before being converted. In sum, the conversion was a largely proportional exchange with modest elements of partial freezing.

Convertible currency deposits and loans were left untouched. As the exchange rate was set at 8 kroons to the German mark, or near the prevailing implicit market rate, the conversion had a negligible impact on balance sheets. This rate also allowed the whole of M2 to be initially backed by gold and foreign exchange reserves, as required by the new Law on the Backing of the Kroon.

Around the date of conversion, Estonia reached payments agreements with Russia, Ukraine and some other ruble zone states. These envisioned the establishment of a system of inter-state correspondent accounts, first between the respective central banks (much as within the ruble zone), and eventually through direct correspondent links between commercial banks. The holding of non-resident ruble accounts by Estonian non-banks, and the actual flow of rubles across Estonia's frontier, would likely be precluded.

Post-reform monetary and exchange rate policy

The new macroeconomic policy regime has three key elements;

a) A fixed exchange rate of the kroon to the German mark;
b) The emission of new central bank money according to a 'currency board' rule enshrined in law; and
c) A commitment to fiscal responsibility.

This package has been designed to produce a stable, convertible currency and to meet the three criteria noted above; simplicity, restrictiveness, and the inclusion of guarantees. Monetary policy is simplest under fixed exchange rates. Of all emission rules under fixed exchange rates, the simplest (and the best guarantee of convertibility) is the adopted 'currency board' rule, which strictly ties new emission of kroons to the growth of Bank of Estonia's foreign reserves.[25] This resembles the successful Argentine monetary policy regime since April 1991 (*Financial Times*, 14 May 1992).

The regime is restrictive in that it precludes any fiduciary issue by the Bank of Estonia and thus limits the ability of the government to run budget deficits. Up to now, Estonia has maintained budget balance or surplus, even in an environment in which its narrow interests would have been served by fiscal profligacy (Van Arkadie and Karlsson,1992).

This is encouraging for the future, but the likely growth of political pressures as economic reforms begin to bite, means that legal 'firewalls' such as the currency board rule will add credibility to the government's promise to keep the budget in balance. A future IMF standby agreement will add further external guarantees. However, a proposal by Hanke, Jonung and Schuler (1992) to introduce external guarantees via a significant Swedish role in a currency board has not been adopted.

Appropriate to Estonia's small economic size, the new Foreign Exchange Law envisions full current account convertibility and free repatriation of invested foreign capital. At the same time, it resembles the Polish and Czechoslovak laws in requiring eventual repatriation and surrender of all enterprise foreign exchange earnings, restricting future payments into domestic foreign exchange accounts, and maintaining some controls on capital movements.[26]

Results

The introduction of the kroon was successful in the following ways;

a) The kroon immediately became the sole internal means of payment, with the possible exception of some border regions;
b) After the technical problems of the initial days had been sorted out, the kroon became fully convertible for current account purposes;
c) The initial fixed exchange rate relative to the German mark has been rigidly maintained;
d) The Bank of Estonia has experienced a significant reserve inflow, equal to almost one-fifth of high powered money in the first month alone (*Baltic Independent*, 31 July 1992, p. 4); and
e) The move to a single means of payment has stimulated commerce and increased the level of competition in the domestic retail sector.

These successes came with the disappointment of even lower real incomes, as the introduction of the kroon was accompanied by tax increases designed to ensure its stability (*Baltic Independent*, 3 July 1992, p. 4). The expected decrease in inflation was initially not evident. Most important, the new payments system with the ruble zone got off to a cumbersome start, either due to technical problems or to conceptual faults in the design.

Relevance for other ex-Soviet states

The Estonian model is only one of many possible ways to achieve monetary independence. The two-step approach of Latvia, where the experience with the second step of moving to a single legal tender has been quite favourable, is one possible alternative.[27]

While other states wishing to leave the ruble zone will scarcely use either model without adjusting for their specific situation, most of the Estonian package (including the currency board rule for future emission) could be transferred in full. The one important exception is in the initial full backing of the money supply, which adds to the credibility of the currency board rule. The Baltic States are now being returned gold reserves which they had accumulated before the Soviet occupation, and which were held in trust by Western governments (*Baltic Independent*, 22 May 1992, p. 7). While these sums do not appear to be very large, the current small size of the real money stocks in these countries means that these gold reserves can fully back their currencies. To adopt a similar arrangement, most other ex-Soviet states would first have to solicit funds, most likely in conjunction with an IMF programme.

Conclusions

That the ruble zone will continue shrinking is clear. If the historical experience with the end of empires is any indication, it may eventually disappear. Whether the process leading to greater monetary independence will be orderly or chaotic remains unclear, yet matters a great deal. This will depend on the initiatives put forth in the near future by Russia, the other ruble zone countries, and the international financial organizations.

A destructive breakup could result from one of two factors. The first and most senseless would be a fight over seignorage, particularly when it involves governments desperate to fill a budgetary financing gap. Only Russia can avoid this outcome by continuing to distribute enough cash to other ruble zone countries to mitigate these concerns.

The second scenario is a series of tit-for-tat grabs for assets and defaults on liabilities, leading to a confrontational monetary reform and a breakdown of economic relations. The potential for conflict is heightened by the fuzzy boundary where monetary reform ends and the overall splitting of assets and liabilities (gold, debt, military hardware, environmental liabilities, reparations, etc.) begins. For instance, Russia's freezing of another state's bank deposits could lead that country to undertake monetary reform by incremental emission, which could in turn precipitate a breakdown of inter-state payments.

As the returns from avoiding this outcome are huge, there should be interest on all sides to approach the coming currency reforms in a sober and imaginative fashion, with a readiness to make mutual concessions. Russia's unfreezing of most bank deposits, combined with the reforming country's pledge to collect or erase most ruble assets and liabilities, would be one possible starting point.

The international financial organizations will have a crucial role in ensuring an orderly process of monetary reform. They can act as neutral 'referees', using their financial and other influence to guide both sides towards 'good behaviour'.

The most important step in ensuring a positive outcome is a recognition by all sides that the present ruble zone is dead. Attempts to resurrect it with only minor modifications would be as futile as breathing life into the USSR, Yugoslavia or the CPSU. These efforts can lead only to a more chaotic and confrontational breakup, and a shattering of expectations on all sides.

References

Dohan, Michael R. (1991) 'Comment' in J. Williamson, ed., *Currency Convertibility in Eastern Europe*. Washington: Institute for International Economics

Garvy, George (1977) *Money, Financial Flows, and Credit in the Soviet Union*. Cambridge, MA: Ballinger

Hanke, Steve H., Lars Jonung and Kurt Schuler (1992) *Monetary Reform for a Free Estonia: A Currency Board Solution*. Stockholm: SNS Förlag

Hansson, Ardo (1992) 'The Emergence and Stabilization of Extreme Inflationary Pressures in the Soviet Union' in Anders Åslund, ed., *The Post-Soviet Economy: Soviet and Western Perspectives*. London: Pinter Publishers

—— (1991a) 'The Importance of Being Earnest: Early Stages of the West German Wirtschaftswunder'. (Working Paper, UNU/WIDER, No. 94.) Helsinki.

—— (1991b) 'Monetary Reform in a Newly Independent State: The Case of Estonia'. Processed, October.

Horsman, George (1988) *Inflation in the Twentieth Century*. New York: St. Martin's Press

International Monetary Fund (1991) *Exchange Arrangements and Exchange Restrictions Annual*. Washington: IMF.

Ishiyama, Yoshihide (1975) 'The Theory of Optimal Currency Areas: A Survey', *IMF Staff Papers*, 22, July, pp. 344-83.

League of Nations (1926) *Financial Reconstruction of Austria*. London: Constable & Co.

Lenin, Vladimir (1960) *Collected Works*, Volume 26. Moscow

Nurkse, Ragnar (1946) *The Course and Control of Inflation: A Review of Monetary Experience in Europe after World War I*. Geneva: League of Nations

Van Arkadie, Brian and Mats Karlsson (1992) *Economic Survey of the Baltic States*. London: Pinter Publishers

Yeager, Leland B. (1981) *Experiences with Stopping Inflation*. Washington: American Enterprise Institute for Public Policy Research

Notes

1 This paper was written while the author was Research Fellow at the World Institute of Development Economics (WIDER) of the United Nations University, Helsinki. I am deeply grateful to the authorities in the Republic of Estonia for providing the opportunity to actively observe and participate in the preparation of its monetary reform, and for the many insights which this has given. Particular thanks go to the Prime Minister, Mr. Tiit Vähi, and the President of the Bank of Estonia, Mr. Siim Kallas. The views expressed here are mine alone. I am also grateful to Prof. Jeffrey Sachs, Dr. Boris Pleskovic and Dr. Rudolf Jalakas for many insightful conversations. Financial support of the Finnish International Development Agency (FINNIDA) is gratefully acknowledged.

2 In a much quoted passage, Lenin (1960, p. 106) writes, "A single State Bank, the biggest of the big, with branches in every rural district, in every factory,

will constitute as much as nine-tenths of the socialist apparatus. There will be country-wide bookkeeping, country-wide accounting of the production and distribution of goods; this will be, so to speak, something in the nature of the skeleton of socialist society."

3 For a survey of monetary reform plans in each former Soviet republic, see *Financial Times*, 31 July 1992, p. 2.

4 One exception is the circulation of Bank of Scotland notes in the United Kingdom, but as these are fully backed by Bank of England notes at an irrevocable exchange rate, they give no real sovereignty. Hongkong has an independent monetary policy while remaining a British colony, but its vast geographic distance from the U.K. clearly distinguishes it from the ruble case.

5 For an overview of the recent political and economic evolution in the Baltic States, see van Arkadie and Karlsson (1992).

6 These include the absence of exchange risk in trade between members, and the elimination of the cost of exchange conversion. For an extensive discussion of 'optimal currency areas', see Ishiyama (1975).

7 See *The Economist*, 6 June 1992, p. 93. This precariousness and susceptibility to political pressure is common to all transformations of such a magnitude. For an analysis of these pressures in post-World War II western Germany, see Hansson (1991a).

8 For a description of the cash shortage in the Baltic States, see *Baltic Independent*, 3 April 1992, p. 1.

9 This includes the development of domestic institutions for economic management and the reorientation of foreign trade. For example, the Baltic States will develop close links with their Nordic neighbours, while the Central Asian states will develop natural ties with their Turkish and southern neighbours.

10 As noted, it would still be unclear whether the chosen exchange rate would be appropriate for each ruble zone state individually.

11 For a description of the evolution of these inflationary pressures, see Hansson (1992).

12 For more, see Van Arkadie and Karlsson (1992).

13 This phenomenon was also observed in several episodes of extreme inflation during the early 1920s. During the German hyperinflation, complaints about a cash shortage led the Governor of the Reichsbank to express the hope "that installation of new high-speed currency printing presses would overcome the supposed shortage of money." (Yeager, 1981, p. 56). The Soviet hyperinflation exhibited a shortage of coins and monies of small and medium denominations (Yeager, 1981, p. 73).

14 In that episode, it has been estimated that 78 currencies circulated simultaneously (Horsman, 1988, p. 91). During the German hyperinflation, around 2000 'unorthodox monies' circulated, including surrogate currencies issued by provinces and municipalities, (Yeager, 1981, pp. 14-15).

15 The premium of cash over account rubles could be taken as an indicator of the severity of the shortage. This appears to have increased around the time when Russia announced plans to free prices at the end of 1991, i.e. when inflationary expectations would have increased. The premium largely disappeared in May, at a time when the first signs of slower inflation began to emerge.

16 For overviews of the emission of ruble substitutes in the Baltic States, see *Baltic Independent*, 8 May 1992, p. 5 and *Baltic Observer*, 7 May 1992, p.1.

17 One harmful effect of the premium on cash over account rubles is the distortion it can cause in accounting. On paper, both types of rubles are given equal value and added together, yet their market value is different. If government revenues contain relatively more account rubles than do expenditures, which is likely, a budget may appear to be in balance but actually be in defict. To acquire the additional cash, the government would have to pay a premium on its account rubles which is not reflected in the accounts.

18 See Yeager (1981), pp. 72-78, Horsman (1988), pp. 89-99, and Dohan (1991). In fact, the chervonets as an eventually successful and familiar currency reform seems to have a strong influence as a role model.

19 There is evidence of similar confusion during the chervonets period. Horsman (1988) cites the Russian economist Yurovsky as saying, "The quantity of depreciating currency in proportion to the total was insignificant, but its presence was sufficient...to reduce the national economy to a state of havoc."

20 For a comprehensive description of monetary policy in the old Soviet system, see Garvy (1977).

21 This happened in the early stages of the Slovene reform, where overvaluation of the official exchange rate made the new tolar poorly convertible into Western currencies, the refusal of Yugoslavia to accept Slovene payments led to a barterization of Yugoslav trade, and a relatively loose monetary policy led to high (albeit lower than Yugoslav) inflation rates.

22 A comprehensive overview of relevant experiences can be found in Nurkse (1946), Yeager (1981) and Horsman (1988). The strongest analogy is with the collapse of the Austro-Hungarian Empire after World War I, where most of the new national currencies (including those of Austria, Hungary and Poland) experienced hyperinflation before being stabilized. The economic crisis in Austria, which dramatically resembles that of Russia today, was resolved by initial stabilization of the currency and restoration of fiscal balance. For more, see League of Nations (1926).

23 This may be the most persuasive reason for a common currency solution, as a multi-national central bank may be better able to resist pressures coming from any single member government.

24 For extensive descriptions of the conversion, see *Baltic Independent*, 26 June 1992. For a description of the new Currency Law, Foreign Exchange Law, and Law on the Backing of the Kroon, see *Baltic Observer*, 14 May 1992, p. 2.

25 For a description of the operation of a currency board, see Hanke, Jonung and Schuler (1992).

26 For an overview of exchange control regimes, including in Central and Eastern Europe, see IMF (1991).

27 For a brief overview of the Latvian reform, see *Baltic Independent*, 10 July 1992, p. 1.

11 New Banks in the Former Soviet Union: How Do They Operate?[1]

Simon Johnson, Heidi Kroll and Mark Horton

Introduction

Commercial banks are prominent among the new forms of business that have emerged and spread rapidly in the former Soviet Union as a result of reforms introduced under perestroika. Permitted only since 1988, commercial banks already number over 2,000. The rapid growth of these banks has raised questions about their economic consequences. In light of the sharp deterioration in macroeconomic performance which coincided with the banking boom, it is not surprising that the existing literature has tended to emphasize the dysfunctional aspects of commercial banks. Two negative views are frequently expressed.

The first view argues that these banks are a means for former communist party elites (the nomenklatura) to convert political power into economic power. One observer has even asserted that the nomenklatura control commercial banks (Rumer 1991, p. 21.) If correct, this view implies that the banks continue the previous allocation of power under a new guise, and probably preserve some negative economic features of the old planning system.

The second view holds these new banks are too closely tied to groups of firms through cross-ownership of shares. These ties are interpreted not as strengthening competitiveness of industrial groups, as in the German or Japanese model, but rather as allowing state enterprises to maintain soft budget constraints, as in the Yugoslav model (International Monetary Fund, Volume II, p. 115). Because these banks continue to lend at low nominal interest rates while inflation rises, they also stand accused of providing implicit subsidies to privileged enterprises and of contributing to inflationary pressures.

Previously there was almost no published data about these new commercial banks, aside from some aggregate numbers, and as a result rival interpretations of bank behavior were based on anecdotal evidence.[2] There has been almost no serious academic work on these issues.[3] This paper is the preliminary report of a project designed to collect a systematic set of data and evaluate rival hypotheses about commercial bank behavior in the former Soviet Union. Our goal is to explain what information can be collected by interviewing banks, and to suggest ways in which banking behavior in the former Soviet Union can be interpreted.

Because organizing empirical research in the former Soviet Union is difficult, we chose to begin our investigation by interviewing commercial banks in one city — Kiev, capital of Ukraine. According to the National Bank of Ukraine, in summer 1991 there were 14 registered commercial banks in Kiev, and 30 in the whole of Ukraine.[4] In August 1991 two registered Kiev banks were not actually in operation,[5] so the 12 banks we interviewed represented the whole population of operational commercial banks in that city.[6] We are currently in the process of obtaining more updated information on these banks, and our follow-up enquiries in winter 1991-92 indicate the basic situation and structure of Ukrainian commercial banking remains unchanged. However, because the macroeconomy remains unstable and our next round of data collection is not complete, in this paper we will concentrate on the evidence from summer 1991.

In addition to presenting a unique data set, this paper offers an alternative interpretation of banking behavior. Because of the legacies of the traditional "monobank" system and the way this system was reformed after 1987, the environment in which the new commercial banks operate makes it very difficult and costly for them to screen prospective borrowers, monitor their performance, and enforce debt payments. Interestingly, although our sample includes independently founded banks as well as those founded by groups of state enterprises, all these banks have very similar institutional structures for operating in this environment. We argue that these structures are sensible ways to reduce the transaction costs inherent in banking operations. Our evidence does not refute existing explanations for bank behavior, but it does introduce a substantially new and positive element. It also suggests several promising directions for future theoretical and empirical research concerning banks in post-communist countries.

This argument and supporting evidence are presented in the next three sections. The second section identifies some key structural attributes of the current banking environment and traces them to the reorganization of the traditional monobank system after 1987. The third section examines the profiles of commercial banks in Kiev, and shows that, irrespective of how they were formed, all of them lend to and are owned by state organizations. Using this background, the fourth section offers a transaction-cost interpretation for the behavior of commercial banks. The fifth section deals with the one important aspect of banking which cannot be explained in terms of transaction costs — low nominal and negative real interest rates. The final section summarizes the main conclusions of the study.

The banking environment

The present banking environment in the former Soviet Union has three distinctive features. First, the credit market is dominated by large state banks. Second, there is a scarcity of publicly available information on firms, and consequently it is difficult for any bank to assess a borrower's credit-worthiness. Even if credit histories did exist, the recent radical changes in economic conditions probably mean they are not good predictors of future creditworthiness. Finally, existing laws do not provide an adequate legal basis for making secured loans. All three conditions are legacies of the monobank system under central planning and the way this system was partially reformed since the late 1980s.

A basic feature of the financial system in the classical central planning system was the integration of all commercial banking operations in a single monobank.[7] Until 1987, the State Bank (Gosbank) was the sole bank responsible for managing the accounts of state enterprises and for issuing them short-term credit to finance inventories and working capital. A system of savings banks was fully subordinate to Gosbank, and the only other banks, the Construction Bank (Stroibank) and the Foreign Trade Bank (Vneshtorgbank), were specialized and did not compete with Gosbank.

In an economy where real economic activity was controlled by detailed production and supply plans drawn up in physical terms, banking played only a supportive role. The enterprise financial plan was formed as the monetary counterpart of the physical plan, in large part so that Gosbank could monitor and control enterprise plan fulfillment. Credit was extended for specific purposes in accordance with the plan through a system of segregated accounts earmarked for specific plan targets. Money and credit were passive in the sense that they supported fulfillment of centrally-determined plans rather than influencing economic activity directly.

In such circumstances, there was no need for Gosbank to be concerned with risk appraisal or the availability of legal means for securing debt. While official Soviet doctrine held that credit should be secured and repayable, in practice the criterion for extending credit was not the borrower's profitability or credit-worthiness, but instead whether a particular transaction was provided for in the plan. As long as the latter condition was met, credit was made available almost automatically (Garvy 1977, pp. 115-116). There were provisions in the existing body of civil law authorizing the use of property to secure loans, but they excluded the lion's share of productive assets by stipulating that enterprises, buildings, equipment and other productive assets owned by the state could not be seized to satisfy the claims of creditors.[8]

In 1987, the banking system was reorganized by creating three new specialized banks alongside the two existing ones (On the Improvement, 1987). The result was a two-tiered banking system consisting of Gosbank and five specialized banks: the Bank for Foreign Economic Relations (Vneshekonombank), created out of Vneshtorgbank; the Industrial Construction Bank (Promstroibank), created out of Stroibank; the Agro-Industrial Bank (Agroprombank); the Bank for Housing, Municipal Services and Social Development (Zhilsotsbank); and the Savings Bank (Sberegatel'nyi Bank, or Sberbank), which had a monopoly on individual savings accounts. A central aim of the reorganization was to transfer commercial banking operations from Gosbank to the specialized banks. The specialized banks were charged with providing loans and taking deposits in their respective sectors, leaving Gosbank to manage the total supply of money and credit and to coordinate the banks' activities.

Since 1990, there has been a process of commercializing the specialized state banks by converting them into joint-stock companies. Agroprombank and Zhilsotsbank were converted into joint-stock banks in the second half of 1990 (Zakharov 1992, p. 126; Mirimskaya and Arkhangelskaya 1991), and new banking legislation adopted in December 1990 targeted Promstroibank for conversion by the end of 1991.[9] Parallel with the process of commercialization, the specialized banks started to split up along geographical lines from 1990, and their branches were progressively reorganized as independent commercial banks at the republic, regional and local levels (International Monetary Fund 1991, Vol. 2, pp. 111- 113; Shatalov 1991, pp. 25-26; Zakharov 1992, p. 126).

Confusingly, the specialized banks are now generally referred to as commercial banks and lumped together with private commercial banks. Unlike the specialized banks, however, most commercial banks did not emerge from Gosbank, but were formed independently. The emergence of private commercial banks began with the 1988 Law on Cooperatives, which authorized the formation of cooperative banks to serve the financial needs of cooperatives. The first such banks opened in September and October 1988, and by the end of 1988 there were 34 commercial banks in the Soviet Union. This total rose to 225 by January 1990, and 1500 by May 1, 1991. In the fall of 1991, there were 2,250 commercial banks, with 3,500 branches throughout the former Soviet Union (USSR Business Reports, October 15, 1991).[10]

Similar developments also occurred in Ukraine, but with a lag of several months compared with Moscow. Table 1 shows that new commercial banks began to form in Kiev during 1989; the first to be registered was Ukrinbank, on January 24, 1989. Four of the banks in our interview sample were formed during 1989, and seven during 1990.[11] In addition, a new National Bank of Ukraine was established in May 1990, and became operational in 1991.[12]

While the structure of the banking system has changed rapidly since 1987, complementary changes in the legal basis for securing loans have been slow to occur. As noted above, existing laws placed severe restrictions on the use of productive assets owned by the state as collateral. Recent legal changes, including provisions of the "Principles of Civil Legislation of the USSR and the Republics" (Osnovy, 1992, p.25) and a new Russian Federation law "On Pledge" (O Zaloge, 1992), ostensibly allow loans to be secured not only by pledges of any productive asset, but also by pledges of property rights over such assets.[13] The practical effect of these changes, however, remains to be seen. By the time the "Principles of Civil Legislation of the USSR and the Republics" was to have taken effect on January 1, 1992, the Soviet Union no longer existed.

The Law on Pledge was approved by the Russian Supreme Soviet in early January 1992 (Grigor'ev 1992), but one Russian banker complained in a newspaper interview published shortly thereafter that there was still no enforcement mechanism in place for putting the law into effect (Chto 1992), and the law did not formally take effect until the following June (Kopylova 1992). The fundamental problem, however, is that the current structure of ownership in the former Soviet Union is extremely muddled. While the Law on Pledge allows the assets of state enterprises to serve as the basis for securing loans, implementation of the law is complicated by the existence of various restrictions on the transferability of state property (Pevzner 1992).

As a result of the reforms outlined above, the commercial banking industry in the former Soviet Union now has a dual structure consisting of a few enormous state banks and many relatively small commercial banks. In banking, as in many other parts of the economy in the former Soviet Union, the old structures have disintegrated, and new institutions — commercial banks — are emerging. But these institutions work in idiosyncratic ways, which are hard to understand using only published sources. In order to comprehend the full effects of the dominance of large state banks, the lack of any information market about borrowers, and the weak legal structure, it is necessary to interview commercial bank managers. The principal findings from these interviews are described in the next three sections.

Bank profiles

This section describes the important characteristics of commercial banks in Kiev. In particular, we report the quantity and quality of resources employed in these banks and find most banks are very similar. However, while almost all banks began with very similar "endowments", there is evidence that some have subsequently performed better than others.

We can divide Kiev commercial banks into three categories: those which emerged out of Gosbank, those founded primarily by a ministry or by a group of enterprises under one ministry, and those founded as "independents". Despite these significantly different origins, our interviews revealed strong connections between all new commercial banks and existing state structures — state enterprises, ministries and in some cases even state banks.

As Table 1 indicates, in three cases the interviewee stated the bank had been formed directly out of former state specialized banks: Perkombank from the Syretsk bank of the all-Union Promstroibank, Vidrodzhennya also from Promstroibank, and Ukrsotsbank from Zhilsotsbank.[14] Four banks were founded primarily at the initiative of a government ministry: Ukrinbank by the Ukrainian Council of Ministers, Ukrstrombank by the all-Union Construction Ministry, Ukrmezhvuzbank by the Science Department of the Ministry of Higher Education, and Ukrsnabbank by the all-Union Gossnab.[15] Legbank was formed by 11 state enterprises, the majority of which are producers of clothing.

In contrast, several banks were founded more independently, although all of them have state enterprises as significant shareholders. Kiev Cooperative Bank and the Ukrainian Bank for Commercial Development were both founded on the initiative of their respective chairmen. INKO Bank was founded in April 1990 as the Kiev branch of Mosinkombank, a large independent commercial bank based in Moscow, but broke away in December 1990.[16]

We should emphasize that these are almost all relatively small banks. Table 2 shows the number of employees by bank in summer 1991. With the exception of Ukrsotsbank — a former state bank — the highest number of workers was 115 in Ukrinbank. In nearly all the banks there was a

Table 1 KIEV BANKS
Date of Foundation and Founders

Date of Foundation	Gosbank	Founders Ministry	Independent
1989			
January		Ukrinbank	
February		Ukrstrombank	
April			Kiev Coop.
July		Legbank	
1990			
April			Bank INKO
1st half year		Ukrmezhvuzhbank	
May			Kiev Narodnii
June			Ukrainian Bank for Commercial Development
October	Ukrsotsbank		
November	Perkombank		
November		Ukrsnabbank	
Unknown	Vidrodzhennya		

Source: Interviews.

high level of guidance and control by the president and chief executive officer, frequently referred to simply as the "chief". In one case the president was proud to claim personal responsibility for around two-thirds of the bank's profits.

Initially we thought banks more closely connected to Gosbank and ministries would tend to have older chairmen. However, there appears to be no such pattern. Banks which emerged out of the state monobank tend to have slightly older chairmen: 52 years old (1 year's experience in the banking system) at Vidrodzhennya, 41 years old (19 years in banks) at Perkombank, 37 years old (16 years in banks) at Ukrsotsbank. Banks founded by ministries had chairmen with the following characteristics:

189

Table 2 UKRAINIAN COMMERCIAL BANKS: Bank Source of Hiring

Bank		Interview Date	Employees (Current)	Source of Hiring
1	Bank INKO	1-Aug-91	50	Only recently began to hire from state banking sector.
2	Kiev Cooperative Bank	23-Jul-91	48	Recommendations from former employees. Former state bank employees are considered only for positions such as cashiers or bookkeepe
3	Kiev Narodnii Bank	30-Jul-91	34	Hire based on professional abilities and personal character.
4	Legbank	24-Jul-91	16	Hire known people. Hire only "smart, young" state bank employees.
5	Perkombank	10-Jul-91	12	From Promstroibank, other state banks.
6	Vidrodzhennya	31-Jul-91	32	Not older than 40 years; bank education and foreign language.
7	Ukr. Bank for Comm. Dev	.2-Aug-91	35	Hire based on professional abilities and experience, reliability and possibility of additional study.
8	Ukrstrombank	31-Jul-91	25	Twenty percent from old state banking system; eighty percent from other sources, such as Ministry of Finance.
9	Ukrinbank	1-Aug-91	115	Most specialist are from the ol state banking system, found through interview and recommendation process.
10	Ukrmezhvuzhbank	11-Jul-91	5	N/A
11	Ukrsnabbank	6-Aug-91	29	Ninety percent from old syste hired on the basis of expertise "diplomacy," and "commerci soul."
12	Ukrsotsbank - Kiev	9-Jul-91	850	Former state bank.
	Total		1251	
	Total w/o Ukrsotsbank		401	
	Average		104	
	Average w/o Ukrsotsbank		36	

Source: Bank Interviews. Summer 1991. Kiev, Ukraine, USSR. Mark A. Horton.

50 years old (33 years in banking) at Ukrmezhvuzbank, 39 years old (15 years in banking) at the Ukrainian Bank for Commercial Development, 30 years old (9 years in banking) at Ukrsnabbank. The more independent banks had chairmen aged 33 years old (2 years in banking) at Kiev Cooperative Bank and 37 years old (16 years in banking) at Kiev Narodnii Bank.

There is a pattern in the number of years which interviewees have worked in banks — although the average number of years in banking system was 14, there was a bimodal distribution. In six banks, we interviewed eight directors with an average of 22.3 years in the banking system, while in the other six banks we interviewed six directors with an average of 2.9 years in banking. However, the second group is quite mixed — it contains the chairmen of former state banks, ministry-founded banks and independent banks.[17]

The similarities in personnel in the three types of banks appear to outweigh the differences. All top bank management have professional training in banking. Almost all the bankers which we interviewed were graduates of the Kiev Institute of National Economy.[18] Interviewees in the two largest independent banks, Ukrinbank and Bank INKO, were trained as engineers and worked outside the banking system, but they also have had training as "financial specialists."

Table 2 does indicate some differences in the hiring practices of different kinds of banks. Independent banks and some ministry-founded banks said they preferred to hire people based on close personal contacts or references, with the additional requirement that people not be tainted by having worked "too long" in the former monobank. Bank INKO only recently began to hire former state bank employees for "technical positions", while Kiev Cooperative Bank's policy is to hire such people just for fairly basic work, such as being a cashier.[19] In contrast, Perkombank and Ukrotsbank — formed from Promstroibank and Zhilsotsbank — hire from state banks without reservations. Of course, experienced bankers are only found in the state system, but some commercial banks are evidently more discerning in their hiring than others.[20]

As Table 3 shows, each of these banks has less than 100 owners. Banks with relatively few owners include ministry-founded Legbank (15 owners) and Ukrmezhvuzbank (12 owners), but also Perkombank (20 owners) which was formed from a branch of Gosbank, and the independently-founded Kiev Narodnii Bank (35 owners). Ukrinbank, which was ministry-founded, had the most owners (95), while the independent Bank INKO had 92. There may be a pattern revealed by these numbers: the five Ministry-founded banks have an average of 37 owners each, while the four independent banks average 64 owners. Unfortunately, our sample is too small and too local for us to know whether this pattern

Table 3 UKRAINIAN COMMERCIAL BANKS: Ownership Concentration

		Ownership Capital (Rubles)	Number of Owners	Capital/ Owner (Rubles)
1	Bank INKO	86,874,000	92	944,283
2	Kiev Cooperative Bank	21,000,000	50	420,000
3	Kiev Narodnii Bank	15,000,000	35	428,571
4	Legbank	22,000,000	15	1,466,667
5	Perkombank	40,000,000	20	2,000,000
6	Vidrodzhennya	82,000,000		
7	Ukr. Bank for Comm. Dev.	35,000,000	80	437,500
8	Ukrstrombank	25,000,000	22	1,136,364
9	Ukrinbank	46,300,000	95	487,368
10	Ukrmezhvuzhbank	7,000,000	12	583,333
11	Ukrsnabbank	45,000,000	20	2,250,000
12	Ukrsotsbank - Kiev	500,000,000		
	Total	925,174,000	441	
	Total minus Ukrsotsbank	425,174,000	441	
	Average	77,097,833	44	1,015,409
	Average minus Ukrsotsbank	38,652,182	44	1,015,409

Source: Bank Interviews. Summer 1991. Kiev, Ukraine, USSR. Mark A. Horton.

would hold more generally in the former Soviet Union.

Table 3 also shows the capital per owner ratio for each bank. This ratio was highest for Ukrsnabbank (ministry-founded) followed closely by Perkombank (former state bank). Capital value was less than one million rubles per owner in all three banks which we have characterized as independent. However, it was also below a million rubles for the ministry-founded Ukrainian Bank for Commercial Development and Ukrinbank.

Table 4 shows the growth in nominal ownership capital for these banks from their formation to summer 1991.[21] In most cases this growth was rapid, ranging from 24 percent in Bank INKO to 462 percent in Ukrsnabbank. However, it should be remembered there was substantial inflation over this same period, and growth rates of less than 50 percent may represent a fall in real values.

There was definitely real growth in capital value for five banks: Kiev Cooperative Bank, Vidrodzhennya, Ukrstrombank, Ukrinbank and Ukrsnabbank. Four of these fast-growing banks had very strong ministerial ties, with the exception being Kiev Cooperative Bank. This is sug-

Table 4 UKRAINIAN COMMERCIAL BANKS: Growth of Ownership Capital

	Bank	Interview Date	Initial owner-ship capital	Date of initial ownership capital (1)	Current ownership capital (2) in roubles	Number of months in operation	Overall growth of ownership capital	Monthly growth of ownership capital
1	Bank INKO	1-Aug-91	$70,000,000	1-Apr-90	86,874,000	16	24.11%	1.36%
2	Kiev Cooperative Bank	23-Jul-91	3,500,000	1-Apr-89	21,000,000	28	500.00%	6.61%
3	Kiev Narodnii Bank	30-Jul-91	10,000,000	18-Oct-89	15,000,000	21	50.00%	1.95%
4	Legbank	24-Jul-91	16,366,550	1-Apr-91	22,000,000	4	34.42%	7.68%
5	Perkombank (3)	10-Jul-91	N/A		40,000,000			
6	Vidrodzhennya	31-Jul-91	15,000,000	1-Jul-90	82,000,000	13	446.67%	13.96%
7	Ukrainian Bank for CommercialDevelopment	2-Aug-91	22,000,000	19-Jun-90	35,000,000	13	59.09%	3.64%
8	Ukrstrombank	31-Jul-91	8,100,000	1-Feb-89	25,000,000	30	208.64%	3.83%
9	Ukrinbank (4)	1-Aug-91	15,000,000	24-Jan-89	46,300,000	30	208.67%	3.83%
10	Ukrmezhvuzhbank	11-Jul-91	N/A		7,000,000			
11	Ukrsnabbank	6-Aug-91	8,000,000	1-Jan-91	45,000,000	7	462.50%	27.99%
12	Ukrsotsbank - Kiev (5)	9-Jul-91	N/A		500,000,000			
	Total		167,966,550		925,174,000	162		
	Total minus Ukrsotsbank		167,966,550		425,174,000	162		
	Average		27,994,425		77,097,833	18		
	Average minus Ukrsotsbank		27,994,425		38,652,182	18		

Source: Bank Interviews. Summer 1991. Kiev, Ukraine, USSR. Mark A. Horton.

Notes: 1   Day of the month not specified in interview given as first day of month.
2   "Current Ownership Capital" is the amount reported during interview.
3   Perkombank was formed from a branch office of Promstroibank.
4   Ukrinbank has approval from the National Bank of Ukraine to sell up to 100,000,000 roubles of ownership capital.
5   Ukrsotsbank was formed from Kiev branch of Zhilsotsbank in October 1990.

gestive, but not conclusive evidence that banks with closer ties to well-funded ministries tend to grow faster.[22] We have too few observations to feel comfortable trying to draw any more general inferences from this evidence.

In conclusion, although we have collected a considerable amount of data about Kiev's commercial banks, we can find only small differences between banks in terms of the labor and capital they employ. Most of these banks are quite similar, particularly in the way they remain closely linked to the state sector, although there is some evidence that banks with closer ties to ministries tend to have grown faster. As the next section shows, these banks are also remarkably similar in the institutional forms they have adopted.

Transaction costs

Based on the banking environment described in the previous sections, our reading of the Western theoretical literature on banking suggests four types of transaction costs would be important in Kiev. Each cost is the result of some form of asymmetric information which, although it exists in a Western market economy, is probably a much worse problem in the current banking environment of the former Soviet Union. In addition, the lack of an adequate legal framework imposes severe constraints on the types of contracts which can be devised to deal with asymmetric information.

First, adverse selection means it is necessary to screen loan applicants, and this is a costly undertaking (Stiglitz and Weiss 1981). Potential borrowers may have an incentive to misrepresent their type, and claim they intend to repay even when they do not. Second, moral hazard implies the need to monitor borrower performance, because *ex post* there is an incentive to claim to be unable to repay a loan. However, it is costly to collect information about borrowers' actual profits. Third, it may also be costly to collect payments owed even, particularly as there is no well-developed contracts or bankruptcy law in the former Soviet Union.[23] Fourth, there are also costs to investors associated with monitoring whether a bank is performing properly (Calomiris and Kahn 1989) and whether other investors in the bank will withdraw their funds (Diamond and Dybvig 1983). Given that in the former Soviet Union, investors in banks are firms which could plausibly lend directly to other firms, investors need to consider all four types of transaction costs.

How do Kiev commercial banks screen potential loan customers and attempt to minimize the costs of dealing with adverse selection? One obvious way is by lending primarily to firms connected with the banks' owners. Banks rely on personal contacts to obtain information about borrowers. This is somewhat different from the usual (Anglo-American) view of how banks should operate, namely at arms'-length from borrowers and requiring the borrower to put up collateral. However, making arrangements through personal contacts or bank owners makes sense in Kiev because it is hard to arrange collateral for loans or to litigate if there is a default.

Interviewees in commercial banks said they wanted to have loan collateral, and prefered the pledge of tangible goods, but only when the borrower has clear ownership rights.[24] In fact, for most suitable assets — such as buildings and land — ownership status is unclear. Interviewees informed us there is not yet a Ukrainian law on collateral, and they regarded its absence as a problem. A further indication of this difficult legal situation is that in July 1991 the National Bank of Ukraine was unable to tell us how long a lawsuit would take in the case of loan default.

In practice, most loans are "secured" by a letter which is a written pledge to repay and which has unclear legal status. Nevertheless, interviewees did not report a single case of default by a borrower, and nor did we hear any suggestion that loans do not really have to be repaid. These commercial banks are profit-making businesses, and they protect themselves by being very selective in choosing to whom they lend.

For example, some borrowers are small enterprises formed by bank owners, while others are firms which want to buy equipment from bank owners. One bank described a system in which a large state enterprise acts as co-signer on a loan to ensure repayment.[25] The director of this bank also said he can use ministerial contacts to lobby for subsidy payments to enterprises which would otherwise default on their loans. These are all ways to address adverse selection and monitoring problems.

Most commercial bank loans have short maturity, usually 3-6 months, and the majority of credits are explicitly intended to finance a trading operation or the manufacture of scarce goods, such as food, furniture or housing. Commercial banks do not lend to individuals.[26] Nor, with the exception of former state banks, do they usually provide long-term investment credits.[27] By concentrating on financing for projects which promise quick profits, commercial banks do not directly deal with the monitoring problem, but they reduce the probability the borrower will genuinely be unable to repay. These banks regard an unpaid debt as extremely unusual, and would probably make a special investigation of the circumstances. In addition, by offering to roll-over credits, the bank provides an incentive for the borrower to be honest — so he can borrow in the future.

We should also stress that real interest rates on loans are negative and have been so at least since mid-1991. Borrowing from a commercial bank is extremely profitable as long as an investment project pays at least a zero real rate of interest. Until real interest rates become positive, we would not expect to see firms defaulting on their loans.

Each commercial bank is owned by and lends to a group of firms, and rarely looks for customers outside that group — for example, by advertising.[28] The commercial bank provides a way for these firms to pool their resources, increase the range of projects which they can fund, and also share the benefits of cheap refinance credit from the National Bank of Ukraine. But if banks perform this role, we still need to know how banks monitor lenders *ex post*, how they collect on debts, and how owners monitor the banks.

Western theoretical literature has linked the form of contracts involving banks with ways in which *ex post* monitoring costs are reduced. The conventional view is that it makes sense for banks to obtain funds through short-term deposits, and advance funds in the form of debt. However, for Kiev banks we find commercial banks' liabilities are mostly equity, while their assets are primarily short-term debt.[29] How can this be an efficient contractual arrangement?

It is fairly obvious why banks do not advance funds by buying equity, because shares in the former Soviet Union have a number of limitations. Table 5 shows that commercial banks have a high proportion of state firms among their customers, and it remains time-consuming and costly for state firms to issue shares. It is easier for most state enterprises to obtain outside financing by borrowing. In cases where state enterprises have issued tradeable shares, there is usually no secondary market, and frequently an enterprise stipulates that its shares can be sold only back to the enterprise itself — this is known as a "closed" joint stock company. Even when outside investors hold shares, managers usually retain strong control over the operation of the company and are difficult to replace.[30] Therefore, buying equity is only desirable if the investor intends to make a long-term investment, and has some viable way to force managers to act in shareholders' interests. By itself, equity in Ukrainian state enterprises cannot be used to control managers.[31]

In contrast, short-term revolving credits from a commercial bank are relatively easy to start and to terminate. Although these credits do not help the bank to know the actual performance of firms, they do provide regular checks on whether a firm is willing to comply with its obligations. Presumably, both adverse selection and moral hazard problems are further reduced by lending to firms connected with the banks' owners, as long as the latter have access to inside information about borrowers' performance or are able to punish recalcitrant borrowers by cutting

Table 5 UKRAINIAN COMMERCIAL BANKS: Customers by Sector

	Bank	No. of Owners	No. of customers	Percentage state customers	Percentage non-state customers	Percentage of customers from Kiev	Sectors represented
1	Bank INKO	92	500	90	9	80	Transport, furniture, trading.
2	Kiev Cooperative Bank	50	800	10	90	65	Consumer goods, repair, machinery production, services, entertainment.
3	Kiev Narodnii Bank	35	170	40	60	90	Construction, including construction materials, agriculture, timber, ship building.
4	Legbank	15	60	N/A	N/A	90	Light industry (30%), trading operations (60%).
5	Perkombank	20	100	N/A	N/A	N/A	Electronics, commercial trading.
6	Vidrodzhennya	N/A	210	N/A	N/A	N/A	Building renovation.
7	Ukr. Bank for Comm. Dev.	80	200	50	50	50	Scientific institutes, telecommunications.
8	Ukrstrombank	22	200	100	0	5	Building materials production (80%), agriculture and intermediate trading (20%).
9	Ukrinbank	95	1000	N/A	"Most"	70	Technology; consumer goods, timber, oil.
10	Ukrmezhvuzhbank	12	8	N/A	N/A	N/A	Educational institutions.
11	Ukrsnabbank	20	60	30	70	30	Building materials production, food products, associations, exchanges, newspapers.
12	Ukrsotsbank - Kiev	N/A	7500	N/A	N/A	N/A	Many sectors, including housing (3%).
	Total	441	10808				
	Total w/o Ukrsotsbank	441	3308				
	Average	44	901	53	47	60	
	Average w/o Ukrsotsbank	44	276	53	47	60	

Source: Bank Interviews. Summer 1991. Kiev, Ukraine, USSR. Mark A. Horton.

off supplies or evicting them.

If equity has so many unsatisfactory features, why do banks obtain finance by issuing shares? Part of the answer lies with the nature of equity shareholdings in the former Soviet Union. For example, one interviewee provided us with details on the shareholding arrangement of his bank which has two types of shares: simple shares, and privileged shares. Privileged shares give a fixed return, irrespective of the bank's profitability, but cannot account for more than 10 percent of all outstanding shares. Simple shares pay dividends which vary with bank profits. However, there is an important drawback. If a shareholder is dissatisfied and wants to sell his shares, he must give right of first refusal to existing shareholders and the bank itself.[32]

These contractual arrangements give a great deal of power to insiders, particularly to managers (Johnson and Kroll 1991). In the case of most state industrial enterprises, shares do not provide a viable way for outsiders to control pre-existing stakeholders, and this makes it difficult to attract new investors. However, new commercial banks are different because they do not have a pre-existing set of stakeholders with a strong claim on profits. Because there are relatively few "inside" shareholders in commercial banks, issuing shares is a feasible way to obtain funds from outside investors.

But this still does not fully answer the question of how shareholders monitor bank management. We know commercial banks have large boards of directors on which all of their owners are represented. Table 6 shows that in every case for which we have data, each shareholder has a seat on the board of directors and this board meets 1 to 4 times a year.

On the surface these numbers are surprising — for many banks more people sit on the board of directors than work as employees! But in most cases the board of directors serves only a general oversight function. In effect, it is a shareholders' meeting in which bank managers must report what they have done.

More detailed monitoring of executive decisions is delegated to the Bank Council, which comprises the largest shareholders. As Table 6 also shows, in those cases for which we have data, Bank Council meetings are quarterly. It makes sense that a few shareholders — those with the most to lose — specialize in monitoring bank management.

All our explanations of how commercial banks limit transaction costs show this institution relies on personal contacts, which together constitute networks for obtaining and sharing private information. These networks tend to be based on previous business contacts, and it is not surprising most banks do business with firms in only a few sectors.[33] As Table 7 indicates, new commercial banks provide a feasible institutional arrangement for related firms to pool their resources, and for state firms

Table 6 UKRAINIAN COMMERCIAL BANKS: Ownership and Board Size

	Bank	Number of owners	Size of bank board of directors	Board of directors meetings/year	Size of bank council	Bank council meetings/year	Percent of board represented on council
1	Bank INKO	92	92	2	7	4	7.61%
2	Kiev Cooperative Bank	50	50	1	7	4	14.00%
3	Kiev Narodnii Bank	35	35	4	5	N/A	14.29%
4	Legbank	15	15	N/A	4	N/A	26.67%
5	Perkombank	20	20	1 or 2	5	N/A	25.00%
6	Vidrodzhennya	N/A	N/A	N/A	N/A	N/A	N/A
7	Ukr. Bank for Comm. Dev.	80	80	2	11	4	13.75%
8	Ukrstrombank	22	N/A	N/A	N/A	N/A	N/A
9	Ukrinbank	95	N/A	N/A	N/A	N/A	N/A
10	Ukrmezhvuzhbank	12	N/A	N/A	N/A	4	N/A
11	Ukrsnabbank	20	20	N/A	12	4	60.00%
12	Ukrsotsbank - Kiev	N/A	N/A	N/A	N/A	N/A	N/A
	Total	441	312		51		
	Total w/o Ukrsotsbank	441	312		51		
	Average	44	45		7		
	Average w/o Ukrsotsbank	44	45		7		23.04%

Source: *Bank Interviews. Summer 1991. Kiev, Ukraine, USSR. Mark A. Horton.*

to build financial relationships with nonstate firms. In our assessment, there are strong grounds for considering the contractual forms associated with these new banks to be — in some specific senses — efficient.

Interest rates

There is one important element of commercial banks' behavior which cannot plausibly be explained in terms of transaction costs: their interest rates. In summer 1991, commercial banks' loan rates were in the range of 15-20 percent per annum. Most deposit rates were less than 10 percent. By November 1991, loan rates had risen to 25-30 percent (Matvienko 1991). But although it is hard to know the precise rate of inflation during 1991 — because shortages of goods mean official price statistics are misleading — it is evident these lending rates were negative in real terms. Why do commercial banks charge negative real interest rates?

The explanation for this aspect of bank behavior must lie with government monetary policy and with the legal restrictions on interest rates. Throughout 1991 interest rate controls existed at least on paper. In November 1990, the all-Union government capped interest rates on one-year deposits at 8 percent and 10 percent for one to three-year deposits. Loan rates were limited to 10 percent for one-year credits, and 12 percent for between one and three-year credits. However, banks could find ways to partially circumvent these controls — for example, by claiming that loans were "unsecured", which allowed interest rates to rise to 20 percent, and by increasing their commissions (Golubovich 1991).

In November 1991, the National Bank of Ukraine was lending to commercial banks at the incredibly low rate of 8 percent per year (Matvienko 1991), and in January this rate was still only 15 percent (*Euromoney* 1991), while inflation easily exceeded one hundred percent per year. Does the National Bank of Ukraine effectively control the loan rates of commercial banks? Our discussions with the National Bank of Ukraine on this matter were puzzling. While bank officials refused to state that there were official limits on interest rates, they hinted at informal limitations, either in the form of limits on prudent business — decisions made by the banks to keep rates low so as not to discourage customers — or alternatively, efforts by banks to keep rates down so as to avoid implementation of formal credit controls by the National Bank of Ukraine. The fact that all commercial banks regularly borrow from the National Bank probably means they are not inclined to step out of line with official interest rate policy.

From our interviews we know state enterprises can borrow at low

Table 7 UKRAINIAN COMMERCIAL BANKS: Owners by Sector

	Bank	No. of owners	Percentage of owners from state sector	Percentage of owners from non-state sector	Sectors represented
1	Bank INKO	92	50	50	2 Ministries, various industry,media, Ukrainian Academy of Sciences
2	Kiev Cooperative Bank	50	30	70	N/A
3	Kiev Narodnii Bank	35	55	45	Construction, publishing, sports organization
4	Legbank	15	N/A	N/A	Chemical production, Clothing production, Ministry of Light Industry
5	Perkombank	20	N/A	N/A	Defense, computer production, software, sports organization
6	Vidrodzhennya	N/A	N/A	N/A	N/A
7	Ukr. Bank for Comm. Dev.	80	70	30	Electronics, shipbuilding, machine production, tourism
8	Ukrstrombank	22	100	0	Enterprises of Ministry of Building
9	Ukrinbank	95	N/A	N/A	Insurance, Industrial construction, Ukrainian Academy of Sciences
10	Ukrmezhvuzhbank	12	100	0	High schools, polytech. institutes, universities
11	Ukrsnabbank	20	50	50	Ministry of Economic Activity, Recycling Authority, Building Supply Enterprises, Red Cross
12	Ukrsotsbank - Kiev		100	0	Meat production, clothing, trade unions, Ukrainian Academy of Sciences, hotels.
	Total	441			
	Average	44	69	31	

Source: Bank Interviews. Summer 1991. Kiev, Ukraine, USSR. Mark A. Horton.

rates from the state banking system or obtain subsidies from min-istries.[34] Most state enterprises are unwilling to pay the "high" interest rates charged by commercial banks. This environment clearly affects the nature of commercial bank customers, who tend to be of three types. First, small enterprises which do not have recourse to state banks or ministries. Second, enterprises which need credit quickly in order to take advantage of an unexpected and short-lived opportunity — such as the purchase of goods on a commodities exchange. Third, state enter-prises which — for reasons best known to themselves — do not wish to rely exclusively on state banks for credit.

Therefore, the most plausible explanation for the low nominal interest rates charged by commercial banks is the availability of cheap loans from state banks. Because commercial banks compete to some extent for clients with state banks, they have to regard the National Bank of Ukraine's interest rates as a benchmark and not raise their loan rates too far above that level. Commercial banks did not appear unhappy with this situation, presumably because this interest rate policy also held down their cost of capital — assuming the opportunity cost for their investors is the interest paid on deposits in state banks.

Commercial banks certainly are able to make respectable profits on the spread between loan rates and the rate paid to investors. This sug-gests that the legal restriction of nominal interest rates, not directly in commercial banks but on their close competitors, accounts for negative real interest rates.

It still remains unclear why commercial banks do not raise both deposit and loan rates, and draw capital away from the state banks — particularly because the opportunity cost for investors might reasonably be considered to be a zero real rate, from investing in inventories of goods. None of our interviewees expressed an interest in doing this. The most plausible explanation is that they fear the National Bank of Ukraine would intervene and set interest rates directly if state banks lost a significant amount of funds. Whether it could and would take such action remains an interesting hypothetical question.

Conclusions

Irrespective of how they were founded, most commercial banks in Kiev tend to behave similarly. They are owned by relatively small groups of connected firms, and they lend to firms closely connected to their own-ers. These banks obtain funding by issuing shares, but most of their assets are in the form of short-term debt. The institutional arrangements of these banks seem well suited to economize on transaction costs in the prevailing credit market conditions of Ukraine. If our interpretation is correct, it suggests these banks may be able to play a positive role in the restructuring of the economy.[35]

One important aspect of banks' operations cannot be explained in terms of transaction costs: their low nominal loan rates. There are two reasons for this level of interest rates. First, these banks receive subsidies from the National Bank of Ukraine in the form of loans at interest rates far below the rate of inflation. One reason for forming a commercial bank must be the expectation of getting these credits. Second, banks' loan rates are also less than inflation, apparently because of the low interest rates charged by state banks and the threat of action by the National Bank of Ukraine if it perceives commercial bank interest rates as "excessive."

Our analysis suggests new commercial banks in the former Soviet Union may serve a more useful economic role than is commonly believed. However, none of our evidence disproves the other two prevailing interpretations mentioned in the introduction. In fact, we showed that banks more closely tied to ministries have enjoyed more rapid growth, and that commercial banks do contribute to inflationary pressure because they use cheap central bank credit. However, we still view both these negative interpretations with caution. In order to argue that the "nomenklatura" is the primary beneficiary from the creation of new banks, we would need a full accounting of precisely who benefits and who loses within different parts of the nomenklatura.[36] And surely inflationary pressure would be almost as bad without commercial banks — probably the volume of cheap central bank credit which flows through state banks would increase. The fundamental cause of inflation lies with government fiscal and monetary policy.

This paper suggests two interesting avenues for further research. The first would be to model the transaction costs involved in banking under the current conditions in the former Soviet Union. It would be useful to derive results in which the efficient institutional structure of banks depended on, among other things, the legal enforceability of contracts, the nature of publicly available information about borrowers, and the nature of available investment opportunities. This might help determine the critical differences in banking environment between the West and the former Soviet Union, and suggest how various policies would change optimal banking arrangements.

Second, more empirical research on the types of contracts used by other banks in the Soviet Union is needed to determine whether our observations and interpretations can be generalized. Furthermore, we need to compare and contrast the institutional arrangements in new commercial banks with those in large state banks. Hopefully, this would throw further light on the question of what constitutes an efficient set of contracts in the difficult economic circumstances of a post-communist economy.

References

Blanchard, Olivier, Rudiger Dornbusch, Paul Krugman, Richard Layard, and Lawrence Summers (1991). *Reform in Eastern Europe.* Cambridge, Massachusetts: The MIT Press.

Calomiris, Charles W. and Charles M. Kahn undated. "The Role of Demandable Debt in Structuring Optimal Banking Arrangements."

Calvo, Guillermo and Fabrizio Coricelli (1991). "Stagflationary Effects of Stabilization Programs in Reforming Socialist Countries: Enterprise-Side vs. Household-Side Factors." Mimeo, February.

"Chto volnuet bankirov? (What Worries Bankers?)" *Ekonomika i zhizn'*, No. 5, February 1992, p. 8.

Diamond, Douglas W. and Philip H. Dybvig (1983). "Bank Runs, Deposit Insurance, and Liquidity." *Journal of Political Economy*, vol. 91, no. 3, pp.401-419.

Euromoney (1991). "Breaking Up is Hard to Do." January.

Garvy, George (1977). *Money, Financial Flows, and Credit in the Soviet Union.* Cambridge, Massachusetts: Ballinger Publishing Company for National Bureau of Economic Research.

Golubovich, Alexey D (1991). "Soviet Banking System: Markets, Services, Regulations." *Russian Business Review*, Vol. 1, pp. 4-5.

Gregory, Paul R. and Robert C. Stuart (1986). *Soviet Economic Structure and Performance.* Third Edition, New York: Harper and Row.

Grigor'ev, Mikhail (1992). "Uchites' prinosit' dobro. V zalog." *Kommersant*, No. 4, January 20-27, p. 25.

Halich, Natalie (1991). "Private Banking." An unpublished memorandum to the Project on Economic Reform in Ukraine. May 2.

International Monetary Fund, The World Bank, Organization for Economic Cooperation and Development, European Bank for Reconstruction and Development (1991). *A Study of the Soviet Economy.* Paris (Study undertaken in response to a request by the Houston Summit). February.

Johnson, Simon and Heidi Kroll (1991). "Managerial Strategies for Spontaneous Privatization." *Soviet Economy*, 7, 4, pp.281-316.

Kopylova, O. (1992), "O zaloge (On Pledge)," *Ekonomika i zhizn'*, No. 26, June, p. 21.

Lipton, David and Jeffrey D. Sachs (1990). "Privatization in Eastern Europe: The Case of Poland." *Brookings Papers on Economic Activity*, 2, pp.293-341.

Matvienko, Vladimir Pavlovich (1991). "We Can Turn Into an Absurd, Self-Destructive State," Interview published in *Verchernii Kiev*, November 18.

Mirimskaya, Olga M. and Olga Yu. Arkhangelskaya (1991). "Soviet Banks: Whom to Deal With?" *Russian Business Review*, Vol. 1, pp.16-18.

Ofer, Gur (1989). "Budget Deficit, Market Disequilibrium and Soviet Economic Reforms." *Soviet Economy* 5, 2: 107-161, April-June.

"O Gosudarstvennom Banke SSSR (On the State Bank of the USSR)," *Ekonomika i zhizn'*, No. 52, December 1990, pp. 16-17.

"O Bankakh i Bankovskoi Deyatel'nosti (On Banks and Banking Activity), *Ekonomika i zhizn'*, No. 52, December 1990, pp. 17-18.

"O vvedenii v deistvie Zakona SSSR `O Gosudarstvennom banke SSSR' i Zakona SSSR `O bankakh i bankovskoi deyatel'nosti' (On putting into effect the Law of the USSR `On the State Bank of the USSR' and the Law of the USSR `On banks and banking activity.'" *Ekonomika i zhizn'*, No. 52, December 1990, pp. 19.

"On the Improvement of the Banking System in the Country and Boosting its Effect on the Enhancement of Economic Activity." Central Committee of the CPSU and the USSR Council of Ministers Resolution 821, July 17, 1987. Translated in *FBIS, Soviet Union: Daily Report*, October 26, 1987, pp.47-52.

"Osnovy grazhdanskogo zakonodatel'stva soyuza SSR i respublik (Principles of Civil Legislation of the USSR and the Republics)," *Vestnik Verkhovnogo Suda SSSR*, Number 0, 1991, pp. 15-39.

"O Zaloge (On Pledge)," *Ekonomika i zhizn'*, No. 24, June 1992, pp. 16-17.

Pevzner, A. (1992), "O zaloge (On Pledge)," *Ekonomika i zhizn'*, Np. 27, July, p.5.

Rumer, Boris (1991). "New Capitalists in the USSR." Challenge, 34, 3, pp. 19-22

Sachs, Jeffrey D. (1991). "Accelerating Privatization in Eastern Europe: The Case of Poland." WIDER Working Papers, WP 92, September.

Shatalov, Sergei (1991). "Privatization in the Soviet Union: The Beginnings of a Transition." Policy Research Working Paper Series, The World Bank, November.

Stiglitz, J. and A. Weiss (1981). "Credit Rationing in Markets with Imperfect Information." *American Economic Review*, 71, pp. 393-410.

Szirmai, Z. ed. (1966). *Law in Eastern Europe* (No. 11). Leyden: A. W. Sijthoff.

Uchitelle, Louis (1992). "The Roulette of Russian Banking." *New York Times*, February 29, 1992.

Zakharov, Vyacheslav S. (1992), "Restructuring of the Monetary and Credit System of the USSR," in David M. Kemme and Andrzej Rudka, eds., *Monetary and Banking Reform in Postcommunist Economies*, New York: Institute for East-West Security Studies.

Notes

1 This paper is the product of a research project funded by a grant to Simon Johnson from the the National Council for Soviet and East European Research. Mark Horton's interview work was generously financed by the Soros Foundation through its support to the Project on Economic Reform in Ukraine at Harvard University's Kennedy School. The authors express their appreciation to Mr. Andrei Burovskii of Kiev Pedagogical Institute, Kiev, Ukraine, who helped coordinate and translate bank director interviews during the summer of 1991.

2 Interesting articles with an anecdotal basis include Uchitelle (1992), and Mirimskaya and Arkhangelskaya (1991).

3 There is some recent literature on banking in post-communist countries, but it deals with Eastern Europe where the situation is quite different. Most of these papers assume that a partially reformed post-communist banking system does not function well, although they differ in explaining precisely how a

weak banking system hurts the economy. Some authors argue an improved banking system is needed to process information about borrowers and to ensure that credit continues to flow to good borrowers (Blanchard et al 1991), while others take a more apocalyptic view, stressing that the lack of a proper banking system may cause a fall in output when the state decides to stop acting as a "lender of last resort" to industrial firms (Calvo and Coricelli 1991).

4   This information was obtained on July 9, 1991, and confirmed in an interview on August 7, 1991.

5   These two were Neftichembank and Arendbank. Neftichembank had only recently been registered and was not yet in operation. The chairman of Arendbank did not turn up for two appointments with us, and we understood this might have been due to recent management changes.

6   Interviewees stated that their banks had branches in Kharkov, Cherkassy, Dneprpetovsk and Chernikov in Central Ukraine, Nikolaev and Kherson in Southern Ukraine. Very few had branches in Lvov, Ivano Frankovsk or Rovno in Western Ukraine, or in the Donetsk region in Eastern Ukraine.

7   The discussion of the monobank system draws generally on Garvy (1977), Gregory and Stuart (1986, pp. 191-193); and Ofer (1989, pp. 112-115).

8   Pledges of property for securing obligations were, and still are, regulated by provisions of the basic civil codes of the various republics. See, for example, the Civil Code of the RSFSR, Articles 98, 101 and 192 to 202 (Szirmai, 1966, p. 36-37 and 58-60).

9   In December 1990, the Supreme Soviet of the USSR adopted new banking legislation, including a Law on the State Bank of the USSR and a Law on Banks and Banking Activity (O gosudarstvennom, 1990, pp. 16-17; O bankax, 1990, pp. 17-18). The resolution that accompanied the legislation provided for the transformation of Promstroibank into a joint-stock commercial bank by December 31, 1991 (O vvedenii, 1990, p. 19).

10 There is a significant disparity in the scale of commercial banking activities between Moscow and other cities. For example, at the start of 1991, Mosinkombank had 50 million rubles in paid-up capital, and assets of around 8,000 million rublies. The Commercial Bank for Innovations also had capital worth 50 million rubles.

11 Bank Vidrodzhennya began operations in 1990, but we do not know when it was formed.

12 A new chairman, Vladimir Pavlovich Matvienko, was appointed in spring 1991, but did not assume full responsibility until September 1991. He was formerly director of Promstroibank in Ukraine. The National Bank of Ukraine is responsible directly to the Ukrainian Supreme Soviet and had founding capital of 1.5 billion rubles and 200 million dollars, obtained not from the budget but from the former Gosbank, Sberbank and Promstroibank (Matvienko 1991). It was formed from the Kiev branch of Gosbank.

13 For a discussion of an earlier draft Law on Pledge, see International Monetary Fund 1991, Volume 2, pp. 244 and 303, footnote 17.

14 Since our interviews were conducted, Bank Ukraina was formed from Agroprombank.

15 Ukrinbank might be considered to have a mixed origins, because its founders

were both the Academy of Sciences and the Council of Ministers. However, because this bank has always had very close ties to the government, we classify here as "ministry-founded".

16 This split occurred following public accusations that the bank was serving as a conduit for exporting Ukrainian capital to Russia. Mosinkombank remains the bank's largest shareholder.

17 Examples for each category are, respectively: Vidrodzhennya, with 1 year; Ukrsnabbank, with 9 years; and Kiev Cooperative Bank, with 2 years.

18 This technical aspect is important: it is harder to become a bank entrepreneur than just an ordinary businessman. Most private businessmen in the former Soviet Union have had no formal management training.

19 INKO has even established an internship and scholarship program with the leading economics university in Kiev (the Institute of National Economy), in order to hire the bright prospects while they are still students.

20 Apparently the commercial banking department has a hard time keeping bright employees, who instead prefer the action and remuneration of commercial banks.

21 Surprisingly, the Ukrainian banking law does not state the minimum capital needed to form a bank. However, we understand that regulations require a commercial bank founded by the state to have 5 million rubles, and a cooperative bank to have 500,000 rubles initial capital. The president of the National Bank of Ukraine has claimed that, "(commercial banks)" capital from shareholders is small and their main capital comes from preferential credits from the National Bank," (Matvienko 1991).

22 The Ministry of Higher Education is not well funded, and this has held back the bank it founded — Ukrmezhvuzbank.

23 This is not a problem which is prominent in the Western literature, because in the West contracts are usually legally enforceable. In principle in the former Soviet Union, it is possible to have a problem collecting on debts even if *ex post* outcomes are completely observable. Presumably, we should regard this as an issue of adverse selection, because what matters is whether the borrower is honest.

24 For example, ownership rights would be clear in the case of a loan made against the security of goods purchased from a commodities exchange.

25 Halich (1991) reports that one bank in Western Ukraine states it will lend to small business if there is a co-signer, and prefers equipment as collateral. If a client defaults on a loan, the bank can legally have a freeze put on all the client's accounts in any bank.

26 Why do commercial banks not lend to individuals? We were told by Alina Anatolevna Glushchenko, assistant head of the Department of Coordination of Commercial Banking Activities at the Ukrainian National Bank, on August 7, 1991: "Banks do not yet serve individual persons as clients, except in taking deposits. This... is due to a lack of space, personnel and papers. However, it is illegal for banks to loan money to individuals. On August 5, 1991 it became legal to loan money to farmers. Individuals must register as farmers with the oblast executive committee".

27 According to the Ukrainian National Bank, commercial banks have issued 4

billion rubles worth of credits but only 100 million have gone to "investment". President Matvienko said, "...money is being poured into short-term purposes, mainly into the resale of goods..." Matvienko also said interest rates, up to 30 percent per year in November 1991, were "too high" and "Naturally, under these conditions, enterprises are not interested in taking long term credits for investment."

28 Bank INKO is unusual because it advertises aggressively and very prominently. Some other banks advertise in newspapers, but others said they did not find advertising useful.

29 There was one notable exception. Ukrinbank bank has an innovative scheme for financing innovation which involves obtaining an equity stake.

30 For example, see the discussion in Johnson and Kroll (1991).

31 There is some evidence banks have taken equity stakes in "small enterprises" which are a different legal form from state enterprises. These are new firms which do not have insiders with strong claims.

32 This resembles a Western partnership more than a Western joint stock company.

33 A good example is the Lis' Bank in Yzgorod. As Halich (1991) reports: "The majority of the stockholders represent timber and furniture enterprises and organizations... The dividends that stockholders and depositors receive can be applied to the purchase of furniture from the various member organizations." (p. 4).

34 For example, in fall 1991 Agroprombank could borrow at 3 percent per annum (Matvienko 1991).

35 It has already been suggested that banks could play a key role in privatization, through acquiring shares and providing the outside ownership which is currently lacking — they are one of the few financial institutions already in existence at the end of communism (Lipton and Sachs 1990, Sachs 1991).

36 This is a complex issue. For example, see Johnson and Kroll (1991).

12 Russia's Balance of Payments Prospects

Peter Boone

A key goal of the Russian economic reform program is integration into the world economy. The government has taken bold measures to begin this process: the exchange rate has been floated for the first time in seventy years, individuals and enterprises are basically free to carry out import and export operations, import customs duties have been temporarily abolished, and all export taxes on non-traditional exports have been removed.

These measures come at a time when Russia's balance of payments situation has reached a critical point. The former USSR government spent all the country's foreign reserves, built up substantial external debt, and permitted key export sectors to decline. This occurred as exports to the CMEA collapsed, and political and economic instability led to capital flight. As a result, the performance of the Russian economy, and the speed and nature of macroeconomic adjustment, is restricted by a severe balance of payments constraint.

This paper examines the causes and implications of this balance of payments constraint, both analytically and empirically. The paper addresses several questions: What are the underlying causes and nature of Russia's current balance of payments situation? How does the balance of payments situation affect key macroeconomic variables (such as the dollar wage, output, the real exchange rate, and the real wage)? How is the tight fiscal situation and effectiveness of import competition related to the balance of payments constraint ? And finally, what are the likely prospects for relaxation of the balance of payments constraint during the immediate several years?

We argue that the announced policies of the Russian government, in combination with the existing measures already taken, should lead to a sharp growth in exports during the next 12 to 24 months. Based on experience from East European countries, and the existing potential for nat-ural resource exports from Russia, it is reasonable to expect that Russian exports could rise by over 60 percent (approximately 28 bn. dollars) from projected 1992 levels during the next two years. These exports would help finance additional annual imports of approximately 29 bn. dollars. Higher imports would ease the fall in output and the real wage, and lead to a sharp rise in the dollar wage from its current low level (approximately $30 per month in June 1992).

The paper is divided into four sections. First, there is an overview of the balance of payments situation in the former USSR from 1985 to 1991. Second, we present a simple analytical framework which highlights the impact of the balance of payments constraint on key macroeconomic variables, and discusses fiscal and competition implications. The third section presents estimates for Russian import financing in 1992 and beyond, and discusses prospects for the future based on specific Russian conditions and experience from other East European countries, and the last section serves as a conclusion.

The reader should beware that the trade statistics presented here remain subject to revision. To analyze the conditions leading up to the Russian reform program, we have chosen to present IMF historical esti-mates of the current account from the former USSR. We adjusted these data to make them comparable over time, and we present dollar figures. There is still considerable debate over what the proper exchange rate should be when converting these data to dollar levels. For this reason, we focus on the qualitative changes in the variables rather than the lev-els.

In the section on Russian import financing we base our analysis upon a forecast for exports and imports in 1992, based on the available data for the first trimester. In this manner we avoid trying to compare 1992 data, reported in dollars, with 1991 data which was converted from rubles to dollars, and which requires assumptions about the share of Russian imports and exports in total trade of the former USSR.

Overview of the USSR BOP from 1985 to 1991

Table 1 presents the IMF's estimates of convertible currency trade, on a transactions basis, for the former USSR in 1985, 1990 and 1991. From 1985 to 1990 the USSR trade balance moved from a small surplus to deficit. Underlying these changes is a rapid fall in oil exports from 1989 onwards, and a growth in imports in the late 1980s aimed at supporting the consumer goods market, and paying for the Afghanistan war. To raise new financing, gold exports were raised well above production levels, and substantial new short and medium term credits were taken. The new credit obligations led to a sharp increase in debt service payments.

From 1990 to 1991 convertible currency exports and imports declined sharply. The main cause of the fall in exports was a 4 billion dollar drop in oil and gas exports, as a consequence of the decline in USSR oil production.

In both 1990 and 1991, the USSR repaid short-term liabilities, financing these payments by spending gross reserves. In 1990 the USSR amortized 10.1 billion dollars in short-term credits, managing this by running down reserves of 7.4 billion dollars. In 1991 they amortized an additional 4.6 billion dollars, partly financed again by spending 1.4 billion dollars from reserves. As a result, by end 1991 gross reserves were only a few days imports.

TABLE 1 BALANCE OF PAYMENTS FOR THE USSR
WITH CONVERTIBLE CURRENCY COUNTRIES
(billions of dollars)

	1985	1990	1991
EXPORTS	27.5	33.6	30.6
IMPORTS	26.3	35.3	28.2
TRADE BALANCE	1.2	-1.7	2.3
NET INTEREST	-0.6	-3.7	-3.6
OTHER NET SERVICES	-1.2	-2.9	-3
GOLD SALES	1.8	2.5	3.4
CURRENT ACCOUNT BALANCE	1.2	-5.8	-0.9

Source: IMF (1991,1992)
Note: The original IMF (1992) report includes East Germany and Finland in 1991 export and import data. These data have been adjusted to make them comparable to 1990.

Table 2 shows the 1990 and 1991 current account balances with the non-convertible countries. These include CMEA countries, and other countries where there are clearing arrangements. As a result of the breakdown of the CMEA trading system, exports declined by 56 percent, and imports fell by 53 percent.

TABLE 2 BALANCE OF PAYMENTS FOR THE USSR:
NON-CONVERTIBLE
(billions of dollars)

	1990	1991
EXPORTS	70.2	39.6
IMPORTS	85.4	40.0
TRADE BALANCE	-15.2	-0.3
NET INTEREST	0.2	-0.2
OTHER NET SERVICES	-0.2	-1.0
GOLD SALES	0.0	0.0
CURRENT ACCOUNT BALANCE	-15.2	-1.5

source: IMF (1992)
note: The original IMF report includes East Germany and Finland in 1991
export and import data. These data have been adjusted to make them comparable to 1990.

Table 3 shows an example of quantity and price declines for various goods from 1990 to 1991. The key point here is that the drop was largely due to volume rather than price changes. According to this data, the cost of the 1991 import and export baskets in 1992 prices each rose by roughly 1 percent. Further, while some of the traded goods were military equipment, or useless machinery, there were also substantial declines in basic food items and other consumer goods.

There is little or no sign, apart from trade in basic raw materials, that this trade was redirected. Even though these decreases in trade are massive in scale, there is no subsequent growth in exports to the convertible currency regions. This pattern, on a sectoral basis, has been pointed out in Rodrik (1992) for Eastern Europe. The implication is that the USSR lost an important source of financing for basic imports when CMEA trade collapsed.

By end 1991 the external debt of the former USSR reached 82.4 billion dollars. The volume of oil exports had fallen by more than half from the high reached in 1988, and debt service obligations in the coming year reached 15.6 billion dollars (9.6 in principal, and 6 interest). Economic and political instability led to capital flight.

This sharp tightening of the balance of payments constraint is reflected in a rapid decline in the dollar wage and the real exchange rate, and further deterioration in general macroeconomic conditions. Table 4 shows the pattern of the dollar wage, using various measure of the exchange rate. In every case the dollar wage falls sharply from the level

TABLE 3 USSR EXPORTS AND IMPORTS FROM ALL COUNTRIES
(price and volume changes by good, comparing 1990 and 1991)

IMPORTS 1991/1990	PRICE	VOLUME	EXPORTS 1991/1990	PRICE	VOLUME
MEAT & MEAT PRODUCTS	1.00	.57	FISH & FISH PRODUCTS	1.17	.64
MILK POWDER	0.99	.81	COKING COAL	1.00	.91
BUTTER	0.72	.65	CRUDE OIL	1.00	.93
POTATOES	0.97	.76	OIL PRODUCTS	0.90	.95
CITRUS FRUITS	1.00	.53	NATURAL GAS	1.07	.87
WHEAT	1.02	.70	IRON-ORE	1.00	.57
BARLEY	1.02	.62	CEMENT	1.00	.56
CORN	0.53	.92	POTASIUM FERTILIZER	1.01	.71
RICE	0.69	.79	NITROGEN FERTILIZER	1.01	.96
TEA	0.99	.80	OTHER RUBBER PRODUCTS	1.00	.01
FLOUR	1.01	.55	SYNTHETIC RUBBER	1.00	.90
SUGAR	1.00	.80	OTHER WOOD PRODUCTS	0.96	.01
OTHER RUBBER PRODUCTS	1.10	.01	ROUND TIMBER	1.00	.75
NATURAL RUBBER	1.00	.41	CUT TIMBER	1.01	.65
SYNTHETIC RUBBER	1.00	.77	PAPER AND CARDBOARD	0.96	.69
PAPER AND CARDBOARD	5.30	.12	OTHER COTTON PRODUCTS	1.08	.01
WOOL	1.00	.94	RAW COTTON	1.08	.72
SOAP	1.17	.87	OTHER FERROUS METAL P	0.99	.01
OTHER FERROUS METALS	1.00	.01	CAST IRON	1.01	.72
ROLLED FERROUS METALS	1.00	.76	IRON ALLOYS	1.00	.91
PIPES	1.00	.74	ROLLED FERROUS METALS	1.03	.64
TRUCKS	0.72	.85	PIPES	1.02	.59
BUSES	0.88	.85	COPPER	0.97	.58
AUTOMOBILES	0.69	.85	ALUMINUM	0.99	.68
FREIGHT CARS	1.00	.87	TRACTORS	1.10	.37
			TRUCKS	1.02	.48
			LIGHT AUTOMOBILES	1.01	.73
			ELECTRICAL PRODUCTS A	0.96	.80
			PLANES AND HELICOPTERS	1.07	.31

Source: Russian Goskomstat
Note: Imports listed here represent 31 percent of the total value of imports in 1990 and 36 percent in 1991. Exports represent 72 percent of all exports in 1990 and 76 percent in 1991. The calculated rise in the cost of the 1991 import basket in 1992 is 1.6 percent. The rise calculation for the export basket

TABLE 4 DOLLAR WAGE AND REAL EXCHANGE RATE

	Real Exchange Rate		Dollar Wage	
	Mkt.	Off.	Mkt.	Off.
1980	1	1	44.1	269.26
1985	1.18	1.22	40.8	239.83
1986	0.95	1.01	51.1	240.62
1987	1.03	0.89	48.3	295.38
1988	1.44	0.85	37.7	341.17
1989	2.70	0.86	21.5	387.16
1990	3.41	0.78	18.5	410.48
1991	5.03	18.84	11.7	494.67
1992 (Apr)	2.05	12.51	21.43	21.43

Source: Goskomstat: Russia in Figures, IMF
Notes:
Mkt: Average Moscow and St. Petersburg cash rate to 1989,
Off: Official Exchange Rate
Wage: Average wage in the economy
Price Index: Retail price index in state stores.
Real Exchange Rate takes exchange rate divided by price index.
Dollar Wage is ruble wage in whole economy divided by the exchange rate index.

of the mid-1980s, and is at an all-time low at the start of 1992. This mirrors the movement in the real exchange rate, which in April 1992, using the parallel market exchange rate, had depreciated by a factor of 2.

Table 5 compares Russian average wages and GDP per capita at the market exchange rate, with recent data from other reforming East European countries. Russia's dollar wage is less than one-seventh the average wage in Poland, and Russian GDP per capita places it at the same level as the IMF's estimate for Mongolia.

This fall in the dollar wage and low value of dollar GDP is directly related to the current balance of payments crisis. The policies introduced by the Russian government could lead to a very rapid and significant improvement in the balance of payments. As we discuss in the next section, this would permit a rise in the dollar wage, dollar GDP, and real exchange rate. These policies will also reduce an important bottleneck in production — the shortage of imported inputs — and therefore further help ease the decline in output and the real wage.

TABLE 5 DOLLAR WAGE AND GDP PER CAPITA IN TRANSFORMING ECONOMIES

		MONTHLY WAGE	GDP PER CAPITA
		(dollars)	
RUSSIA	Apr. 92	22	533
POLAND	Nov. 90	190	2000
CZECHOSLOVAKIA	Mar. 92	160	1800
HUNGARY	Oct. 91	242	
MONGOLIA	Jun. 90	30	550

Source: Data from IMF, Plan Econ, and World Bank.
Notes: Mongolian GDP per capita from 1989. Russian GDP calculated using 10 trillion rubles as annual GDP, and an exchange rate of 125 rb/$

The impact of the balance of payments constraint on output, wages and the exchange rate

In this section, in a simple analytical framework, we examine the links between the balance of payments constraint and key macroeconomic variables. We use this framework to consider how the shocks to the economy discussed above, and the reforms being implemented, have affected and will affect the balance of payments. We also examine the impact of the balance of payments constraint on the effectiveness of import competition, and the implications for fiscal balance.

The framework

Consider an economy where there are two goods: an imported good 'M', and a domestically produced good 'Y'. The production of the domestic good requires imported inputs M_y and labor L. Since the total employment in the economy is assumed to remain fixed, we set L=1. The price of the world good is normalized to 1, and the domestic good price, which we will solve for, is labelled 'p'. Since 'p' represents the price of the domestic good in terms of foreign goods, we call 'p' the (real) exchange rate. The home country exchange rate appreciates whenever p rises, and depreciates when p falls.

Production is determined by a Cobb-Douglas production function:

(1) $Y = a*L^{1-b}*M_y^b$

216

We solve for the optimal allocation of inputs, where 'w' is the (dollar) wage measured in units of the foreign good, and the price of the foreign good is the numeraire = 1. We solve:

(2) $M_y = (p*a*b)^{1/(1-b)}$

(3) $Y = a*(p*a*b)^{b/(1-b)}$

(4) $w = a*(1-b)*(p*a*b)^{b/(1-b)}$

These equations have the following interpretation: An appreciation of the ruble (p rising) means foreign goods are relatively cheaper, producers therefore chose to use more imported inputs. The higher inputs lead to higher output. And, more inputs increase the marginal productivity of labor, so dollar wages can also rise.

During the initial stage after a liberalization of trade, or after a shock to the balance of payments, it will take time for trade flows to adjust to new levels. In particular, exporters must find new markets, learn to deal in world trade, arrange credits and payments procedures, design their products to match customer requirements, etc. For this reason, we assume that exports adjust gradually to profit incentives, and initially are fixed at some predetermined level. Further, for simplicity we assume that exports are proportional to output, so total exports X can be written as $X = x*Y$, where x is the proportion of output which is exported. The remaining portion of output, Y - X, is sold domestically.

Exports increase if export sales are more profitable than home sales. Home sales earn p. Exports earn 1. Therefore:

(5) $X = x*Y$ at time T.

(6) $dx/dt > 0$ if $p < 1$
        < 0 if $p > 1$

where T is time of the liberalization, t is a time index, and dx/dt denotes the partial derivative of x with respect to t.

The last source of foreign exchange is other foreign financing, which we label F. Key components of this are: net interest receipts, net foreign resource transfers, reserve decumulation, and repatriation of capital (reverse capital flight). Each of these items raises F when it increases. For simplicity, we write:

(7) $F = f*Y$

where f is the share of financial flows in output.

In a country which has lost access to world capital markets, total expenditures are limited to domestic incomes plus net financing from foreign sources. We can write total expenditures measured in terms of the foreign good, E, as:

(8) $E = p*(Y - X) + X - M_y + F$

Assuming that total expenditures equal total available funds, then expenditures are the value of total output sold domestically at domestic prices, plus the value of export receipts, less the cost of imported inputs in total production, plus the available financing.

Lastly, we assume that consumers have preferences such that they spend a fixed share of their expenditures, c, on imported consumer goods. This implies that the demand for consumer imports is:

(9) $M_c = c*E = c*[p*(Y - X) + X - M_y + F]$

We want to solve the model to find the equilibrium dollar wage, real exchange rate and level of output as a function of the other parameters. In equilibrium, the demand for consumer and producer imports must equal the supply. But the supply of imports is restricted by the balance of payments condition. This restriction is:

(10) $M = X + F$

Imports must equal total export receipts plus all sources of foreign financing. The equilibrium condition has:

(11) $M = M_y + M_c$

Solving for the real exchange rate, the dollar wage, and output we get:

(12)
$$p = \frac{(1 - c)}{b + c*(1-b-x)} * (x + f)$$

$$\frac{d(\log(p))}{d(\log(x))} > \frac{X}{M}, \quad \frac{d(\log(p))}{d(\log(f))} = \frac{F}{M}, \quad \frac{dp}{da} = 0$$

$$(13) \qquad w = cte* \left(\frac{(1-c)*(x+f)}{b + c*(1-b-x)} \right)^{(1/(1-b))}$$

$$\frac{d(\log(w))}{d(\log(x))} > \frac{X}{M*(1-b)} \qquad \frac{d(\log(w))}{d(\log(f))} = \frac{F}{M*(1-b)}, \quad \frac{d(\log(w))}{d(\log(a))} = \frac{1}{1-b}$$

$$(14) \qquad Y = cte* \left(\frac{(1-c)*(x+f)}{b + c*(1-b-x)} \right)^{(b/(1-b))}$$

$$\frac{d(\log(Y))}{d(\log(x))} > \frac{X*b}{M*(1-b)}, \qquad \frac{d(\log(Y))}{d(\log(f))} = \frac{F*b}{M*(1-b)}, \quad \frac{d(\log(Y))}{d(\log(a))} = \frac{1}{1-b}$$

The interpretation of these results is as follows: A sudden reduction in any of the financing items or exports (e.g. due to loss of access to foreign capital markets, or the collapse of CMEA trade), increases the financing constraint on the balance of payments. This means there are less imports available for production and consumption. The real exchange rate must depreciate, reducing the demand for imports to a level equal to the supply. Since there are less imports available for production inputs, total production falls. This leads to a decline in the dollar wage for two reasons: First, the exchange rate depreciates, so the dollar wage declines. Second, the productivity of labor declines as 'import shortages' cause output declines. It can also be shown that because the productivity of labor falls, and the relative price of imports rises, the domestic real wage measured in terms of the consumer price index also decreases.

The dynamic adjustment of the economy to a shock which causes a temporary drop in exports is illustrated in Figures 1 and 2. The initial tightening of the payments restriction reduces imports, leading to a decline in output and the dollar wage, and a depreciation of the exchange rate. The dollar wage falls by more than the exchange rate, since labor productivity is reduced. This depreciation of the exchange rate makes it more profitable to export than to sell goods domestically, so producers start finding markets abroad. Over time exports rise. As this occurs the balance of payments constraint is reduced, and output, the dollar wage, the real wage and imports increase.

One implication is that the effectiveness of import competition, as

Figure 1

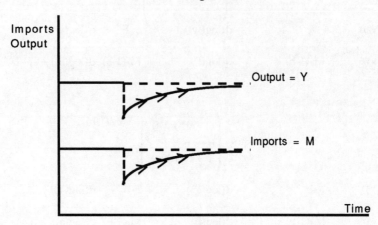

Figure 2

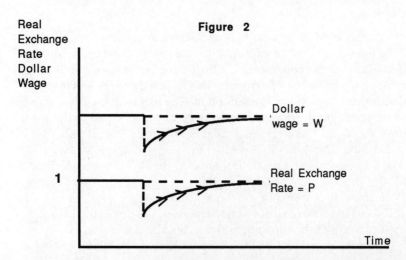

Response of the dollar wage, real exchange rate, output and imports to an exogenous shock which causes a temporary reduction in exports

reflected in the change in the real exchange rate, initially falls after the shock, and then rises as exports adjust and imports increase. In an economy such as Russia, where there is a high degree of monopolization, the balance of payments condition effectively slows restructuring, and limits pricing discipline which would arise from import competition.

Finally, note an important fiscal implication of these results. After a balance of payments shock, the real exchange rate will temporarily 'overshoot,' this means the dollar value of GDP will fall, and then rise as the exchange rate approaches the new equilibrium. If the fiscal authorities are responsible for a fixed payment in foreign currency, such as debt service, then the share of this payment in GDP goes up in conjunction with the balance of payments tightening. This would in general require revising the tax system, or reducing real expenditures.

If the government can receive debt relief or new loans to cover existing payments requirements, it can avoid making relatively large initial changes to the tax system. As the exchange rate appreciates, the dollar value of government revenues will increase (for any tax system which raises a fixed share of GDP) and the government's ability to pay debt service will rise.

Russia's balance of payments and prospects

Prospects for 1992

Table 6 shows our forecast for imports and broad categories of import financing in 1992. Due to very severe problems with the Russian trade data, we have not compared these estimates to 1991 data. Depending on whether we calculate dollar values for trade using official ruble data, or commercial ruble data, the estimated imports here of 40.9 billion dollars in 1992 could be higher or lower respectively than 1991 results. Both sets of data show a sharp fall in Russian exports, particularly to the CMEA countries.

Given these data problems, our strategy in this section is to forecast the change in the balance of payments constraint during 1993 and 1994, based on announced policies, and using rough forecasts of exports and imports for 1992 to determine base levels. The 1992 data has the advantage that all numbers are reported in dollar values, so we no longer need to reconvert figures from rubles to dollars. Nor do we need to calculate the Russian share of exports in 1991.

During the first trimester, Goskomstat reports total exports of 10.6 billion dollars, though the monthly trend shows rising exports, with April alone at 3.1 billion dollars. Based on these figures, and the assumption that non-energy exports will continue to show a rising trend, we esti-

TABLE 6 FORECAST SOURCES OF IMPORT FINANCING TOTAL RUSSIAN IMPORTS

	1992	1993	1994
TOTAL IMPORTS	40.9	56.1	70.4
FINANCED BY:			
EXPORTS	42.0	55.2	70.9
GOLD SALES	1.0	1.2	1.4
NET FOREIGN RESOURCE TRANSFER	5.2	3.0	1.0
DIRECT INVESTMENT	0.2	0.5	1.0
NET FORMER REPUBLICAN FINANCING	0.0	0.0	0.0
CAPITAL FLIGHT	-2.0	2.0	2.0
RESERVES	-2.8	-3.0	-3.0
OTHER	-2.7	-2.8	-2.9

Notes:
1. Exports for 1992 and beyond based on author's projections discussed in text. Net foreign resource transfer assumes that 12.9 billion dollars in new disbursements, and further debt service rescheduling will be provided in 1993.
2. Net foreign resource transfer takes the sum of: net interest; net short, medium, and long-term capital flows; and financing through arrears.
3. Direct Investment and net financing to CIS countries are author's projections. These do not include major capital investments in the eneregy industry which could substantially raise both imports and foreign direct investment.
4. Errors and omissions include 2 billion dollars in capital repatriation annually in 1993 and 1994, and 2 billion in capital flight n 1992.
5. Reserves build-up allows for 2 months imports of gross reserves by end 1994.
6. 'Other' is other net service flows not included above.

mate total exports will equal 42 billion dollars in 1992. This includes an allowance for 2 billion dollars in unrecorded capital flight, and 3 billion dollars in other unrecorded exports where the funds are used to reimport goods (i.e. we assume the official data for the year will understate exports by 5 billion dollars and report 37 billion dollars as total exports).

The second most important source of import financing in 1992 is net foreign resource transfers of 5.2 billion dollars. Some of this financing is conditional on agreement of a stand-by arrangement with the IMF, and incorporates the assistance implied by the announced 24 billion dollars of G7 aid to Russia. The net resource transfer to Russia is much smaller than this 24 billion because: 6 billion of the aid goes to the Russian stabilization fund, 7.2 billion dollars is used to cover arrears or remaining debt service obligations, and another 5.6 billion dollars of assistance is 'unidentified'.

Other financing items in Table 6 are gold sales from current production equal to 1 billion dollars, an accumulation of 2.8 billion dollars of gross reserves as part of the IMF program, and a net services deficit (not including net interest payments) of 2.1 billion dollars.

Based on these estimates, the total imports which Russia will be able to finance in 1992 are 40.9 billion dollars. While we cannot compare this to 1991 data, this estimate for imports certainly implies a very sharp fall from 1990, and a continued tight balance of payments situation through 1992.

Import financing prospects for 1993 and beyond

The government has announced its intention to further liberalize trade and pricing policies in 1992 and 1993, and to implement a policy to stabilize the ruble. The policies include: liberalization of energy prices, and raising energy prices to world levels by spring 1994 (by gradually reducing an export tax on energy products); floating the ruble within narrow bands during 1992; introducing full currency convertibility during 1992; removing all licenses and quotas on export items by 1993 (currently these apply to basic raw materials); and maintaining a monetary and fiscal stance consistent with macroeconomic stabilization.

Based on the experience of East European countries, and the likely demand effects of energy price increases, these policies should lead to an export boom in Russia in the coming years, capital repatriation, and a gradual improvement in direct foreign investment. We examine the main category of financing items separately:

Energy exports. Table 7 shows the production and consumption of oil and oil products in Russia. Table 8 shows the same items for natural gas. As we have already discussed, production of oil has been falling sharply since 1988. The Ministry of Energy forecasts that production will stabilize in 1993 at approximately 400 million barrels annually. Several recent measures have been adopted by the government to achieve this.

The striking fact from these tables is the pattern of consumption. Between 1990 and 1992 both oil and natural gas consumption have remained constant, while GNP is estimated to have fallen 14 percent in 1991, and forecast to fall by 10 percent to 20 percent in 1992. This consumption pattern is a direct result of policy decisions. Quotas for oil

TABLE 7 OIL AND OIL PRODUCTS - PRODUCTION, CONSUMPTION AND EXPORTS

	1990	1991	1992	1993	1994
PRODUCTION	516	461	400	400	425
CONSUMPTION	208	220	215	183	164
EXPORTS	156	91	90	122	166
EXPORTS TO FORMER REPUBLICS	163	150	95	95	95
IMPORTS	11	0	0	0	0
PRICE OF OIL	174	122	116	121	125
VALUE OF NET EXPORTS (bln $)	27	1 11.1	10.4	14.7	20.8

Notes:
1. Source: Ministry of Fuels and Energy, Russia
2. Production projections based on discussions with officials in the Ministry.
3. Assuming a 15 percent decline in oil consumption in 1992, and 10 percent decline in 1993 as Russia moves to world energy prices.
4. All quantities in million tons.

TABLE 8 NATURAL GAS - PRODUCTION, CONSUMPTION AND EXPORTS

	1991	1992	1993	1994
PRODUCTION	643	654	654	654
CONSUMPTION	416	451	406	365
EXPORTS	91	104	149	189
EXPORTS TO FORMER REPUBLICS	139	99	99	99
PRICE OF GAS ($ per mln m3)	113	85	88	92
VALUE OF NET EXPORTS (bln $)	10.3	8.8	13.1	17.4

Notes:
1. Source: Ministry of Fuels and Energy, Russia
2. Production projections based on discussions with officials in the Ministry.
3. Assuming a 10 percent decline in gas consumption in 1992, and 10 percent decline in 1993 as Russia moves to world energy prices.

exports are set by the Ministry of Economy based on its prediction for domestic consumption needs.

During the first year of reforms, Polish oil consumption fell by 13 percent while GDP fell by 12 percent. During 1991, Polish oil consumption is estimated to have fallen approx. 15 percent further, while GDP fell a further 8 percent. This reduction in energy intensity is a natural outcome after the movement to world prices, and given the extremely high energy-intensity of the formerly socialist economies.

In Table 7 we assume that Russia implements a pricing policy for energy which leads to a reduction in oil consumption of 15 percent in 1993 (or approx. one half the estimated decline in GDP in 1991 and 1992) and a 10 percent decline in natural gas consumption. In 1994 we assume the rise in energy price to world price levels leads to a further 15 percent fall in oil consumption, and a 10 percent drop in natural gas consumption.

Based on these forecasts for production and consumption, and assuming that exports of energy to other republics remain at the 1992 levels (after a sharp fall from 1991 to 1992, and in order to buy needed imports for Russia), such consumption declines would free 6.2 billion dollars of oil for export, and 7.1 billion dollars of natural gas. Taking into account price inflation (assuming 4 percent annually), we forecast these policy measures will allow total energy exports to rise by 8.3 billion dollars in 1993, and 9.2 billion dollars in 1994.

Other exports. During 1990 and 1991 Polish exports to OECD countries increased at an annual average rate of 26 percent, Hungary's exports increased at a 23 percent rate, and Czechoslovakia's exports increased at a 26 percent rate. The experience from these countries has shown that reintegration of trade into the world economy proceeds quickly once market incentives for trade are restored. This occurred even during periods of sharp declines in industrial production, and rising energy prices.

In Poland, exports declined initially, and then began increasing 4 months after the reform program was started. The fastest increasing exports were in the metallurgical, electromachinery, wood and textile sectors.

There are several reasons why Russian exports may not gain as quickly as observed in these countries. First, Russia is much larger and farther from Europe, so distances will limit trade. Second, there are still quota and license requirements on raw material exports. Third, the military industrial complex in Russia is much larger than in these other countries, and the prospects for exports in this sector are unclear. Fourth, the undefined relations with other republics, and continued economic instability across the former CIS disrupts trade and production.

TABLE 9 EXPORTS IN 1992 AND BEYOND
(billion dollars)

	1992	1993	1994
TOTAL	42.0	55.2	70.9
of which:			
OIL	10.4	14.7	20.8
GAS	8.8	13.1	17.4
OTHER	22.8	27.3	32.8

Note: assumes growth of other exports at 20 percent per year, and movement of oil and gas prices to world levels

While all these factors may slow the response of trade, the same pattern of export growth to the West is likely to emerge in Russia as in these other countries. Currently Russian trade with the West is a small fraction of GDP (supposing Russia's GDP will equal $2000 per capita after stabilization, Russian exports to the West are approximately 5 percent of GDP) and there is bound to be greater integration. Second, the profit incentive to export, particularly non-traditional goods, must be enormous. Labor costs in Russia are extremely low. Third, quotas on traditional exports of raw materials in 1993 and 1994 will be removed.

Based on these arguments, in 1993 and 1994 we forecast growth of 20 percent per year in non-energy exports (16 percent real and 4 percent inflation). Table 9 shows the pattern of total, energy and non- energy exports during these years.

Net foreign resource transfer. Russia's debt service obligations in 1993 (not including any payments resulting from previously rescheduled debt) equal 8.3 billion dollars. Of this 5.7 is principal, and 2.6 is interest. Another 7.1 billion dollars falls due in 1994. Currently there are no agreements on debt service rescheduling for 1993 and 1994. We assume that net foreign resource transfers decline to 3 billion and 1 billion in 1993 and 1994. This would imply new financing (either through debt relief, or new disbursements) of 11.3 billion in 1993 and 8.1 billion in 1994, plus financing to cover any required payments on previously rescheduled debt. This compares to 16.7 billion dollars of new financing and debt relief planned for 1992, and may understate the total financing which will actually become available.

Based on these assumptions, at the end of 1994, Russia would have a total outstanding debt equal to approximately 70 billion dollars, or one year's exports.

Financing of other countries in the ruble area. The current monetary arrangement between the countries in the ruble area poses a threat to Russia's balance of payments stability. Since each country is able to create base money, and use that money to purchase hard currency or imported goods from Russia, this item could lead to a substantial capital and import outflow. Even once agreement on a monetary union is reached to prevent this, countries in the monetary union are likely to run non-zero trade balances with each other, which will lead to financing items in Russia's balance of payments. We assume this balance is zero currently.

Capital flight. Estimates of underinvoicing and unrecorded exports for Russia in 1991 range from 0 to 15 billion dollars. Officials from the Ministry of Foreign Economic Relations estimate that underinvoicing and non-reporting in 1991 was approximately 4 to 5 billion dollars, and that most of this was used to reimport goods. Capital flight was 1 billion dollars. Other estimates of capital flight are much higher. Currently we have no information on this. For 1991, comparisons of the former USSR statistics for exports with reports from Western importers should permit a more accurate assessment. We assume that in 1992 capital flight is 2 billion dollars. In 1993 and 1994 Russia receives capital repatriation of 2 billion dollars annually as confidence in the banking system is restored and macro-stabilization takes hold.

Foreign direct investment. Taking into account the competition from and experience of Eastern Europe, it is unlikely that Russia will receive substantial foreign investment during the next two years.

Reserves. We allow for 3 billion dollars in reserve accumulation in 1993 and 1994. This raises total reserves to approximately 2 months' imports (not including the stabilization fund) by end 1994.

Imports. Based on these forecasts, the balance of payments situation should substantially improve sometime in 1993. We predict financing for imports could rise by 14.8 billion dollars in 1993 compared to 1992, and a further 14.7 billion dollars in 1994. Two-thirds of this increase is financed by new energy exports alone.

Conclusion

Russia, like other East European countries, has begun its economic reform program in the midst of a critical economic situation. The former USSR disbanded with no reserves, a deteriorating export base, and a large debt burden. The collapse of CMEA trade has further worsened the payments situation. Economic and political instability has led to capital flight, and there is a risk that a breakdown in CIS trade, or misman-agement of the ruble area, could further lead to payments difficulties.

All these factors have contributed to a severe balance of payments dif-ficulty in Russia. Macroeconomic indicators of the shortage of hard cur-rency include a dollar wage equalling approximately 30 dollars per month, or less than one-seventh of the Polish level, a GDP per capita at 550 dollars per person, and an exchange rate which has depreciated by twofold from its level in the mid-1980s.

By contributing to the decline in output, and a decline in the real wage, the balance of payments constraint represents a clear threat to the reform program. The 'artificially' depreciated exchange rate limits the effectiveness of import competition in a highly monopolized economy, and puts fiscal policy in jeopardy if debt service payments are to be met.

In this paper we have argued that the policy program outlined by the Russian government should lead to a sharp improvement in Russia's balance of payments position during the next 12 to 24 months. Macroeconomic stabilization should reduce capital flight and eventually lead to repatriation of capital.

Most importantly, the government's intention to raise energy prices to world levels during the next two years could release at least 13 billion dollars worth of oil and natural gas for export. Unlike other East European countries and members of the CIS, the energy-intensity of the Russian economy has actually increased in 1991 and 1992.

Finally, like other East European countries, the liberalization of the trade regime and the opening of the economy to foreign markets should result in a rapid growth in non-traditional Russian exports to Western nations. Experience from Eastern Europe suggests that growth rates in the range of 15 to 25 percent per year are possible.

All these factors imply that 1992 may be the watershed year for Russia's balance of payments crisis. If the reform program is implement-ed as planned, we can expect rapid improvement in Russia's balance of payments situation during the next year.

Bibliography

International Monetary Fund. (1991) *A Study of the Soviet Economy*. Paris: OECD Publication Services.

International Monetary Fund. (1992) *Staff Report on the Russian Economy*. Washington.

Rodrik, Dani. (1992) 'Foreign Trade in Eastern Europe: Early Results' mimeograph.

Russian State Committee for Statistics. (1991) *Narodnoe khozyaistvo RSFSR v 1990*.g.h. Moscow.

Russian State Committee for Statistics. (1992) *Rossiskaya Federatsiya v tsifrakh*. Moscow.

Index